Mircea A. Tamas

MONEY: THE EVIL EYE

RENÉ GUÉNON AND THE TRADITIONAL SPIRIT

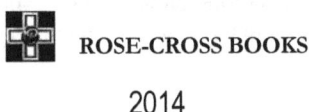

ROSE-CROSS BOOKS

2014

Copyright © 2014 by Mircea A. Tamas

Published by *Rose-Cross Books*
TORONTO
www.rose-crossbooks.com

Printed in Canada   Toronto 2014

Text editing by *Ariana Ananda Tamas*
Cover design by *Imre Szekely*

Library and Archives Canada Cataloguing in Publication

Tamas, Mircea A. (Mircea Alexandru), 1949-, author
    Money : the evil eye : René Guénon and the traditional spirit / Mircea A. Tamas.

Includes bibliographical references.
ISBN 978-0-9865872-3-8 (pbk.)

1. Guénon, René. 2. Tradition (Philosophy). 3. Money-- Philosophy. 4. Philosophy and religion. 5. Symbolism. I. Title.

B2430.G84T34 2014   194   C2014-902120-8

CONTENTS

FOREWORD: René Guénon and the Traditional Spirit — 5

CHAPTER I: The Journey to the Center — 14

CHAPTER II: The Royal Art — 24

CHAPTER III: The Royal Investiture — 35

CHAPTER IV: The Royal Art of Love — 47

CHAPTER V: Solomon and the Royal Art of Love — 64

CHAPTER VI: The Hierarchy of Love — 83

CHAPTER VII: René Guénon and *Mysterium Conscientia* — 96

CHAPTER VIII: *Mysterium Conscientia* and *Kali-Yuga* — 113

CHAPTER IX: The Traditional Mentality — 134

CHAPTER X: Our Days are Numbered — 148

CHAPTER XI: Money before Money — 169

CHAPTER XII: Measure for Measure — 183

CHAPTER XIII: Money more than Money — 203

CONCLUSION: The Templars' Treasure — 216

FOREWORD

RENÉ GUÉNON
AND THE TRADITIONAL SPIRIT

Initially, this work sought to be a second volume and a continuation of the *Free-Masonry: A Traditional Organization*,[1] and in a way it is; yet we soon understood that, even though we had Free-Masonry in mind as a traditional organization still alive in the *Occidens*, the first volume coping with the symbolism of the center and of the Holy Grail has surpassed by far the intended subject, compelling us therefore to rethink this second volume as part of a series depicting the *Traditional Spirit* rather than the Masonry that should belong to this spirit.

We chose the syntagm *traditional spirit* as a challenge to the modern world for which both words "traditional" and "spirit" lost their real meaning; we also chose it, because René Guénon used this expression many times, and, regardless how hostile the contemporary mentality is to his works, there is no doubt that his writings remain essential to the endeavour of reviving this *esprit traditionnel*.

The *Traditional Spirit*, like the Principle itself, is one without a second, universal and everywhere the same[2]: "The real traditional spirit is

---

[1] Rose-Cross Books, 2010.
[2] That's why the competition among various traditional forms is so unwise and harmful to the traditional spirit itself: *mais nous ne sommes pas de ceux qui estiment qu'on peut se désintéresser des atteintes portées à une tradition quelconque, et qui sont même toujours prêts à se féliciter des attaques qui visent une tradition autre que la leur, comme s'il s'agissait de coups dirigés contre des "concurrents," et comme si ces attaques n'atteignaient pas toujours, en définitive,*

always and everywhere essentially the same, whatever apparent form it may take; the various forms that are specially suited to different mental conditions and different circumstances of time and place are merely expressions of one and the same truth; but this fundamental unity beneath apparent multiplicity can be discovered only by those who are able to place themselves in the order of pure intellectuality."[1] The *Traditional Spirit*, no different from the traditional mentality, is what governs and dominates a sacred world, where all activities are ritual and blessed by God, where people participate in a tradition of supra-human origins, expressed by divine doctrines and principles revealed from the beginning of the cycle, where all the indefinite multiple adaptations of the tradition are valid if they are done in keeping with the traditional spirit[2]; the "antitraditional spirit" is what fuels the modern mentality, which has not only invented the profane world, but it also trying to destroy the traditional spirit.[3]

In fact, the existence (and persistence) of the traditional spirit or its expulsion defines the division of the world into *Oriens* and *Occidens*. We

---

l'esprit traditionnel lui-même (René Guénon, *Mélanges*, Gallimard, 1976, p. 231). We are aware of the official view regarding quotations from a foreign language, but in Guénon's case we decided to keep the original text and give an English translation only when it is absolutely necessary; our decision was based on two reasons: our readers are a small exclusive number and usually very knowledgeable of René Guénon's work; any translation would diminish the sense of Guénon's writings.

[1] *Le véritable esprit traditionnel, de quelque forme qu'il se revête, est partout et toujours le même au fond; les formes diverses, qui sont spécialement adaptées à telles ou telles conditions mentales, à telles ou telles circonstances de temps et de lieu, ne sont que des expressions d'une seule et même vérité ; mais il faut pouvoir se placer dans l'ordre de l'intellectualité pure pour découvrir cette unité fondamentale sous leur apparente multiplicité* (René Guénon, *La crise du monde moderne*, Gallimard, 1975, p. 51).

[2] *La tradition permet des adaptations indéfiniment multiples et diverses dans leurs modalités; mais toutes ces adaptations, dès lors qu'elles sont faites rigoureusement selon l'esprit traditionnel, ne sont pas autre chose que le développement normal de certaines des conséquences qui sont éternellement contenues dans le principe* (René Guénon, *Études sur l'Hindouisme*, Éditions Traditionnelles, 1979, p. 23).

[3] *...un esprit vraiment conforme aux principes dont tout dépend, esprit qui est ce que nous appelons l'esprit traditionnel au véritable sens de ce mot, et dont, malheureusement, toutes les tendances spécifiquement modernes sont l'antithèse ou la négation* (René Guénon, *Autorité spirituelle et Pouvoir temporel*, Véga, 1976, p. 11).

prefer to use these Latin words instead of Orient and Occident, because the division does not refer so much to the geographical situation, today when the modern occidental mentality is everywhere, but to a spiritual one[1]; René Guénon chose the syntagm *esprit traditionnel* mainly to characterize the modern world and its lack of such a spirit,[2] in comparison with a sacred "Orient," which is the only one that can still perform the role of keeper and guardian of the traditional spirit.[3]

The gradual break-up with tradition, which became so visible after the obliteration of the Order of the Temple, gave birth to the modern mentality (starting with the Renaissance and the Reformation[4]), and

---

[1] ...*l'antithèse de l'Orient et de l'Occident, telle qu'elle se présente actuellement, ne doit pas être entendue en un sens simplement géographique, mais qu'elle est en réalité celle de l'esprit traditionnel et de l'esprit moderne* (Guénon, *Études sur l'Hindouisme*, p. 200). ...*l'esprit oriental et de l'esprit occidental, qui est en somme la même chose pour nous que celle de l'esprit traditionnel et de l'esprit moderne* (René Guénon, *Le règne de la quantité et les signes des temps*, Gallimard, 1970, p. 16). This modern spirit or lack of the traditional spirit Guénon described as an "antitraditional spirit": "the opposition that at present exists between the Eastern and the Western mentalities... coincides with the opposition between the traditional and the antitraditional spirit" (*l'opposition qui existe actuellement entre l'esprit oriental et l'esprit occidental... est... celle de l'esprit traditionnel et de l'esprit antitraditionnel,* Guénon, *La crise,* p. 55).

[2] And because it does not have it anymore, the modern world denies the existence of such a spirit: *entre l'esprit traditionnel et l'esprit moderne, il ne saurait en réalité y avoir aucun accommodement, et toute concession faite au second est nécessairement aux dépens du premier, puisque, au fond, l'esprit moderne n'est que la négation même de tout ce qui constitue l'esprit traditionnel* (Guénon, *Le règne,* p. 118).

[3] "In the present state of things, the true traditional spirit, with all that it implies, no longer has any authentic representatives except in the Orient" (*dans l'état actuel des choses, le véritable esprit traditionnel, avec tout ce qu'il implique, n'a plus de représentants authentiques qu'en Orient,* Guénon, *La crise,* p. 41) *Ce rôle de conservation de l'esprit traditionnel, avec tout ce qu'il implique en réalité lorsqu'on l'entend dans son sens le plus profond, c'est l'Orient seul qui peut le remplir actuellement; nous ne voulons pas dire l'Orient tout entier... c'est en Orient seulement que subsiste encore une véritable élite, où l'esprit traditionnel se retrouve avec toute sa vitalité... La tradition permet des adaptations indéfiniment multiples et diverses dans leurs modalités; mais toutes ces adaptations, dès lors qu'elles sont faites rigoureusement selon l'esprit traditionnel, ne sont pas autre chose que le développement normal de certaines des conséquences qui sont éternellement contenues dans le principe* (Guénon, *Études sur l'Hindouisme,* p. 22).

[4] René Guénon considered the three "R"s (Renaissance, Reform, Revolution) as the main profanatory agents of the Occident.

implicitly to the modern world and to the antitraditional spirit,[1] and the invasion of the profane viewpoint seemed to accelerate and be in an increasing rush as though the world could not endure its precarious balance anymore and decided to exhaust its inferior possibilities and die, possibilities that themselves felt the lack of time and were in an escalating hurry to fulfill their reign. What is left now in the *Occidens* are some "vestiges of the traditional spirit,"[2] which the current profane educational system tries to sweep away once and for all,[3] while

---

[1] *C'est sur cette rupture avec la tradition que nous devons encore insister, puisque c'est d'elle qu'est né le monde moderne, dont tous les caractères propres pourraient être résumés en un seul, l'opposition à l'esprit traditionnel* (Guénon, *La crise*, p. 97); *la Renaissance et la Réforme sont surtout des résultantes, et elles n'ont été rendues possibles que par la décadence préalable; mais, bien loin d'être un redressement, elles marquèrent une chute beaucoup plus profonde, parce qu'elles consommèrent la rupture définitive avec l'esprit traditionnel* (ibid., p. 29).

[2] René Guénon, *Orient et Occident*, Guy Trédaniel, 1993, pp. 180, 199.

[3] "Profane instruction as it exists in the modern world... is obviously one of those things that exhibit an antitraditional character in the highest degree; one can even say that, in a way, it was devised only for this purpose, or at least that its primary and principal purpose lies in this characteristic, for it is evident that it is one of the most powerful instruments for achieving the destruction of the traditional spirit" (*L'instruction profane, telle qu'elle est constituée dans le monde moderne, et sur laquelle sont modelées toutes les représentations en question, est évidemment une des choses qui présentent au plus haut point le caractère antitraditionnel; on peut même dire qu'elle n'est faite en quelque sorte que pour cela, ou du moins que c'est dans ce caractère que réside sa première et principale raison d'être, car il est évident que c'est là un des instruments les plus puissants dont on puisse disposer pour parvenir à la destruction de l'esprit traditionnel*, René Guénon, *Aperçus sur l'Initiation*, Éditions Traditionnelles, 1992, p. 221). *Partout où les Européens se sont installés, ils ont voulu répandre les soi-disant "bienfaits de l'instruction"... le principal "bienfait" qu'attendent de cette instruction ceux qui l'imposent, c'est probablement, toujours et partout, la destruction de l'esprit traditionnel* (Guénon, *Orient et Occident*, p. 63). *Non contente d'avoir détruit l'esprit traditionnel en Occident ou plutôt d'être née de sa destruction même en vue de parachever cette destruction, l'instruction "scientiste" et "égalitariste" s'attaque à présent à ce qui demeure de cet esprit chez les autres peuples et dans les autres parties du globe. Et à cet égard on peut dire que l'expansion commerciale sous sa forme brutale mais efficace de colonisation a été la grande introductrice de ce mouvement subversif et dissolvant des traditions établies chez les autres, car tout cela est en effet très récent. Le « travail » à ce point de vue peut être divisé en deux grandes phases : travail d'abord "intérieur", pour nous servir des mêmes termes que ceux de ces pages, visant à amoindrir la tradition en Occident – cette tradition qui pendant près de treize siècles et plus n'avait jamais songé à aller détruire ce qu'il y avait de par le monde de traditionnel également – pour lui substituer progressivement quelque chose qui se distingue essentiellement et qui va même à l'encontre de toute vraie tradition ; puis, ce travail intérieur une fois en bonne voie, et ce quelque chose, qui est l'esprit moderne lui-même ou son essence si l'on veut et si l'on peut employer ce terme pour désigner*

"traditionalists"[1] imagine these "vestiges" as futile, which prompts them to ignore any exotericism.[2]

Just because we refer to the "vestiges of the traditional spirit" does not mean that the traditional spirit was actually obliterated; like the Holy Grail or the Center, it did not dissolve, but became hidden[3]; the traditional spirit, like the center, cannot die, since it is beyond change and death, but it can withdraw completely from the world, like the Goddess Justice, waiting for another cycle to begin, "and then there would really be the 'end of a world.'"[4]

Meanwhile, any effort to retrieve the traditional spirit is a perfectly orthodox, traditional and intelligent quest.

---

quelque chose qui n'est que néant et multiplicité, une fois devenu suffisamment important pour absorber la presque totalité des activités et des pensées des peuples occidentaux, travail "extérieur", visant à obtenir le même résultat non plus seulement dans une simple portion du globe, mais dans le monde entier et chez tous les peuples de la terre afin d'arriver à établir ce quelque chose, cette essence dont l'esprit moderne est l'actuelle expression, dans un état souverain de domination mondiale comparable, bien qu'à tous les égards inverse, de celui qui est l'apanage légitime de ce que diverses traditions désignent comme le « Roi du Monde » et qui, dans la tradition chrétienne, est le Christ lui-même (René Guénon, *Florilegium: Oriens et Occidens*, Rose-Cross Books, 2015, p.).

[1] *...ceci vaut également pour le mot même "traditionalisme," qui, comme nous l'avons expliqué, est fort loin d'être synonyme d'"esprit traditionnel," et que nous rejetons absolument pour notre part* (Guénon, *Etudes sur l'Hindouisme*, p. 242).

[2] *Du reste, cette ignorance pratique elle-même, qui consiste à regarder comme inutile ou superflue la participation à une tradition exotérique, ne serait pas possible sans une méconnaissance même théorique de cet aspect de la tradition, et c'est là ce qui la rend encore plus grave, car on peut se demander si quelqu'un chez qui existe une telle méconnaissance, quelles que soient d'ailleurs ses possibilités, est bien réellement prêt à aborder le domaine ésotérique et initiatique, et s'il ne devrait pas plutôt s'appliquer à mieux comprendre la valeur et la portée de l'exotérisme avant de chercher à aller plus loin. En fait, il y a là manifestement la conséquence d'un affaiblissement de l'esprit traditionnel entendu dans son sens général, et il devrait être évident que c'est cet esprit qu'il faut avant tout restaurer intégralement en soi-même si l'on veut ensuite pénétrer le sens profond de la tradition* (Guénon, *Initiation et Réalisation spirituelle*, pp. 71-72).

[3] "The traditional spirit is already tending to withdraw into itself [to become "complicated," – Latin *complicare*, 'to fold together'] and the centers where it is preserved in its entirety are becoming more and more closed and less accessible" (*déjà, l'esprit traditionnel se replie en quelque sorte sur lui-même, les centres où il se conserve intégralement deviennent de plus en plus fermés et difficilement accessibles*, Guénon, *La crise*, p. 154).

[4] *L'esprit traditionnel ne peut mourir, parce qu'il est, dans son essence, supérieur à la mort et au changement; mais il peut se retirer entièrement du monde extérieur, et alors ce sera véritablement la "fin d'un monde"* (*ibid.*, p. 156).

We mentioned "the endeavour of reviving this *esprit traditionnel*," but is such a thing actually possible? What steps should be taken to acquire and re-establish the traditional spirit? Should this be an activity for the public at large, for a small group or for individuals? It is obvious that for such an enterprise the current profane views, such as "political correctness" and "equalitarianism," are impotent; it is also obvious that, from the traditional viewpoint, the idea of "public at large," or even a "group" in the sense of a profane association, has no meaning. Therefore the spiritual activity should be an individual one, with a theoretical study of the traditional doctrines as a first step (and only as a first step), and with the paramount and indispensable second, higher, much higher and complex step, represented by an effective realization; and when we say "theoretical study" we do not mean a scholarly reading based on a vague aspiration to the sacred domain, which leads to a "traditionalist" not a traditional spirit,[1] let alone that reading for educational purposes, out of curiosity, or in a superficial manner, is totally worthless.

Individuals who actually realize the traditional spirit and are able to *prendre conscience* of it, have the necessary vocation to influence the present mentality and to adapt traditional doctrines to the mental conditions of the modern environment.[2] How difficult such a task is and what chances of success would have are questions that nobody could answer affirmatively now, at the end of *Kali-Yuga*.

---

[1] "Unfortunately, 'traditionalism' is not the same as the authentic traditional spirit: because it cannot be, and it is often no more than a tendency, a more or less vague aspiration, presupposing no real knowledge (*Malheureusement, le traditionalisme n'est point la même chose que le véritable esprit traditionnel ; il peut n'être, et il n'est bien souvent en fait, qu'une simple tendance, une aspiration plus ou moins vague, qui ne suppose aucune connaissance réelle*, Guénon, *La crise*, p. 42); *D'ailleurs, pour avoir pleinement l'esprit traditionnel (et non pas seulement "traditionaliste," ce qui n'implique qu'une tendance ou une aspiration), il faut déjà avoir pénétré dans le domaine des principes, suffisamment tout au moins pour avoir reçu la direction intérieure dont il n'est plus possible de s'écarter jamais* (Guénon, *Orient et Occident*, p. 168).
[2] *Si donc de nouvelles adaptations sont requises, ce qui est d'autant plus naturel qu'on a affaire à un milieu différent, rien ne s'oppose à ce qu'on les formule en s'inspirant de celles qui existent déjà, mais en tenant compte aussi des conditions mentales de ce milieu, pourvu qu'on le fasse avec la prudence et la compétence voulues, et qu'on ait d'abord compris profondément l'esprit traditionnel avec tout ce qu'il comporte ; c'est ce que l'élite intellectuelle devra faire tôt ou tard* (*ibid.*, p. 208).

As for us, we decided to tackle the most distinctive feature of the modern world, that is to say, the adulation for money, which is today, no doubt about it, the "evil eye," in comparison with the times when the traditional spirit was alive and when money, under the supervision of spiritual authority, was a sacred support. Moreover, in a traditional society, money was a tool for the Goddess Justice not only to transmit spiritual influence through the symbols it carried, but also to balance traditional activities by providing just and truthful payment with the "true measure" of weight. Similarly, in the "parable of the workers in the vineyard" from the *Gospel*, Jesus Christ used the act of payment to reject the quantitative and materialistic aspects of money and depict the divine reward and justice, beyond the understanding of the human mind; in addition, for operative Masons, "payment" had a hidden symbolism that was transmitted, even without being completely understood, to modern Masonry.[1] The executioner, whose job was a very peculiar one, received a "payment" to confirm that his actions were just, and we have an unexpected illustration in Alexandre Dumas' *Les Trois Mousquetaires*:

> Alors il la fit entrer dans la barque, et, comme il allait y mettre le pied, Athos lui remit une somme d'argent.
> - Tenez, dit-il, voici le prix de l'exécution; que l'on voie bien que nous agissons en juges.
> - C'est bien, dit le bourreau; et que maintenant, à son tour, cette femme sache que je n'accomplis pas mon métier, mais mon devoir. Et il jeta l'argent dans la rivière.

---

[1] René Guénon wrote in a letter to Marcel Maugy (Denys Roman), in October 19, 1948, about the "coin of the Temple" and its use in the Mark Masonry: *D'autre part, il faut faire attention que, dans la* Mark Masonry, *il y a en réalité 2 degrés distincts, ceux de* Mark Man *et de* Mark Master; *en tout cas, le "Mark Master's token" (je ne crois pas qu'on emploie habituellement le mot "Tessera") est bien la "monnaie du Temple" modifiée quant à la forme des caractères comme je vous l'ai dit (j'en ai une ici); la figure de cette même monnaie a été également adoptée comme sceau par la "King Salomon's Temple Lodge," qui est une des LL∴ les plus "sélectionnées" d'Angleterre. Elle représente d'un côté le vase de la manne et de l'autre la verge d'Aaron, qui étaient deux des objets conservés dans l'Arche d'Alliance; la reproduction de la monnaie authentique (avec les caractères de forme ancienne) se trouve dans une des planches de l'ouvrage de S. Munk sur la Palestine (collection univers pittoresque).*

The moment money started to degenerate and gradually became the "evil eye," the traditional spirit in *Occidens* began to disappear (in fact to go into hiding), and René Guénon concluded that this turning point coincided with King Philippe le Bel's double maleficent deeds: the destruction of the Order of the Temple and the debasing of coinage; with Philippe le Bel the doors opened to "humanism," Renaissance, bourgeoisie, the revolution against normal hierarchy (starting with the revolt against the spiritual authority), and the rejection of the West's own tradition:

> *En Europe, nous trouvons aussi, dès le moyen âge, l'analogue de la révolte des Kshatriyas; nous le trouvons même plus particulièrement en France, où, à partir de Philippe le Bel, qui doit être considéré comme un des principaux auteurs de la déviation caractéristique de l'époque moderne, la royauté travailla presque constamment à se rendre indépendante de l'autorité spirituelle, tout en conservant cependant, par un singulier illogisme, la marque extérieure de sa dépendance originelle, puisque, comme nous l'avons expliqué, le sacre des rois n'était pas autre chose. Les "legists" de Philippe le Bel sont déjà, bien avant les "humanistes" de la Renaissance, les véritables précurseurs du "laïcisme" actuel; et c'est à cette époque, c'est-à-dire au début du XIVe siècle, qu'il faut faire remonter en réalité la rupture du monde occidental avec sa propre tradition. Pour des raisons qu'il serait trop long d'exposer ici, et que nous avons d'ailleurs indiquées dans d'autres études, nous pensons que le point de départ de cette rupture fut marqué très nettement par la destruction de l'Ordre du Temple; nous rappellerons seulement que celui-ci constituait comme un lien entre l'Orient et l'Occident, et que, en Occident même, il était, par son double caractère religieux et guerrier, une sorte de trait d'union entre le spirituel et le temporel, si même ce double caractère ne doit être interprété comme le signe d'une relation plus directe avec la source commune des deux pouvoirs. On sera peut-être tenté d'objecter que cette destruction, si elle fut voulue par le roi de France, fut du moins réalisée d'accord avec la Papauté; la vérité est qu'elle fut imposée à la Papauté, ce qui est tout différent; et c'est ainsi que, renversant les rapports normaux, le pouvoir temporel commença dès lors à se servir de l'autorité spirituelle pour ses fins de domination politique. On dira sans doute encore que le fait que cette autorité spirituelle se laissa ainsi subjuguer prouve qu'elle n'était déjà plus ce qu'elle aurait dû être, et que ses représentants n'avaient plus la pleine conscience de son caractère transcendant; cela est vrai, et c'est d'ailleurs ce qui explique et justifie, à cette époque même, les invectives parfois violentes de Dante à leur égard... Mais revenons à Philippe le Bel, qui nous fournit un exemple particulièrement typique*

pour ce que nous nous proposons d'expliquer ici: il est à remarquer que Dante attribue comme mobile à ses actions la "cupidité," qui est un vice, non de Kshatriya, mais de Vaishya[1]*... et c'est pourquoi nous voyons aussi, à partir de Philippe le Bel précisément, les rois de France s'entourer presque constamment de bourgeois, surtout ceux qui, comme Louis XI et Louis XIV, ont poussé le plus loin le travail de "centralisation," dont la bourgeoisie devait du reste recueillir ensuite le bénéfice lorsqu'elle s'empara du pouvoir par la Révolution.*[2]

King Philippe le Bel is a paradigmatic example of incompatibility between the royal function and the individual who was elected to fill it, a disastrous unsuitability that had terrible consequences, because, if in previous ages it was time for a rectification, now, with the *Kali-Yuga* marching to its end, the Occident and its traditional spirit were doomed, and so were the Royal Art, the Holy Love, the integral consciousness and money.

The "traditional spirit" topic is complex, and to be able to converse about "money: the 'evil eye'," we must first establish the traditional background, by separately examining the Royal Art, the Art of Love, the notion of consciousness, traditional mentality and finally money.

---

[1] See the bourgeoisie of medieval Italy.
[2] Guénon, *Autorité spirituelle*, pp. 81-85.

CHAPTER I

THE JOURNEY TO THE CENTER

The journey to the Center, which is the essence of the Royal Art and, *a fortiori*, of the traditional Masonry, should be understood as described by Maximus Confessor who unveiled the symbolism of Abraham's journey to the Center:

> The one who is still satisfying the passionate appetites of the flesh dwells as a maker and worshiper of idols in the land of the Chaldeans. But after some reflection on this matter he becomes aware of behaviour which is more proper to nature, leaves the land of the Chaldeans, and goes to Harran in Mesopotamia, that is, the frontier state between virtue and vice which is not yet purified of the deception of the senses. This is what the word Harran means. But if one looks even beyond the understanding of the good which is suitable to the senses, he will press on to the good land, that is, to the state which is free from all vice and ignorance which a faithful God points out and professes to give as a reward of virtue to those who love him.[1]

As Philo of Alexandria stressed, we must shift from the "macro-city" (macrocosm) to the "micro-city" (microcosm, that is, the self-knowledge, *gnōthi seauton*), which is represented precisely by "Abraham's migration": the emigration from Chaldea to Harran

---

[1] Maximus Confessor, *Selected Writings*, Paulist Press, 1985, p. 153. See our work, *Freemasonry: A Traditional Organization*, p. 233.

signifies the abandonment of idols (the stars) in favour of self-knowledge, which in a first phase is the knowledge of the ego, of the individual being. "Abraham's migration" is a journey of the intellect when this one renounces the consideration of the world being God, and starts to acknowledge its ego, with the body and the senses; and then, in a higher phase the intellect concentrates on itself, leaving Harran and discovering the one and only God; and Abram becomes Abraham.

Clearly, this journey is a spiritual realization – a genuine one – and not some vague moral achievement and sentimental gratification, as many Masons so proudly believe. There is no reason to be sarcastic or even to show a condescending indulgence with regard to such a belief: the modern mentality is what it is and it cannot be anything else today, which could mean that our present work is a *vox clamantis in deserto*; however, as long as the world and the cycle exist, there is no total *desertum* and nothing is for nothing.

René Guénon was asked many times what such a journey to the Center means in our modern times, what initiation and spiritual realization represent for the modern man, questions that prompted him to write a series of articles, collected later in two essential volumes, *Aperçus sur l'initiation* and *Initiation et réalisation spirituelle*; although Guénon's articles brought many clarifications and important specifications, they also created new questions, uncertainties, confusion and even opposition.

After René Guénon explained the difference between sacred and profane, between the western and eastern mentality, between esotericism and exotericism, between initiation and religion, after he highlighted the function and importance of spiritual influence and of metaphysical knowledge, after he exposed the counterfeit antitraditional, pseudo-spiritual and pseudo-initiatory societies and currents, a fissure into the modern mentality started to develop and a sincere desire for true initiation emerged in the Occident. Yet Guénon, in his articles about initiation, curtailed the enthusiasm of many, stipulating a number of restrictions and, with his uncompromising and categorical style, stated three fundamental initiatory conditions, corresponding to the *potential–virtual–actual* triad: the "qualification," composed of some inherent possibilities in the individual nature; the "transmission" of a spiritual influence (inside a traditional organization to which the neophyte has to belong), representing the "illumination" that awakens the dormant possibilities; the "inner work" through which, and with the help of some external "supports," the being passes from degree to degree along the initiatory hierarchy, ultimately reaching Liberation, Pure Consciousness and the Supreme Identity.[1]

Probably, those who studied Guénon's work (which triggered in them the quest for initiation) thought they were qualified (complying with the first condition) by their very desire to follow an initiatory path, which, of course, was a false supposition, while the third condition was too vague to worry them. However, the second of these three conditions has been a great hardship for those seeking initiation and was received with consternation. As Guénon often said, the West was completely subjugated by the profane point of view and there were no effective and accessible initiatory organizations left for the possible candidates. Masonry was the sole initiatory organization that has survived in the West, but even this one was facing difficult times; therefore, westerners who discovered they had vocation for Tradition and wanted to pass from theory to effective realization found themselves in an impossible situation.

For this reason, all kinds of subterfuges were used to circumvent the categorical conditions for initiation that René Guénon imposed.[2] Some tried to demonstrate that the Christian religion is not only exotericism, but also esotericism, and that the religious rites have initiatory powers (Schuon, Borella, etc.); others tried to change the exception into rule, stating that "spontaneous initiation" is at hand or "self-initiation" is acceptable (Evola). This unrest about initiation persisted in the present days and the confusion with regard to initiation did not diminish, on the contrary. There are opinions suggesting that

---

[1] René Guénon, *Aperçus sur l'Initiation*, Éditions Traditionnelles, 1992, p. 34.
[2] In fact, Guénon did not impose these conditions; he only exposed them.

initiation through the Internet and letters is possible, or that reading Guenon's work can replace initiation, or that initiation is somehow similar to an academic course.

The disarray surrounding initiation, fuelled also by pseudo-spiritualists and pseudo-traditionalists' phantasmagorias, is a victory of the adversary, which, as suggested by Ananda K. Coomaraswamy, found a home into man's "soul." Hence, when we tackle initiation, we should ask, paraphrasing Ramana Maharshi, "who wants to be initiated?" All too often, the desire for initiation is an impulse of the ego, which is far from being qualified in spiritual matters. For example, traditional fairy tales mention initiatory qualifications from the start, when the older brothers are rejected and only the youngest (the hero) is accepted for the journey. Such an examination is necessary to select the candidates worthy of initiation, leaving no room for egos to decide. The initiatory qualification is an indispensable condition, neglected today in the Occident, and its non-observance leads to an imaginary pseudo-initiatory journey that can sometimes have devastating effects. For this reason, normally, the entrance in an initiatory organization is possible only after the neophyte's qualifications are checked, which stresses the necessity of being affiliated to an initiatory organization (the second initiatory condition).

In fact, the attachment to an initiatory organization is not only a necessary condition, but it also designates the very initiation, in a strict etymological sense, and this attachment has to be real and effective to allow the transmission of spiritual influence[1]; as we said, it is not enough for an individual to simply want to enter an initiatory organization, but, first and foremost, he must be accepted by that organization after his initiatory qualifications are verified, and, of

---

[1] Even in the Christian exotericism this condition is a necessity, despite the fact that, today, many hypocrite and ignorant people try to excuse their absence in the church by saying that they pray directly to God. The Hesychast monk, Peter of Damascus said that "the holy Baptism and the holy Eucharist cannot be done without the priests."

course, the initiatory organization, in order to be authentic, has to be the actual keeper of spiritual influence.[1]

Yet, even assuming that a neophyte has the needed qualifications and was initiated in a genuine traditional organization, that is, he successfully fulfilled the first two conditions, he is still far away from being what is commonly known as an "initiate." An initiate is not an "adept," since he is an individual who just embarked on a spiritual path; he is a new-born to whom it was transmitted, through the initiatory rites, the spiritual influence kept and guarded by that specific organization, which corresponds to a virtual "realization." The neophyte is, even in an etymological sense, a "new plant," but at a germinal stage. If the soil is rich (that is, if, indeed, the initiatory qualifications were correctly identified), it could be expected that the planted seed in this soil (the initiation) will grow and become a glorious tree (the spiritual realization). In various traditions, the comparison with the seed or the grain allows one to understand the initiatory process. Obviously, the seed, to become a mature plant, needs favourable conditions (water, light, etc.); similarly, the initiate must travel a long way to be able to pass from initiation to spiritual realization, using all the supports he can get.

The journey from initiation to spiritual realization represents the third initiatory condition, stated by René Guénon. Too often, today, initiation is confused with spiritual realization and many think that, once initiated, they no longer have to make an effort, since, once initiated, they automatically become perfect spiritual masters. The difference between initiation and spiritual realization is significant and therefore some initiates may cover the first few stages of the journey, but they fail miserably before completion. Of course, it is easy for the ego to deceive and arrogantly suggest that the initiate is now an adept, thereby protecting its domination, while the Self is dormant.

---

[1] We cannot stress enough the paramount importance of the spiritual influence. Today, more than ever, the writings about sacred subjects ignore that the spiritual influence is a *sine qua non* in defining the traditional organizations, the initiation, the saints and the adepts, and so on.

Moreover, the ego will tempt initiatory travelers to boast that they are initiates. No true initiate, who has indeed covered a spiritual path, will ever describe himself as a perfect initiate; therefore, the neophyte who was just initiated in a genuine traditional organization and in whose heart the seed of spiritual influence was planted has no reason to speak highly of his status, but he must understand that he has just entered Janus' gate. Even in the case of some famous exceptions, there was a hiatus between "illumination" and "perfection" (understood as ascendant and descendent realization). Saint Paul, after his illumination on the road to Damascus, disappeared for three years in Arabia and only after that did he return into the world; Ramana Maharashi spent years at Arunachala and only then did he return to Tirunavamalai.

The development of the present human cycle brought us in the *Kali-Yuga*, and due to this "fall" we need initiation.[1] In the "Golden Age," there was no reason for initiation. Right now we are at the end of the *Kali-Yuga*, and that is why there are so many difficulties – some insuperable – with regard to initiation and spiritual realization. As René Guénon explained, because today the profane point of view invaded the world, the neophyte needs, more than ever, "supports" to help him travel along the initiatory path or just to aid him escape the profane. That is the role of exotericism. There are people who think that today we no longer need to participate in exoteric rites, that initiation and pure contemplation are sufficient; that is yet another illusion about initiation. Today, more than ever, exotericism is necessary as one of the supports for spiritual realization; modern individuals live a significant part of their lives overwhelmed by profane activities and the Templars could be a good example for them. The Templars filled their life with exoteric rites (sacerdotal and chivalric) as a support for their initiatory spiritual realization. Modern men are in even greater need of participating, effectively and sincerely, in exoteric rites, which will save them from the profane mentality. It is difficult to understand why today, in the West, there is such a gulf between

---

[1] René Guénon, *La Grande Triade*, Gallimard, 1980, p. 13.

exotericism and esotericism. For example, the savage opposition between the Church and Masonry is well known; the Greek-Orthodox Church and the Catholic Church have a blind repulsion for anything related to Masonry.

René Guénon, in all his work, considered that, for the West, Masonry has remained a genuine initiatory organization, despite its decadence, which means that Masonry is a true exponent of esotericism and of the initiatory domain. Of course, the problem is not the Masonry itself, but the Masons. A victim of the counter-initiatory forces, Masonry has decayed inevitably, and today, in its lodges, it is possible to achieve only virtual realization or virtual (speculative) initiation. Masonic initiation has to comply with the three conditions discussed above; obviously, nowadays, the first condition is almost inexistent. Reghini said, "not any profane may become a Mason, and not any Fellowcraft may become a Master Mason."[1] Yet, in most cases, individuals accepted in Masonry have a profane and antitraditional mentality, while the lodges have been turned into some sorts of clubs, either having moral and humanitarian objectives, or imitating the Royal Society of London. The passage through the initiatory degrees is often only a formality and occurs in a rush, whereas the many years needed for an operative mason to be promoted are forgotten. Moreover, today Masonic proselytism is on the rise, seeking to attract as many new members as possible, as if quantity matters. Guénon wrote:

> the real remedy for the present decadence of Masonry, and the only one, no doubt, would be (…) to change the Masons' mentality or at least of some of them, who are capable to understand their own initiation.[2]

For Masonry, the quality of its members is key, since the passage from initiation to spiritual realization is accomplished not with the

---

[1] Arturo Reghini, *Les Nombres Sacrés*, Archè, 1981, p. 172.
[2] René Guénon, *Études sur la Franc-Maçonnerie et le Compagnonage*, Éditions Traditionnelles, 1980, I, p. 246.

guidance of a spiritual master, but during an initiatory collective work. In an article, written at the end of his life, in 1949,[1] Guénon underlined that Masonry is a genuine initiatory organization and explained that the Masonic initiation consists of both personal effort, which is indispensable, and initiatory collective work, as the spiritual influence or the spiritual "presence" operates through the Masons of the lodge. For this "presence" to operate efficiently, it is necessary to have a qualified "frame" or "collective body," otherwise, as the spiritual center hid underground, so would the spiritual "presence," and only something virtual would remain.

Only the present degeneracy of the world allowed such a multiplication of the Masons. Of course, this is a sign of the times, since we are more and more influenced by pure quantity. Even if there were significantly fewer Masons, and miraculously the candidates were accepted based on their initiatory qualifications only, the modern world with its profane perspective would remain a great danger and a serious obstacle. Therefore, Masonry has to consider the exoteric domain and Masons must participate in exoteric rites, the way operative Masons and the Templars participated in the past. The *Old Charges* clearly stipulated that an operative Mason had to go to church and follow the religious rites. Also, the pilgrimages, which in the past were part of the Royal Art, should represent one of the objectives of any Mason. But how many occidental Masons accomplish today such a pilgrimage? How many Masons understand the fundamental importance of spiritual "supports" for their initiatory journey, made possible by Masonic initiation?

What we are saying here does not intend to direct the Mason (or any other initiate) toward an illusory eso-exotericism. René Guénon explained as clearly as possible the difference between exotericism and esotericism; he also showed the correlation between these two domains, exotericism being the skin and esotericism the kernel. It would be a mistake, therefore, to think that, today, an initiation could

---

[1] *Travail initiatique collectif et "présence" spirituelle*, in *Initiation et Réalisation spirituelle*, Éditions Traditionnelles, 1980.

disregard the exoteric rites or that exotericism is sufficient for perfect spiritual realization.

The symbolism of the "golden chain" (*Aurea catena Homeri*), mentioned by Homer,[1] is well known, and so is the symbolism of the "chain of light," mentioned by Dionysius the Areopagite.[2] If we consider, from one point of view, this chain as being the spiritual influence of a non-human origin, which operates through both exoteric and esoteric rites, we will be able to understand the difference between the nature of the exoteric and the esoteric domains, considering that, in the former, the communication with the supra-individual states of the being occurs by pulling the golden chain and assimilating its vibrations, while in the latter the initiate climbs the golden chain higher and higher, actually taking possession of each link, one after another. Both the exoteric and the esoteric rites carry spiritual influences (and not only psychical ones), but as we see, the difference between these two types is fundamental. On the other hand, the exoteric rites allow us to be attached to the golden chain and to participate in its vibrations, which already is a significant gain. It is true that esotericism is not limited by any exotericism, and Masonry is considered to have a universal character, but, in a natural way, the esoteric domain has to be covered and protected by an exoteric skin, which represents a starting point.[3] From this "starting point," located symbolically on the circumference of a circle, the neophyte "enters" the lodge, "travels" along a radius, reaching the center of the circle, and from there rises along the vertical axis: these are precisely the three steps of Masonic initiation (corresponding to the three degrees, Entered Apprentice, Fellowcraft, Master Mason) called *Initiation – Passing – Raising*.

---

[1] *Iliad* VIII, 18-26.
[2] *The Divine Names* III.1. See also *The Everlasting Sacred Kernel*, Rose-Cross Books, 2002, pp. 13-4.
[3] Even though Masonry has this universal nature, it does not mean that a Mason could shift from a traditional form to another during his initiatory journey.

There is, though, a major "alarm" regarding the survival of a traditional organization in the present days. The representatives of the Church ask, with genuine bewilderment, why someone would need an "initiation" when there is "salvation" through religion; why would someone need duplicated rites and a redundant path to God. On the other hand, the Mason could ask the same questions: why someone would need religious rites and religious participation, when this someone already is initiated in a traditional form; even worse, we see Masons having no idea why initiation and spiritual realization are really necessary and thinking of initiation in a distressing profane way.

In fact, what is lost for the majority of Masons is the "traditional spirit," and this is the main difference between what we call *Oriens* and *Occidens*. For us, the "traditional spirit" is the central and essential characteristic of a genuine Masonry and of an authentic Chivalry, and our goal is to unveil this "traditional spirit" as the indispensable quality for an initiatory organization.

René Guénon said:

> *L'esprit traditionnel, de quelque forme qu'il se revête, est partout et toujours le même au fond; les formes diverses, qui sont particulièrement adaptées à telles ou telles conditions mentales, à telles ou telles circonstances de temps et de lieu, ne sont que des expressions d'une seule et même vérité; mais il faut pouvoir se placer dans l'ordre de l'intellectualité pure pour découvrir cette unité fondamentale sous leur apparente multiplicité.*[1]

This "traditional spirit" must be assimilated if we want to really understand the Free-Masonry as a traditional organization, and therefore we have to learn the true meaning of the Royal Art, of the Templars' Treasure, of money, of the art of measuring, of the Consciousness and of the Art of Love.

---

[1] René Guénon, *Recueil*, Rose-Cross Books, 2012, p. 4.

CHAPTER II

THE ROYAL ART

At the end of his work, *The Monarchy*, Dante concluded:

> Perciò l'uomo ha avuto bisogno di una duplice guida in vista di un duplice fine: cioè del sommo Pontefice, per guidare il genere umano secondo gli insegnamenti della rivelazione all vita eterna, e dell'Imperatore, per indirizzare il genere umano secondo gli insegnamenti filosofici alla felicità temporale. ... Cesare dunque si rivolga a Pietro con quel rispetto che il figlio primogenito deve al padre: affinché, illuminato dalla grazia della luce del padre, possa irradiarla con più efficacia sul mondo terreno, al quale è stato preposto da Colui solo che è guida di tutte le cose spirituali e temporali.[1]

Dante describes without equivocation the hierarchical relationship that must exist between the spiritual authority and the temporal power: the worldly king is the son, the pope is the father,[2] and both serve and obey the supreme authority, God. Dante also suggested that, initially,

---

[1] Dante, *Monarchia*, Garzanti, 1999, pp. 145-147. "Wherefore a twofold directive agent was necessary to man, in accordance with the twofold end; the Supreme Pontiff to lead the human race to life eternal by means of revelation, and the Emperor to guide it to temporal felicity by means of philosophic instruction... Wherefore let Caesar honor Peter as a first-born son should honor his father, so that, refulgent with the light of paternal grace, he may illumine with greater radiance the earthly sphere over which he has been set by Him who alone is Ruler of all things spiritual and temporal."

[2] For the modern mentality, these specific words "king" and "pope" are scary, which only proves how troubled this mentality is.

these two branches were united in the Lord of the World, whose model for Christianity is Jesus Christ.

In his *Le Roi du Monde*, René Guénon explained in detail this archetypal hierarchy (the Lord of the World, the Priest, and the King), stressing that these three represent, first and foremost, cosmic functions and universal principles, and they can be found on earth only as applications and projections; in other words, any earthly king is merely a "trace" of the *principial* King and can be identified with the *principle* only if he is able to surpass his individual state. This situation represents an "ideal" case, which functioned without too many errors in the first ages of the present cycle, but, at the end of *Kali-Yuga*, it appears like a heavenly perfection, and for the medieval Occident only Christ was a true illustration of the Lord of the World.[1] The conflict between the emperor and papacy (the Investiture Controversy for example) in Christian Europe, was a vivid expression of the confusion created by this title of "emperor," but this revolt against the papal authority unveils not only a confusion of titling, but also a serious misunderstanding about the normal hierarchy of functions.

Guénon wrote that the supreme function (the Lord of the World or the Emperor of the World, which comprised the two powers, sacerdotal and temporal) was absent in the social organization of medieval Europe,[2] and, indeed, the emperor was only a king endowed with the temporal power, which meant that he was under the spiritual authority of papacy. Even though some commentators tried to present Dante as a promoter of the "imperial idea," an attentive reading of his work leaves little doubt: Dante was in favour of a normal hierarchy,

---

[1] At the beginning, when man lived in a godly unity, castes and functions were not yet differentiated, and there was a "spontaneous" high spirituality (René Guénon, *Autorité spirituelle et pouvoir temporel*, Éditions Didier et Richard, 1930, pp. 14-15, 17-18). Only later, with the evolvement of the cycle, the unity was broken and the two powers, sacerdotal and temporal, were separated, with their two Arts; they were still in harmony and complementing each other, but in *Kali-Yuga* we see the opposition growing and the revolt spreading. However, there was revolt even in the "Golden Age" as we mentioned in our *Free-Masonry*.

[2] René Guénon, *Le Roi du Monde*, Gallimard, 1981, p. 17.

where the temporal (or "imperial") power would be subordinated to the papal authority, and his support for Emperor Henry VII of Luxembourg – who mysteriously died at the time when the Order of the Temple was destroyed[1] – does not represent anything other than his support for a unified Christian traditional society at a temporal level.[2]

During the Roman Empire, the *Imperator* was also *Pontifex Maximus*,[3] that is, *Dominus Mundi*,[4] which means that not only was he above all worldly kings (as interpreted later), but he also united the two powers (*rex* and *sacerdos*), as well as *Oriens* and *Occidens*. As Christian traditional society developed, kings and emperors battled to regain the fullness of the Roman emperor's function, without legitimacy, since the spiritual authority rightfully belonged to papacy.[5] Moreover, for an individual to actually "realize" this high function, he would have had to abandon the profane viewpoint and fulfil a complete spiritual initiation, "royal" and "sacerdotal," but it is well known that even Roman emperors did not qualify for the function, since their "nature" was frequently too corrupt, considering the times – that is, the end of *Kali-Yuga*. The same is true for the royal and sacerdotal functions in the post-Roman era (in Europe), where any individual designated to perform these functions

---

[1] René Guénon, *L'ésoterisme de Dante*, Gallimard, 1981, p. 55.
[2] Dante's animosity regarding some popes refers to their error of intervening in the temporal domain, instead of shepherding the spiritual one. The same way Dante put his hopes in Emperor Henry VII, Shakespeare and other "Hermeticists" and "Rosicrucians," after the disappearance of the Virgin-Queen Elizabeth, were hopeful about Prince Henry, the son of King James I, who, unfortunately, died when he was only 19; the hopes shifted then towards Henry's sister, Elizabeth, who married Frederick V, the Elector Palatine (Yates considered this wedding an illustration of the Rosicrucian Alchemical Wedding), and who triggered the start of the Thirty Years War (at the end of which the last Rose-Cross left Europe). See Frances A. Yates, *Shakespeare's Last Plays: A New Approach*, Routledge and Kegan Paul, 1975, pp. 17 ff. and Frances A. Yates, *The Rosicrucian Enlightenment*, Routledge and Kegan Paul.
[3] Guénon, *Le Roi*, p. 17.
[4] Frances A. Yates, *Astraea*, Penguin Books, 1975, p. 5.
[5] The distinction between the two powers was already stated by Christ: "So give back to Caesar what is Caesar's, and to God what is God's" (*Matthew* 22:21). In Islam, there was a strong tendency to surpass this distinction.

should have first completed the "royal way" (the *Lesser Mysteries*, in king's case) or the "sacerdotal way" (the *Greater Mysteries* in the priest's case); however, all too often there was a sizeable discrepancy between the individual as such and the function he was supposed to execute, and rarely did anyone complete a real initiation or even a virtual one.[1]

Although we mentioned two initiations, a "sacerdotal" and a "royal" one, these are not two independent ways, as some people may think, since the latter is subordinated to the former, both being harmonically integrated in a supreme unity,[2] which means that, for a tradition to be regular and complete, it has to contain both initiations in its esoteric kernel, that is, the *Lesser Mysteries* ("royal initiation") and the *Greater Mysteries* ("sacerdotal initiation"), these two representing not two separate ways but two stages of the same initiation.[3] For the modern mentality, it is almost impossible to actually grasp the real significance of anything related to the sacred domain, and, after the end of the Thirty Years War, the deterioration, deformation, and disorientation of this mentality, together with an actual weakening and distortion of the brain, evolved so quickly that it is hard to believe that, in such a short time, the Christian traditional society was not only forgotten but maliciously and falsely labeled as the "dark ages."

The *Lesser Mysteries* refer to the development of the possibilities of the human state considered in its entirety, and seek to restore the "primordial state"; the *Greater Mysteries* manage the realization of the supra-individual or supra-human states, leading to the final Liberation, to a supreme state, devoid of limitations and conditions; as we saw, the first objective is related to the royal function and the second to the sacerdotal function. When we say "realization" we mean, in Guénon's terms, taking possession of a state or states, an actual seizing, not like

---

[1] If, at the beginning of this human cycle, the "nature" of the individual was in concert with his function and no initiation was needed, at the end of the same cycle, in the majority of cases, there was a flagrant disagreement between "nature" and "function"; however, if there was a discrepancy, the "function" continued to be valid and maintain its powers.
[2] René Guénon, *Aperçus sur l'initiation*, Éditions Traditionnelles, 1992, pp. 254 ff.
[3] *Ibid.*, p. 248.

acquiring a new house, iPod, and so on, but like being born again with a new consciousness, this taking into possession implies in fact a gradual expansion of the consciousness, first "horizontally," then "vertically," with the help of faculties that are asleep in the common man.[1] In addition, the sacerdotal and royal initiations allowed a qualified being to assimilate the principles of a sum of applications contained by the corresponding functions, and these applications were known under the concise names of "sacerdotal art" and "royal art."[2]

The domain of the *Greater Mysteries* is "metaphysical" or "supra-natural," while the domain of the *Lesser Mysteries* is "physical" or "natural,"[3] which explains without equivocation the responsibilities of the spiritual authority and of the temporal power. In traditional India, the guardians of the "sacerdotal art" were the *Brâhmans*, whereas the *Kshatriyas* administered the "royal art"; however, there was also a third caste with *dwija* (twice-born) members, and these *Vaishyas* had access to the *Lesser Mysteries* and to the "royal art," which allowed them to establish close contacts with the *Kshatriyas*, even though, in their case, the initiation was based on practising a métier.[4] It is important to note, in the special case of the métier of builders, in a traditional rather than a profane or decayed society, these artisans were building temples and cathedrals and their initiatory métier was part of the "sacerdotal art."[5]

---

[1] We can understand, at least theoretically, that for the modern man, with a distorted mind, the necessary faculties are often not only asleep, but completely obliterated.
[2] *Ibid.*, pp. 249-250.
[3] Again, we have to abandon the modern mentality if we want to understand the words "physics" and "nature" as they were used by Aristotle; they signify the formal world, the cosmos, and the individual states.
[4] For that reason the expression "royal art" was used and kept till today by Masonry (*ibid.*, p. 251).
[5] See René Guénon, *Formes traditionnelles et cycles cosmiques*, Gallimard, 1970, p. 96: *l'expression de "lieu très éclairé et très régulier," que cette dernière [Masonry] a conservé, semble bien être un souvenir de l'ancienne science sacerdotale qui présidait à la construction des temples.* See also René Guénon, *Symboles fondamentaux de la Science sacrée*, Gallimard, 1980, pp. 262-263, where Guénon mentions the *Royal Arch Masonry*, with its initiatory "exaltation" *from square to arch*, that is, from "royal" to "sacerdotal" art, even though in the end the "sacerdotal" aspect vanished, as a sign of the times. In our *Free-Masonry: A Traditional Organization*, we suggested the direct involvement of the

The fundamental initiatory Masonic formulas represent precisely a heritage transmitted by the "sacerdotal art." From a Hesychastic perspective, sin is defined as "the scattering of the soul's energy, i.e. of the *nous*, to things and its separation from the heart,"[1] and Meister Eckhart said about the purified soul: "The soul is purified in the body in order to reassemble what was scattered"; in Masonry, the task of the Masters consists of "spreading the light and gathering what is scattered."[2] This gathering of what was scattered is achieved in the Center, when the *Lesser Mysteries* are completed and when all the differences will disappear, which means that all the various functions will be reintegrated to their primary unity and the "royal art" will be absorbed into the "sacerdotal art," which will be *The Art* purely and simply.

We could say, from the perspective of the cosmic cycles theory, that, before or at the beginning of the "Golden Age," man, in a total possession of his state (considered in its entirety), was at the same time in possession of the sum total of the possibilities corresponding to all the functions, in a "complicated" mode, before their differentiation. The birth of the various functions occurred, together with the "fall" from the "primordial state," in a posterior and inferior phase, when human being lost the possession of some of these possibilities, but still was conscious of their existence, and only when the decline reached a critical point, this consciousness or conscience was lost and a initiation became necessary allowing man to recover, together with this consciousness, the "primordial state" for which this consciousness was an inherent characteristic.[3]

---

spiritual authority in the building of medieval cathedrals. Finally, as Hocart said, "in India every occupation is a priesthood" (A. M. Hocart, *Caste*, Methuen & Co., 1950, p. 16).

[1] Hierotheos, *Orthodox Spirituality*, Birth of the Theotokos Monastery, 2002, p. 35.

[2] Guénon, *Symboles fondamentaux*, p. 301: *rassembler ce qui est épars*.

[3] By initiation and spiritual realization, the neophyte becomes "conscious" of the "primordial state" and its possibilities, which allows him to consciously participate in all its operations and applications, since he now retrieved the integral and omnipresent consciousness, which is incomparable with regard to what the modern man calls "consciousness." We intend to converse about the consciousness

The initiatory process does not stop with the restoration of the "primordial state,"¹ because the *Lesser Mysteries* are just a preamble of the *Greater Mysteries*, and therefore genuine initiation implies ascension beyond the origin of humanity to the very origin of the spiritual influence or *barakah*.² As a result, questioning about the historical source of an initiation, together with that of (traditional, evidently) arts, métiers, and sciences, is pointless, since all these are united in the "primordial state," beyond any differentiation, and, from there, they are fastened to the divine sphere, because only in this way each of them is able, in its proper domain, to consciously collaborate to perfect the design of the Great Architect of the Universe.³

In every traditional civilization, all human activities are considered essentially derive from the divine and immutable principles, which underlines the immense and irreconcilable difference between the sacred and profane mentalities, and explains how the arts, métiers, and

---

separately, but it is important to mention here that some modern authors seem to have no clue about what consciousness really is, and they continue to believe in what modern psychology teaches them about this notion.

¹ The objective of the religious "salvation" is also the "primordial state," yet mostly understood as a salvation of the posthumous human being from re-entering the *samsâra*, and because this salvation is offered to everybody, regardless of qualifications, there are elements of passivity and of "unconsciousness" that, with the decline of the cycle, became increasingly obstacles and adversities.

² *Nous traduisons par "influence spirituelle" le mot hébreu et arabe* barakah; *le rite de l'"imposition des mains" est un des modes les plus habituels de transmission de la* barakah, *et aussi de production de certains effets, de guérison notamment, au moyen de celle-ci* (Guénon, *Autorité spirituelle*, 1930, p. 80). Indeed, Guénon stressed, there is no veritable initiation, even of an inferior or elementary rank, without the intervention of a "non-human" element, which is precisely the spiritual influence regularly communicated with the initiatory rites (René Guénon, *Mélanges*, Gallimard, 1976, p. 77). This statement is fundamental and indispensable to grasp, even superficially, what initiation and sacred rites represent.

³ Guénon, *Aperçus sur l'initiation*, pp. 251-252, *Mélanges*, pp. 76-77. We insist: the term "consciousness," used by Guénon, has almost nothing to do with what is understood today from a moral or psychological point of view. In fact, as Michel Vâlsan showed, Guénon used this term as corresponding to the Sanskrit *chit*, *chaitanya*, and which have several meanings, including "intelligence," "intellect," "knowledge," "memory," "thinking" (Michel Vâlsan, *Remarques préliminaires sur l'Intellect et la Conscience*, ET 372-373, 1962).

sciences could provide an initiatory support through the Royal Art. In a traditional civilization, the human activity is "transformed" and, instead of being reduced to what is corporeal and most superficial (so characteristic for the profane viewpoint), it is integrated in the traditional trend and represents for the perpetrator a means to participate in the Tradition.[1] In the Christian Middle Ages, for example, all the activities and gestures, even the most common ones, were "religious" or part of the "religious" mentality (requiring no detailed or analytical explanation), since, in a traditional society, the sacredness was not "lived" in a "digital" and quantitative way, but continuously and qualitatively. Religion or, beyond a particular society, tradition did not occupy a specific place, without relation to the daily activities, as it happens today, when even the most diligent "churchgoers" separate their religious gestures from their everyday actions. For traditional man, social life was part of the sacredness and nothing was viewed as profane; thus, there was no difference between "artisan" and "artist," both representing a genuine *artifex*.[2]

Consequently, the diverse activities and métiers were entitled to constitute supports for an authentic initiation, supports that operated effectively in a traditional society where, in comparison with today's Great Disarray, each individual carried out a function, activity or métier that was in full concert with his own nature and inner vocation, with his "self," and so long as this accordance existed he could contribute to the natural order of the universal manifestation.

During the evolvement of the present cycle, the castes emerged precisely because of the need to accord the "function" with the

---

[1] As René Guénon and Ananda K. Coomaraswamy stressed, "the distinctive characteristic of a traditional society is order" and *Ce que nous appelons une civilisation normale, c'est une civilisation qui repose sur des principes, au vrai sens de ce terme, et où tout est ordonné et hiérarchisé en conformité avec ces principes, de telle sorte que tout y apparaît comme l'application et le prolongement d'une doctrine purement intellectuelle ou métaphysique en son essence; c'est ce que nous voulons dire aussi quand nous parlons d'une civilisation traditionnelle* (Ananda K. Coomaraswamy, *Traditional Art and Symbolism*, Princeton Univ. Press, 1986, p. 290, René Guénon, *Orient et Occident*, Éditions Didier et Richard, 1930, pp. 235-236).

[2] Guénon, *Mélanges*, pp. 71-72.

"nature," because different "natures" had to correspond to different "functions"; heredity played a secondary role, but normally a métier was transmitted from father to son, and so was the royal function, which did not mean that the idea of "caste" was based on heredity but on each person's "vocation," which explains how the Dalai-Lama is selected; especially at the end of the cycle this normality was lost and the heredity was forcibly imposed, regardless the "nature" of the individual. In a regular traditional society, only individuals with the appropriate "nature" were qualified to be builders, or priests, or flutists; and only then did an activity or a métier constitute a support for an actual initiation, this one translating, after all, the inner "nature" of the neophyte.

Something similar took place in a sacred wedding. Through initiation, that is, through the transmission of spiritual influence, some latent possibilities hiding in the being's inner self were awaken; this transmission used rites that had as support a métier or an activity. By awakening these possibilities and by their effective and complete realization, the being assimilated and attained the integral consciousness and actual and effective knowledge of the principles corresponding to the activity or the métier used as support, becoming perfectly conscious of and actually knowing the "secrets" of the métier. Thus, if the initiatory lore and knowledge emerged, for the initiate, when practising the activity or métier used as support, this support-art, in its turn, would become the domain of application of this knowledge, which assured a perfect wedding between the interior and the exterior.[1] Likewise, through royal initiation, a knight arrived – by a magisterial control of the chivalric art – at a conscious realization of what he had until then performed somehow instinctively (because of his "nature").[2] Through a suitable initiation, the traditional arts and sciences reached perfection when the initiate became conscious of them as applications of the principles.

The traditional arts and crafts gradually connected the initiate to the

---

[1] *Ibid.*, p. 75.
[2] Only now the qualificative "magisterial" makes sense.

initiatory knowledge, following an ascending journey that, once accomplished, allowed its applications to be perfect and exact arts, which explains expressions like "sacerdotal art" and "royal art" with regard to the *Lesser Mysteries* and the *Greater Mysteries*,[1] since the initiation is no *Deus ex machina*, but an art of managing the spiritual influences, based on positive scientific laws and rigorous technical rules.[2]

For medieval Christian traditional society, the Royal Art is the art that has to be considered first, even though we should be aware of the symbolism found in Dante's *Divine Comedy*, and of the hermetic expressions *albedo* and *rubedo* as the main phases of the Great Work; therefore, without discarding the possibility of an initiation into the *Greater Mysteries*, we ought to view Earthly Paradise as the highest degree accessible to medieval Christian esotericism and as a realization of the Royal Art. After the disappearance of the Order of the Temple, the initiatory degree called Rose-Cross also targeted the accomplishment of the *Lesser Mysteries*; the Rosicrucian initiation, inspired by the Rose-Cross, was attached to Christian Hermeticism, which belonged to the domain of the Royal Art. Furthermore, Alchemy, which could be defined as the "technique" of Hermeticism, was indeed a "royal art," being close to *Kshatriya's* "nature."[3] The pilgrimage also, from an initiatory viewpoint, belonged to the Royal Art, the initiatory journeys (as those found in fairy tales) referring to the

---

[1] *Ibid.*, p. 104.
[2] Guénon, *Aperçus sur l'initiation*, p. 104. For Coomaraswamy, the "royal art" is precisely *karma yoga* (Ananda K. Coomaraswamy, *Autorité Spirituelle et Pouvoir Temporel*, Archè, 1985, p. 124).
[3] Guénon, *Aperçus sur l'initiation*, pp. 259, 262. About Hermeticism as *Ars Regia*, see also Julius Evola, *Le Mystère du Graal*, Éditions Traditionnelles, 1984, p. 224; however, Evola, as usual, distorted the traditional point of view, considering the Royal Art to be strongly connected to "heroic reintegration" (p. 226). For Evola, "*Ars Regia*, the royal art, proves the existence of a secret initiatory current, with virile, 'heroic' and solar characteristics" (p. 234); in addition, Evola understood neither Masonry nor the Christian quality of the Templars.

Kshatriya's domain.[1] Finally, Free-Masonry, as we know it today, kept the expression "royal art" to describe the Masonic Art.[2]

---

[1] René Guénon, *Études sur la Franc-Maçonnerie et le Compagnonage*, Éditions Traditionnelles, 1980, I, p. 59.
[2] Guénon, *Aperçus sur l'initiation*, p. 251.

CHAPTER III

THE ROYAL INVESTITURE

The various applications of the Royal Art, whether pilgrimage, the Orders of Chivalry or Freemasonry, the Rose-Croix or Hermeticism, are based on ritual actions of divine origin; exoteric rites, as well as fairy tales that are relics of the Royal Art, may suggest, by analogy, what the metaphysical rites or the initiation rites could have been as essence of this Art. As the name indicates, the rite involves a perfectly orderly set of actions that follows some immutable rules, which requires an authentic code of precepts that must be fulfilled for rites to be effective. The rites observe an unambiguous hierarchy, the metaphysical and the initiatory ones[1] being situated at the supreme level; nonetheless, the rites, having an eminently symbolic nature, allow for their analogue transposition from one domain to another, but there must be a clear distinction between metaphysical, religious and social rites, each being effective in their own field and cannot be mixed randomly.

The rites are vehicles (Skr. *vâhana*) of superior influences through which the man's life is linked, directly or indirectly, to the Principle,[2]

---

[1] The main purpose of the initiatory rites is the inner purification of the neophyte, where the "purification of ignorance" is fundamental; however, the initiatory rites are only adjuvants, the personal effort and the metaphysical *gnosis* representing the principal part.

[2] Generally speaking, rites connect the being to the levels above that belong to other states of existence, and even though this is not always a conscious communication, it still operates, using some subtle modalities of the individual, modalities to which the majority of human beings cannot transfer their centre of consciousness anymore.

without them humankind becoming a decayed society, severed from the divine and sacred realm.[1] The authentic rites were present in all the domains of traditional civilizations, both exoteric and esoteric, and this common characteristic was the consequence of a "non-human" element present in all these domains.

Initiatory rites, of all the rites, present for us a special interest; they, by their nature, are suitable for a select few, while the exoteric rites are meant for the public at large, and this, not because of some jealous, human, arrogant and selfish rules, but because they cannot be fully operative and effective without a properly qualified receiver. Take, for example, Masonry today: even though the initiatory rites are still operating, many of the receivers are completely unqualified subjects and therefore the force of rites is wasted; as a result, the "initiatory secret" is not even close to what the profane world foolishly believes it is.

All rites are necessarily and naturally made of symbols[2]; the gestures made, the words spoken, the diagrams traced, all the elements of the rites, without exception, are symbolical, and we could see the rites as symbols "put into operation,"[3] in action, every ritual gesture being an "active" symbol.[4]

The rites – we said – observe an unambiguous hierarchy, based on a "non-human" element as a common characteristic, which explains why the modern opinion claiming the existence of two separate and

---

[1] We could say that without rites there is no initiation, because rites constitute the essential element in transmitting spiritual influence and attaching the neophyte to the unbroken initiatory chain (René Guénon, *Aperçus sur l'Initiation*, Éditions Traditionnelles, 1992, p. 109).

[2] Guénon, *ibid.*, pp. 115-119.

[3] We prefer the word "operation" (even though in English it has lost its essential meaning), because it is related to Hermetical *Great Work*, *Grand Oeuvre* (Lat. *opus / opera*).

[4] See, as examples, the *mudrâs* of the Hindu tradition and the *grips* of the Western initiatory organizations. The wedding rite-symbol represents what René Guénon called the "theory of gesture," a theory that has to be understood from a traditional perspective, that is, as one that is essentially a realization, an operation by which the spiritual influence is "fixed" within the being, ready to operate an initiatory transmutation.

independent initiations, a Sacerdotal and a Royal one,[1] of equal value, is an obvious error, generated by a human factor, confused and tangled in its egocentric ropes; in fact, they are two different hierarchical degrees of one and the same initiation. *In principio*, before the castes emerged, the two functions, Sacerdotal and Royal, did not exist separately and distinctively, but were united beyond castes in their common principle, the Lord of the World. Only later in humankind's terrestrial cycle did castes become visible and, with them, the two functions ranked not artificially and arbitrarily, but in accord to the inner nature of human being, *Brâhmanas* being superior to *Kshatriyas*, as knowledge is above action and metaphysics above physics, and consequently the *Greater Mysteries* (the Sacerdotal initiation) are on top of the *Lesser Mysteries* (the Royal initiation), which means that any tradition must contain both degrees of initiation in its esoteric aspect, in order to be complete and regular.

Consequently, the Royal Art corresponds to the *Lesser Mysteries* and to the cosmological doctrines, while the Sacerdotal Art is associated to the *Greater Mysteries* and to the pure metaphysical level. As René Guénon pointed out, Hermeticism, for example, cannot represent an exhaustive traditional doctrine, because it envisages a cosmologic knowledge,[2] which explains why its exoteric or esoteric rites often allude to the doctrine of cosmic cycles and to the change of cycles, not to say that the initiatory symbolism is in perfect accord with the cosmologic one; therefore the initiatory dictum, found also in the Masonic ritual, "to gather what is scattered" is applicable to the cosmologic process, because to pass from one cycle to another means to gather the manifestation in the Center (Principle) (the "complication," Brahma's inspiration), and then to produce it again (expiration, explication), to "scatter" it.[3]

---

[1] The outer expression of the Royal initiation is the Royal investiture, part of the Royal Art and indispensable for the Chivalry to function normally and regularly.
[2] *Ibid.*, p. 261.
[3] However, considering the total harmony that must exist, in Hermeticism there are two phases, *albedo* and *rubedo*, which are reflections of the *Lesser* and *Greater Mysteries*.

The Royal initiation, like in the case of Râma, is a wedding between the royal neophyte, the knight, and the Knowledge, Sophia, *Madonna Intelligenza*,[1] this "feminine" characteristic reflecting the "feminine" quality of the Royal Art itself, as illustrated in the Hindu tradition, where we find a symbolic wedding between the priest and king, with the priest as husband and the king as wife[2]; the royal initiate, feminine in rapport to *Sacerdotium*, needs a target of a similar nature, which will be the Virgin, the Widow or the Bride.[3]

Accordingly, the "wedding" between the *Sacerdotium* and *Regnum* illustrates the Royal Investiture, operating the transmission of the "divine mandate" to the king, and only because of this "wedding," the king is able to be the guarantor of harmony, fertility and wealth in his kingdom.[4] No doubt, the deep meanings of Royal Investiture can be found in all traditional societies, because the idea of universal sovereignty, reflection of the Lord of the World's function, and of

---

[1] See our *Free-Masonry: A Traditional Organization*, Rose-Cross Books, 2010, p. 251. In the *Râmâyana*, Sîtâ is the divine Maiden, Sophia, and *Madonna Intelligenza*.
[2] Ananda K. Coomaraswamy, *Spiritual Authority and Temporal Power in the Indian Theory of Government*, Munshiram Manoharlal Publishers, 1978, p. 23.
[3] Ananda K. Coomaraswamy compared the king with a woman and explained that the main common characteristic is that "both are 'devoted'"; the king is a *bhaktâ*. "It is by no means an accident, or merely historical 'development' that 'the doctrine of *bhakti*' should have been so little emphasized in the Upanishads and so much in BG. For it is the Way of Gnosis (*jnânamârga*) that pertains to the Brâhman and the emotional Way of Devotion (*bhaktimârga*), which is also a Way of Sacrificial action (*karmamârga*), that pertains to the King. The relation of a vassal to a feudal lord, which is also that of the *Regnum* to the *Sacerdotium*, is essentially one of 'loyalty' (a word that better than 'devotion,' perhaps, conveys the meaning of *bhakti*), and that is precisely the relation of the woman to the man... We can see all this as clearly in the connection of European Chivalry (*kshatram*) with devotional mysticism, and in the corresponding Sufi devotional literature, with its 'Fidèles d'Amour,' as in India" (*ibid.*, p. 64).
[4] Of course, the king's "divinity" is not his own as man, "but that of the principle that overrules him and of which he is not the reality, but the living image, instrument and puppet" (*ibid.*, p. 84); only because of that, we can say that the fertility and the life of the kingdom depends on the king.

supra-human origin, is fundamental, unique and the same regardless of nation, geographical area or time.[1]

For the modern mentality, the notion of king, like many others, has lost any traditional meaning and often even the modern kings no longer understand their function[2]; the only possible way to decipher its sense is the initiatory and traditional perspective, which means that we must refer to the metaphysical point of view, recognizing the primacy, eternity and immutability of the supreme Principle, One-without-the-second, and only then, accepting that the world itself is a pure nothing, that what makes the world exist is the Principle from where it receives all reality, will we comprehend the imperial function.

The Lord (Emperor) of the World is the Principle's projection in the Center of the World, being one and unique. With the decline of humanity, the Primordial Tradition has separated into secondary traditions, all valid, and so the Emperor has multiplied into kings and emperors, similar to the apex of a cone, which has projected itself in the center of the base circle, and this center, in turn, projected itself in innumerable points on the circumference. The king is, therefore, an image of the Principle for a specific society, he is, similarly to the Principle that guarantees its legitimacy, the one making the world function, and for this reason, in various traditional societies, the king was considered the guarantor of harmony, wealth, and health, the regulator of the seasons, of rain and heat, he was the one who ensured a good harvest; the king supervised the calendar, the rites and all the sacred elements of life, for the king, as stated by the Hindu and Chinese traditions, is the pivot or pole in the center of the wheel that spins because of his beneficial presence.

---

[1] "The sky does not have two suns, the earth does not have two sovereigns," it is said in the Far-Eastern tradition.
[2] "The ideal king is a Dharmarâja, an incarnation of justice, and the fertility and prosperity of the country depend upon the king's virtue... Thus, in Iranian mythology, earthly kingship (divine right) is plainly established and dependent upon a kingly glory, *hvarena*, 'made by Ahura Mazda,' and overshadowing every legitimate king" (Ananda K. Coomaraswamy, *Yakshas*, Oxford University Press, 1993, p. 115).

Moreover, the king and his people were one, for people represented the multiplicity emerged from One, but intimately connected with It, as the waves are related to the sea itself; therefore, if the king was healthy, people prospered, but if the king became unjust or wicked, the people decayed and the kingdom died. The rites performed by the king, including those related to his funeral, comprised the whole population, for the king was the whole people[1]; suffering and desolation occurred either when the king forgot that he is subject to the divine authority, becoming a rebel, or when people forgot that they are multiplicity linked to Unity and, like Medusa's snakes, broke away from the king.

The Lord of the World relates to *dêva-yâna*, the way or the gate through which he receives divine grace, the heavenly blessing and the supreme approval to reign over a new *Manvantara*, and this scenario should be present in all the traditions to give legitimacy to the royal power; therefore, the king is somehow identified with the gate, the cave or the house, the Egyptian "pharaoh," for example, suggesting a "big house" (that is, palace) and the Turkish "Sublime Porte" (*Bâbiâli*, "High Gate") representing the sultan and his empire. Nonetheless, the name "pharaoh" never served as title for the Egyptian king, because he was usually called "Horus Mighty Bull, Beloved of Maat," "Lord of the two ladies (the twofold country)," "Son of Ra," which illustrates his divinity and his divine paternity, and the fact that he is an *avatâra* by birth[2] and invested by the gods as Lord of the World.[3] The pharaoh was the Sun, the vicar (Latin *vicarius* = "substitute, deputy") of the Principle on earth, the successor of Osiris; the Egyptian king was not an individual, but the embodiment of a principle, of a divine function

---

[1] For the ancient Turks, the killing of the sovereign in battle meant the death of people; hence, the old chivalrous tradition to bring the fight only to the leaders, one's defeat signifying the surrender of all army. In addition, let us not forget that the king is identical to the standard, so if the flag was captured that meant the "death" of the king and his people.
[2] He was considered an *avatâra* of Amon, with the blessing of Ra; his birth was identified with the birth of a god.
[3] Like Zeus, the new-born king was nursed with milk by the Hator cows.

manifested in the world, each pharaoh being attached to the unbroken chain of kings, heirs of the legendary Menes, through this chain the double power, sacerdotal and temporal was transmitted.[1] The pharaoh's Royal investiture meant a change of cycles, at which time the world was regenerated, the chaos that accompanied the death of the old king being transformed in order and equilibrium: "The whole country, enjoy! The happiest times arrived. A master rose over all the land... the overflows are abundant, the days are long, the night hours are accurate, the moon returns regularly"; the world's harmony was directly dependent on the king's condition, and therefore, because at the end of the cycle the king turned into a dragon while the manifestation fell under the power of infernal forces (fed by the most inferior possibilities of existence, which are now prevailing), periodically, like the Cretan king Minos, the pharaoh celebrated the Jubilee feast (*Heb-Sed*), when he died and was born again. The pharaoh was priest and king: the priests officiated in temples only delegated by him; the pharaoh fulfilled the rites; he founded the temples, for gods invested him with the universal authority.[2]

We insist on presenting the example of Egyptian royalty because there is a strong misconception, generated by the modern mentality, with respect to people's lives in ancient Egypt, because the profane historians depicted a false image of an absolute king oppressing a population of slaves, forced to build pyramids. In fact, there was nothing profane in the Egyptian life, and like in other traditional

---

[1] Similarly, in ancient Greece: "At the head of this company of priests and priestesses was the august figure of the high priest, the representative of Zeus on earth and the living embodiment of the god... As the representative and human embodiment of Zeus, the priest-king of Dodona naturally lived in the Prytaneum, the 'primitive palace of the Dodonaean king,' beside the sacred hearth of Zeus" (Charles Bertram Lewis, *Classical Mythology and Arthurian Romance*, Oxford Univ. Press, 1932, pp. 36-37).

[2] René Guénon stressed that, in ancient Egypt, the king was considered to belong, it seems, to the sacerdotal caste, because he was initiated in the *Mysteries*, as Plutarch confirmed it in his *Isis and Osiris* (René Guénon, *Autorité spirituelle et Pouvoir temporel*, Les Éditions Véga, 1976, p. 35). The true Royal investiture raises the king to priesthood.

societies, the main goal of the whole country was "liberation," and the pharaoh was the saviour[1]; all the funeral rites applied first and foremost to the pharaoh, because his successful posthumous journey guaranteed the salvation of all the people.

At the Royal investiture, the Egyptian priests represented the gods, thus the pharaoh was anointed by the spiritual authority, a reflection of the supreme Principle, and accordingly, any legitimate investiture implied the intervention of the sacerdotal power. Similarly, in the Hindu tradition, the king's coronation meant his "anointment" by the *brâhmanas*, who were the keepers of the spiritual knowledge and of the sacerdotal authority; the Royal investiture contained various significant rites, among which we should mention the visits of the "royal chaplain" (*brâhmana*) to various dignitaries to assure their association to the new reign, an illustration of the initiatory formula "to gather what was scattered." At a superior level, a universal one, this "gathering of what was scattered" is equivalent to the "absorption of the waters" back to their source (as described in a Romanian legend) and was performed by the same *brâhmana*, who gathered in a wooden vessel waters from Ganga and from each and every sacred river of India, from oceans and lakes, from fountains and ponds, and then he mixed them with honey, *ghrta* (or *ghî*, clarified butter), and the liquid from a cow in the process of giving birth.

This last ingredient suggests that the investiture was, like in the case of other important rites, a death and a new birth, which is explicitly shown in the ritual Hocart described when he presented the Royal investiture in Fiji.[2] Moreover, like in the case of the multiple states of the being, this death and birth pair implied continuity from a state to another, in this particular situation from the previous king to the new one, a continuity very much treasured, even by the usurpers, because it

---

[1] We could compare the Egyptian doctrine with the Christian one, where Christ was the saviour of the whole mankind and through his crucifixion everybody was redeemed.
[2] A. M. Hocart, *Kingship*, Watts & Co., 1941, pp. 36-37, 45.

represented the uninterrupted chain linked to the Center and through which the spiritual influence and the divine mandate was transmitted.[1]

For this reason, Rome for example proclaimed itself the successor of Troy; therefore Byzantium, the first Christian capital-city, considered itself the successor of Rome, the Byzantine emperor denying Charlemagne and Otto I of the title of "universal sovereign."[2] The division of the Christian Church in two permitted Rome to emerge as a renewed spiritual center, reborn from its ashes, and consequently, to anoint the Western kings and emperors, who claimed to be the heirs of the Roman emperors, defying the Byzantine emperors. In fact, each traditional form has the duty to deem itself as the only valid and orthodox form, and its king as the only legitimate sovereign, the same as each point of the circumference, reflecting the unique center of the circle, appears to be the only authentic point.

The Royal investiture followed strict rules, like the one stipulating the location where the ritual had to take place; obviously, the Royal investiture was an exoteric expression of the Royal initiation, and therefore it had to reproduce the initiatory journey to the Center, which for the Christian world, could be embodied by Constantinople, Rome or other centers. The Byzantine basileus had to fulfil a ritual

---

[1] In the ritual of the investiture of the Byzantine emperor, the patriarch of Constantinople, the supreme sacerdotal authority, after he anointed the future basileus with chrism and put the crown on his head, gave him the *okakia*, a silk bag filled with earth taken from the graves, as a reminder of his mortal nature as an individual, but also as a sign that the individual is dead and the emperor as function is born. It is interesting to note that, when the future basileus has arrived at Hagia Sophia, a senator handed out to the crowd some special kind of bread, each piece containing three coins: one of gold, one of silver and one of bronze (which corresponded to the three castes from the Hindu tradition, representing the *dwija*, "twice-born") (we see the symbolic importance of money).

[2] Generally speaking, the new king considered himself the essential successor, not only the formal one, of the previous king, which illustrated the uninterrupted transmission of the divine mandate. Symbolically, the former king continued to live in the new king, not as an individual but as a function, and likewise, any spiritual center had to be connected to the uninterrupted chain through which the divine influences were transmitted; therefore, the new kings and the new secondary centers always strove to have a "mythical genealogy."

voyage to the center of the center, that is, Hagia Sophia of Constantinople; Charlemagne traveled to Rome, where on Christmas Day,[1] Pope Leo III crowned him *Imperator Romanorum* in Saint Peter's Basilica (while Charlemagne knelt at the altar, see the picture below); similarly, the French kings went for the investiture to Reims,[2] the spiritual center of the Franks.[3]

France also considered itself the successor of Rome, and when Clovis, at the end of the fifth Century, became a Christian, he implied that baptism enabled him to be the heir of the Roman emperors. The sacred chrism, kept in the Holy Ampulla and received directly from heaven, made the French king to consider himself primary "Lord of

---

[1] It was not only a spatial journey to the center, but also a temporal one, to the solstitial gate. Clovis was also baptized at Christmas.
[2] The legend says that Reims was founded by Remus' soldiers.
[3] Clovis was baptized at Reims, and that is where the Holy Spirit descended bringing the sacred oil for Clovis' baptism. This oil, safeguarded in a sacred vessel called "la Sainte-Ampoule," was kept in the cathedral of Reims and was used to anoint the French kings. It was said that the holy oil was inexhaustible, the Holy Ampulla regaining its fullness after each anointment.

the World," invested with the supreme function, and only secondary king subordinated to the spiritual authority of the pope.[1]

From all this, the most essential element for the Royal investiture appears to be the holy oil, the chrism, and the main reason is its fire-like characteristic, symbolizing for the Christian tradition the Holy Spirit, but also in Islam there was a similar significance: "the Prophet – a *hadîth* says – when he was in *ihrâm* (state of sacralization) anointed himself with aromatic oil"; as Ibn 'Arabî said, the oil is an extension of light.[2]

The anointment symbolizes the transmission of a spiritual influence, indispensable in any genuine rite[3]; but, associated with this, equally essential is the death and the new birth taking place during the Royal investiture, where these two elements (the transmission of the spiritual influence and the death, followed by a second birth) reflect the composition of the initiatory rites, since they are the core of any initiation:

---

[1] Yet order must prevail, that is, obedience and well-regulation should be mandatory elements for both *Sacerdotium* and *Regnum*, as Christ stressed in two of his teachings: first, when he accepted to be baptized by John the Baptist; second, when he gave to Caesar what belonged to Caesar. Some historians tried to defend the French kings' revolt against the sacerdotal power, pointing out that the sacred oil came directly from heaven and not from the pope, but this fact only endorsed their independence regarding other emperors (for example, Charles V of France did not permit the German emperor to enter Paris on a white horse, but only on a black one) and certainly would not allow any insubordination to the spiritual authority, and for this reason the bishop of Reims anointed the future king. It is true that the rite of anointment somehow raised the king to a "supra-human" level, making him a "sacerdotal-like" being (and a thaumaturge); also, in 1089, Pope Urban II officially endorsed to the bishops of Reims the right to anoint the future kings of France, because the oil of "Clovis' baptism" came from heaven.

[2] Surat an-Nûr is well known: "Allâh is the Light of Heavens and Earth. His light is like a niche within which there is a lamp, the lamp is within a glass, the glass as if it were a pearly [white] star lit from [the oil of] a blessed olive tree, neither of the east nor of the west, whose oil would almost glow even if untouched by fire. Light upon light. Allah guides to His light whom He wills."

[3] Another ancient rite permitting to transmit a spiritual influence is the "imposition of hands": "And Israel stretched out his right hand, and laid it upon Ephraim's head, who was the younger, and his left hand upon Manasseh's head, guiding his hands wittingly; for Manasseh was the firstborn" (*Genesis* 48:14).

For the keys of hell and the guarantee of salvation were in the hands of the goddess, and the initiation ceremony itself took the form of a kind of voluntary death and salvation through divine grace... I came to the boundary of death and after treading Proserpine's threshold I returned having traversed all the elements; at midnight I saw the sun shining with brilliant light; I approached the gods below and the gods above face to face and worshipped them in their actual presence. Now I have told you what, though you have heard it, you cannot know. So all that can without sin be revealed to the understanding of the uninitiated, that and no more I shall relate.[1]

In the Christian tradition, the exemplary Royal investiture is the "Coronation of the Virgin," with Saint Mary kneeling in front of Jesus, and we will see in the next chapters, in accord with the traditional spirit, how the "Love of the Virgin" is part of the Royal Art and what the act of kneeling means[2]:

---

[1] Lucius Apuleius, *The Golden Ass*.
[2] "Coronation of the Virgin" – painting by Fra Angelico, Musée du Louvre. There are other "Coronations" by Fra Angelico at Uffizi and San Marco, Florence.

CHAPTER IV

THE ROYAL ART OF LOVE

The diminishment of the Royal Art's contents, and its reduction today to the Masonic Art exclusively, should not stop us from recalling lost components, like the Chivalric Art, which was the main constituent of the Royal Art in the times when the traditional spirit reigned effectively. We already had the chance to describe the Chivalric Art, when we thoroughly deciphered the symbolism of the Grail tales and of *Râmâyana*,[1] where the woman as *Madonna Intelligenza* played a major initiatory role, and we will have other opportunities in future volumes, which allows our current discourse to be restricted to just a few considerations regarding the symbolism of Love, an inexhaustible subject, it is true, but unavoidable in the *oikonomia* of the present work.

It must be strongly stated that the Royal Love, like the Sacerdotal Knowledge (that included the Love), had God as supreme goal, and, of course, *Madonna Intelligenza*, as Its face, was part of this goal[2]; even though it seemed to be a contradiction between the chivalric love, as propagated by the troubadours of Occitania, and the pious love of the monks, we should have no doubts that the goal was the same, and

---

[1] See our *Free-Masonry: A Traditional Organization, The Center and the Holy Grail*, Rose-Cross Books, 2010.
[2] René Guénon specified that, in some cases, the same symbols represented both the Virgin Mary and Christ, and the solution to this enigma is the relation between *Shekinah* and *Metatron* (René Guénon, *Aperçus sur l'Ésotérisme chrétien*, Éditions Traditionnelles, 1983, p. 64).

only an antitraditional mentality could suggest a profane type of love; nonetheless, the human society at the end of *Kali-Yuga* was far from perfect, which imposed a hierarchical difference between the religious or exoteric love and the initiatory one, even though they often used the same language.[1]

---

[1] When the gap between the official Church and the initiatory organizations became too wide, *jargon* was used as in the case of the *Fedeli d'Amore*. Boccaccio and Rabelais employed the abuses regarding "love" to cover up their esoteric data, criticizing at the same time the decadence of the medieval Christian civilization, the way St. Bernard and Dante did. However, the opinion that a genuine initiatory organization could oppose the exoteric establishment is totally wrong, and suggestions like the one describing the Templars fighting the Church are malevolent. René Guénon explained how esotericism is not contrary to "orthodoxy" (not even against the religious one), because it is above the religious viewpoint; consequently, even if the word *Amor* is the reverse of *Roma*, it does not mean that initiatory love is the antithesis of Rome, but only that *Roma* is a visible image, reversed like in a mirror (like the *per speculum in Ænigmate* of Saint Paul). Mr. Valli's confusion, Guénon added, between esotericism and "heterodoxy" is surprising since he understood that *Fedeli d'Amore*'s doctrine was not at all "anti-Catholic," but it was, like the one of the Rose-Cross, rigorously "catholic." Valli also accepted the opposition between *Amor* and *Mors* as illustrating the conflict between *Fedeli d'Amore* and the Church: *la Chiesa carnale e corrotta, detta convenzionalmente "la Morte"* [Death] *o "la Pietra"* [Stone, Peter] *e che è dipinta come avversaria della setta dei "Fedeli d'Amore" e come occultatrice di quella Sapienza santa che i "Fedeli d'Amore" perseguono sotto la figura della donna*, even though he underlined that *la Morte* or *la Pietra* is the "corrupted and carnal church" (the clergy of this corrupted church was *un "clergé" exotériste qui ne possède que la lettre et s'arrête à l'écorce de la doctrine. – Selon l'ordre hiérarchique normal, l'initié est au-dessus du "clerc" ordinaire (fût-il théologien), tandis que le "laïque" est naturellement au-dessous de celui-ci*, Guénon, *Aperçus sur l'Ésotérisme chrétien*, p. 84). In fact, an initiatory mentality is needed to understand that, as Guénon explained, in this association *Amor-Mors*, first, the death should be the "initiatory death," and second, *A-mor* (like in Sanskrit *a-mara, a-mrita*) symbolizes the "immortality" (Guénon, *ibid.*, pp. 60-61, 66-67). Similarly, St. Bernard of Clairvaux did not condemn the Church, which was for him the Bride of Christ, but only some of its servants: "Let the clerics, let the ministers of the Church, who are guilty of impious conduct in their benefices, be filled with fear. Discontented with the stipends that ought to suffice them, they sacrilegiously retain the surplus income that is meant for the upkeep of the needy; they are not afraid to squander the sustenance of the poor in pandering to their own pride and luxury. They are guilty of a double wickedness: they pilfer the property of others and prostitute the goods of the Church to serve their lusts and vanities" (*Sermon 23, On the Song of Songs*; see also Guénon, *Saint Bernard*, Éditions Traditionnelles, 1984, p. 8); and, even stronger: "This world has its nights – not few in number. I say the world has its nights, but it is almost all night, and always plunged in complete darkness. The

In the legend of the Grail, the Knights worshipped the Virgin; the Order of the Temple and Saint Bernard of Clairvaux had a special veneration for "Our Lady" Virgin Mary; and the Teutonic Knights belonged to the "Order of Our Lady," but we should not forget that such an extraordinary love did not suggest a disregard for Jesus Christ or God, as some exponents of the infrahuman mentality fantasized, more or less wittingly, and it is enough to remember that the battle cry of the Templars was "Vive Dieu, Saint Amour," and their device "Non nobis Domine, non nobis, sed Nomini Tuo da gloriam."[1] Regarding the Virgin Mary, Nennius, the Welsh monk of the 9th century, said about King Arthur, "The eighth battle was in Guinnion fort, and in it Arthur carried the image of the holy Mary, the everlasting Virgin, on his shield, and the heathen were put to flight on that day, and there was great slaughter upon them, through the power of Jesus Christ and the power of the holy Virgin Mary, his mother"; Gawain, "the courteous knight," "had that queen [Queen of Heaven]'s image etched on the inside of his armoured shield"[2]; and, as the legend says,

---

faithlessness of the Jews, the ignorance of pagans, the perversity of heretics, even the shameless and degraded behaviour of Catholics – these are all nights. For surely it is night when the things which belong to the Spirit of God are not perceived" (*Sermon 75*). St. Bernard, Dante and the *Fedeli d'Amore* blamed the "corruption" within the Church, a "corruption" leading to "solidification," similar to the hardening of the Pharisees and Sadducees' hearts, in the time of Christ; therefore, *Amor* was beneficent in comparison to *Pietra* (stone; Peter) (Luigi Valli, *Il linguaggio segreto di Dante e dei "Fedeli d'Amore"*, Optima, 1928, p. 240), not to say that, as we mentioned, the initiatory domain is above the religious one. About this "corruption" Guénon said: "the Medusa's head, which changes the men in 'stones' [Greek *petra*] (a word that plays a very important role in the *Fedeli d'Amore*'s language), represents the corruption of the Wisdom" (*Aperçus sur l'Ésotérisme chrétien*, p. 62).

[1] "Not for us, Lord, not for us, but to Thy Name give glory." Guénon stated: *Ce sens profond de l'"Amour," en connexion avec les doctrines des Ordres de chevalerie, pourrait résulter notamment du rapprochement des indications suivantes: d'abord, la parole de saint Jean, "Dieu est Amour"; ensuite, le cri de guerre des Templiers, "Vive Dieu Saint Amour"; enfin, le dernier vers de la Divine Comédie, "L'Amor che muove il Sole e l'altre stelle"* (Guénon, *ibid.*, p. 66).

[2] *Sir Gawain and the Green Knight*, Penguin Books, 1968, p. 50.

Saint Bernard received milk (a symbol of spiritual knowledge) from Virgin Mary's breast.[1]

Many churches and orders dedicated their love to the Blessed Virgin, and the Knights Templar in particular, but it is expected to see this love raised to pure knowledge, when, from an initiatory viewpoint, the Virgin is *Madonna Intelligenza*. As there were interminable discussions about the differences between courtly love and devotional

---

[1] It took place, it is said, in 1146, at Speyer Cathedral. Ananda K. Coomaraswamy gave to this "miracle" a strictly metaphysical significance, that of a formal adoption and "It would, moreover, accord with all that we know of St. Bernard as the exponent of a doctrine of *deification* [which for Nicolas Cusanus, as he explained in *De filiatione Dei*, is the divine filiation], to suppose that the 'miracle' had an especially appropriate application to him in this sense" (see *The Virgin Suckling St. Bernard*); and Coomaraswamy, giving other examples of symbolic suckling (Juno, offering her breast to Hercules, who is showed in a half-kneeling position), stressed the meaning: it is an adoption, implying a new birth and a resurrection (in the case of Hercules), and it is also a gift of immortality; "it is a matter of initiation, second birth, and recognition" (*ibid.*). René Guénon wrote about St. Bernard: "He liked to name the Holy Virgin *Notre-Dame*; under his influence, this name was generally used after that. St. Bernard was a genuine 'knight of Mary' and he considered St. Mary his 'dame,' in a Chivalric sense" (*Saint Bernard*, p. 20). Speyer Cathedral (photo MAT):

love,[1] so there were on the difference between love and knowledge; yet we should stay away from these types of discussions, while bearing in mind that for the supra-individual journey all the "human" elements (human love, devotion, memory, reason, etc.) are ineffectual. Coomaraswamy tried to elevate *bhakti-mârga*, the "way of dedication," to the level of *jnâna-mârga*, the "way of gnosis,"[2] admitting though a distinction that "is certainly not without meaning insofar as it corresponds to one of mysticism from gnosticism, that is, of devotional faith and religious exercises from initiatory teaching and metaphysical practice."[3]

Let us repeat what we said before:

---

[1] However, in the 13th century, it was obvious that the majority of *chansons pieuses* were paraphrases of *chanson courtois* and *chansons de femme*, and their subject was almost exclusively the Virgin Mary (even those texts about Christ or God were often fused with Mariological poems); *amour courtois* (courtly love) was considered a mediation between St. Bernard's spirituality and the cult of the Blessed Virgin Mary, both influenced by the lyric tradition of the troubadours (see Mark Everist, *French Motets in the Thirteenth Century: Music, Poetry and Genre*, Cambridge Univ. Press, 2004, p. 131). As usual, the initiatory data were used at a lower level by exotericism, and then, with the fall of the cycle, were debased by the profane world. "The influences of the initiatory world descend to the profane world, but the reverse is not possible, because a river never goes uphill, back to its source; that source is the 'fountain of learning,' which is so often mentioned in the poems studied here [of the *Fedeli d'Amore*], and which is generally described as located at the foot of a tree, which, of course, is none other than the 'Tree of Life'; the symbolism of the 'Garden of Eden' and of the 'Heavenly Jerusalem' must find its application here" (Guénon, *Aperçus sur l'Ésotérisme chrétien*, p. 59).

[2] Shankarâchârya, the greatest and most intellectual exponent of nondualistic (*advaita*) metaphysics, was at the same time a *bhakta* and a *jnânî*, Coomaraswamy specified. We should add what Dante said: "Ladies that have intelligence of Love" (*Donne ch'avete intelletto d'amore*) (*Divine Comedy*, *Purgatorio* XXIV).

[3] *Metaphysics*, Princeton Univ. Press, 1977, *Bhakta Aspects of the Âtman Doctrine*, p. 387. "A perfected Gnosis necessarily involves a Beatification" (p. 396). René Guénon wrote to Coomaraswamy: *Pour ce qui est de bhakti, vous avez tout à fait raison en ce qui concerne le sens originel; mais, dans les époques plus récentes, le sens de "dévotion" ne paraît-il pas malgré cela avoir prévalu, avec la prédominance de l'élément sentimental qu'il implique comme vous le dites très justement?* (Letter of September 5, 1935); and, twenty years previously: *Ce ne peut pourtant pas être à l'ordre intellectuel; et j'avoue bien volontiers n'avoir jamais pu comprendre ce que Spinoza voulait entendre par "amour intellectuel," une telle expression me paraissant foncièrement contradictoire* (Letter to Noële Maurice-Denis Boulet, February 16, 1919) (René Guénon, *Fragments Doctrinaux*, Rose-Cross Books, 2013, p. 243).

It is interesting to compare the name of the Near-Western and Middle-Western churches. In Western Europe, cathedrals are usually called "The Church of Our Lady," or in French, *Notre Dame*. Orthodoxy praised the Virgin equally, calling her 'the Mother of God,' the Orthodox icons with the Mother of God being famous. There are also churches bearing the name "Mother of God," yet the most important church was called *Hagia Sophia*. Obviously, "Holy Wisdom" is the equivalent of *Notre Dame*. In the Middle Ages, in Western Europe, the Virgin was a symbol for esoteric spirituality, she was *Madonna Intelligenza*. Much earlier, in the Near-West, the divine Sophia became part of the Christian tradition, expression of an esoteric core. Yet only secondarily "Holy Wisdom" was in the Near-West an equivalent for the Mother of God; in the first place, it represented Jesus himself, as *Logos*.[1] "Wisdom has built herself a house, she has erected her seven pillars"[2]; in the same way, Constantinople on its seven hills was the "city of wisdom" and the Orthodox Church was the house of God's Wisdom. The Holy Sophia came down as Jesus, the first earthly "house of wisdom" being the Mother of God, the Virgin, the holy womb of the *Logos*. An old Syriac manuscript presented an icon of the Mother of God carrying Jesus inside an oval form (the World Egg), the Virgin having king Solomon at her right and Holy Wisdom at her left.[3] Solomon himself is an emblem of Wisdom, being considered the wisest king and the builder of the Temple. And his name is related to Peace.[4]

The involvement of Solomon is not a coincidence; Gawain's shield, with the Virgin Mary's image etched on the inside, is also described as "the shield with its shining gules, with the Pentangle in pure gold depicted theron… [the Pentangle] is a symbol which Solomon conceived once… and it is endless everywhere, and the English call it, as I have heard, the Endless Knot."[5]

---

[1] John Meyendorff, *Byzantine Hesychasm*, Variorum Reprints, London, 1974, pp. 259 ff.
[2] *Proverbs* 9:1.
[3] Meyendorff 263.
[4] *The Wrath of Gods, The Near West*, ch. XI.
[5] *Sir Gawain*, p. 49. The "endless knot" looks like this:

However, before we follow St. Bernard's teachings regarding Solomon and the Art of Love, and before we look into Solomon's love for the "strange woman," we would like to present a 19th century Christian Orthodox icon of the Mother of God[1]:

René Guénon was asked: "Is it correct to call the double triangle or the five-pointed star the 'Shield of David'? I heard this name applied to two symbols without distinction, which is then the 'Seal of Solomon'?" He answered: "The Kabbalists call the double triangle equally 'Seal of Solomon' and 'Shield of David,' and also 'Shield of Mikaël' (Mikael-Malaki, 'My Angel,' that is, 'The Angel in which My Name is'); equally, in Arabic, it is designated as 'Khâtem Seyidnâ Suleymân' and 'Dir'a Seyidnâ Dawûd.' None of these designations can be properly applied to the five-pointed star, the pentalpha or pentagram of the Pythagoreans, which is the Masonic blazing star. This last one, in its general significance, is a 'microcosmic' symbol, while the double triangle is a 'macrocosmic' symbol. There is another Arab symbol, called 'Ugdat Seyidnâ Suleymân' or the 'Knot of Solomon,' whose meaning is very similar to the Seal of Solomon's, in connection to the Hermetic adage: 'As above, so below'" (*The Speculative Mason*, 1935, Volume XXVII, pp. 77-78); see René Guénon, *Recueil*, Rose-Cross Books, 2013, p. 297, where Guénon gives the diagram of the knot:

[1] From our collection.

This type of icon derives from the one known as *Theotokos Oranta*,[1] designated so because the early Christians[2] (and others before them) used to pray standing, with the elbows close to the sides of the body and with the hands outstretched sideways; the type presented above is usually called the *Theotokos of the Sign* (Our Lady of the Sign).[3] The fame of the *Theotokos Oranta* (or the *Theotokos of the Sign*) developed in the Byzantine Empire, where the Mother of God became so central that Constantinople metaphorically changed to *Theotokoupolis* (the "City of Mother of God").[4]

---

[1] *Orans* ("praying") comes from Latin *os*, "mouth," and relates to *oratio*, "speech," *oratus*, "prayer" (and, to English *oral* and *orator*).
[2] Frescoes of the *Theotokos Oranta* have been found in the catacombs, dating back to the 4th Century (see the catacomb of Calyxtus, or the cemetery of St. Agnes).
[3] It is considered to depict Isaiah's prophecy: "Therefore the Lord himself shall give you a sign; Behold, a virgin shall conceive, and bear a son, and shall call his name Immanuel" (*Isaiah* 7:14).
[4] About Constantinople and the Mother of God see also our work *The Wrath of Gods*. Some Byzantine icons are legendary for their spiritual powers, like, for example, the *Theotokos Nicopeia*, which was taken from Constantinople during the Fourth Crusade and now resides in St. Mark Cathedral, in Venice. One of the most illustrious Byzantine icons was the so called *Theotokos of Blachernae*, where Blachernae is a quarter of Constantinople with the church of Mother of God (*Theotókos tón Blachernón*) as a place of pilgrimage and a major Marian shrine, a church that was second-most important after Hagia Sophia and – we should stress – built near a sacred spring (*hagiasma*) (about the symbolism of the Fountain of Life see René Guénon, *Symboles fondamentaux de la Science sacrée*, Gallimard, 1980, p. 109 and Ananda K. Coomaraswamy, *What is Civilisation?*, Lindisfarne Press, 1989, the special article called *Khwâja Khadir and the Fountain of Life*). *Theotokos of Blachernae* was said to have protected Emperor Heraclius in his campaign against the Persians (see about Heraclius our *Free-Masonry: A Traditional Organization*, 2010, pp. 182-185), but nobody knows what type of icon this was, *Orans* or *Hodegetria*; it seems that originally it has been a *Theotokos Oranta* (as it can be seen on coins and seals), which disappeared during a fire that destroyed the church in 1434 (a similar fire destroyed, in 1194, the Romanesque basilica of Chartres, which was the center of the cult of Mary in France, if not in Western Europe, and the fire and disappearance of the relics – the main relic was the shirt that the Virgin Mary was said to have worn at the birth of Christ – were considered as a sign of divine wrath, when the Virgin had abandoned her shrine; the miraculous recovery of the relic was therefore interpreted a sign from the Virgin that "she wanted a new and more beautiful church to be built in her honour"; see our *Free-Masonry*, p. 183). The *Theotokos of Blachernae* miraculously reappeared on Mount Athos, but as *Hodegetria*; there is, nonetheless, a different

The symbolism of the outstretched hands is universal, and the religious explanation is a part of it, translating the same fundamental and primordial idea accurately expressed in the Daoist *Book of Huang Di*, the mythical Yellow Emperor, where it is said: "everything [in the universal manifestation] is covered by Heaven and supported by the Earth."[1] The "supporter" is also a "receiver," because the outstretched hands describe a container, a chalice ready to receive the spiritual influences, the indispensable "light" and "rain" needed by the "ten thousand beings."[2] There are other remarkable aspects worthy of

---

legend describing how a Constantinople widow discovered the icon in her house, and we should make a note that it was a widow who recovered the icon. As example, we present a coin from Emperor Constantine IX Monomachus (year 1042):

[1] The Free-Masonry preserved the formula as a sign of the Entered Apprentice, where the hands are held horizontally in front of the body, palms apart and facing each other, the right hand covering and the left supporting. René Guénon said at the beginning of the third chapter of his *La Grande Triade*: "'Heaven covers, Earth supports' [*Le Ciel couvre, la Terre supporte*]: this is the traditional formula that defines, with the greatest accuracy, the roles of these two complementary principles, and symbolically defines their positions, respectively above and below [*supérieure et inférieure*], in relation to the 'ten thousand beings,' that is, to the totality of universal manifestation." In Orphism, the god Phanes is born from the World Egg as Universal Man, the Egg being the Zodiac; the superior half of the World Egg, which is Phanes' hood, represents *Tian*, Heaven that covers, and the inferior half is *Di*, the Earth, supporting the god, who symbolizes *Ren*, the Mediator and the Grand Triad's middle term (see our *About the Yi Jing*, p. 91).
[2] The both famous "sign of Tanit" and the Egyptian Geb's image distinctly show the hands suggesting this idea of "supporting" and "receiving."

contemplation, including the question "is Shakti, Prakriti or Geb (or Fu Xi, the master of the square) the supporter-receiver?" but we intend to direct our exposé to the geometrical symbolism of the 19th century icon shown above, which is in accord with René Guénon's discourse about the symbolism of Janus Bifrons and the solstitial gates, based on this description from the Masonic ritual:

> in every well regulated and governed lodge there has been a certain point within a circle, which circle is bounded on the east and the west by two perpendicular and parallel lines, representing the

About the "light" and "rain," René Guénon wrote: "light and rain both have a 'vivifying' power that well represents the action of the influences in question... It is important to note that light and rain, when they are considered from this point of view, are not only related to the heavens in a general way, but more especially to the sun... In very different times and places and even into the Western Middle Ages, the sun has often been represented with two kinds of rays, straight and undulating by turns... Each of the four vertical and horizontal rays is constituted by two straight lines forming between them a very acute angle, and each of the four intermediary rays is made up of three undulating parallel lines... the double radiation is the light and the rain" (*Symboles fondamentaux*, pp. 361-363); see as illustration this sun as Christ from one of Goa's churches (photo MAT):

anniversary of St. John the Baptist and St. John the Evangelist, who were perfect parallels, as well in Masonry and Christianity.[1]

We don't suggest a new interpretation for the above icon of the *Theotokos of the Sign* with the intent to contest its religious sense or to unveil a secret message; what we suggest is a fundamental geometrical symbolism, very visible, which, at one time, provided the Christian sacred art and thinking with traditional support in expressing its

---

[1] William Morgan, *Freemasonry Exposed*, pp. 47-8; "Our Brethren add that, 'this circle is embordered by two perpendicular parallel lines, representing Saint John the Baptist and Saint John the Evangelist, and upon the top rest the Holy Scriptures' (an open book)" (Albert Pike, *Morals and Dogma of the Ancient and Accepted Scottish Rite of Freemasonry*, Charleston, 1871, p. 16); the diagram of the circle with the two tangents is also given in Oswald Wirth, *La Franc-maçonnerie rendue intelligible à ses adeptes* (see the *Fellowcraft Book*). Prichard mentioned from the beginning the syntagm "Lodge of St. John" that refers to the Johannite aspect of the Masonry (Samuel Prichard, *Masonry Dissected*, Poemandres Press, 1996, p. 9). René Guénon wrote: "In relation to the two Saints John and their solstitial symbolism, it is of interest to consider a symbol which seems peculiar to Masonry in the Anglo-Saxon world, or which at least has only been preserved in that Masonry: this is a circle with a point in the centre, placed between two parallel tangents; and these tangents are said to represent the two Saints John. In fact, the circle here is the annual cycle, and its solar significance is made more evident by the presence of the central point, for this same figure is also the astrological sign of the sun; and the two parallel lines are tangents of the circle at the solstitial points, which they thus define as 'limit-points' [*marquant ainsi leur caractère de « points-limites »*], these points being in fact bounds beyond which the sun can never pass in the course of its journey; it is because the lines thus correspond to the two solstices and can also be said to represent precisely the two Saints John… In this special case, therefore, a certain modification has been brought to the general symbolism of the annual cycle, one that is easy enough to explain, for it is obvious that it could only have been introduced by an assimilation established between the two parallel lines and another double symbol, that of the two columns; these columns, which by their nature can only be vertical, have thereby, as well as by their being situated respectively to the North and South, an actual relationship with the solstitial symbolism, at least from a certain point of view" (*Symboles fondamentaux*, p. 255). In a letter to Marcel Maugy (Denys Roman), of September 16, 1948, René Guénon drew the symbol:

specific teaching, without its primeval meaning being affected[1]: we can see the two tangents (the outstretching hands), the circle, and Christ as the central point. From a Masonic viewpoint, we may well accept the hands as emblems of the two columns and the Mother of God as the Widow.[2]

In a Romanian fairy tale, there is a curious expression, like an incantation: "In the evening, maiden/ Over night, mommy/ In the morning, little widow," which suggests one and the same woman, the image of the Feminine Principle, as Aditi, Shakti, Shekinah, Virgin Mary or Prakriti.[3] From a supernal viewpoint, the Widower or the Widow, as they often are found in fairy tales and myths, represents the

---

[1] When René Guénon established a link between the Holy Grail and the Sacred Heart of Christ, his universal view was contested, and he answered, among other things, that "It is of little importance that Chrestien de Troyes and Robert de Boron did not see in the ancient legend (of which they were only the adapters) all the significance contained in it; this significance was really there, nevertheless [*cette signification ne s'y trouvait pas moins réellement*], and we claim only to have made it explicit without introducing anything 'modern' whatsoever into our interpretation" (*ibid.*, p. 46).

[2] We saw Guénon mentioning the "assimilation established between the two parallel lines and another double symbol, that of the two columns." He even compared the two tangents and the two Masonic columns with the pillars of Hercules, saying: "In the geographical representation that places these two pillars on either side of the actual straits of Gibraltar, it is obvious that the pillar situated in Europe is the column of the North, and the one situated in Africa is the column of the South" (*ibid.*, p. 256); and, in the following footnote, Guénon referred to the coin's symbolism: "A representation of the pillars of Hercules can be seen on ancient Spanish coins, in which they are joined by a kind of streamer [*banderole*] on which the motto *non plus ultra* is inscribed; …the usual sign of the American dollar is derived from this figure. But here, all the importance has been given to the streamer, which originally was only an accessory and which has been changed into the letter S whose form it approximated, while the two columns which constituted the essential element were reduced to two parallel strokes, vertical like the two tangents to the circle in Masonic symbolism, which we have just explained; this is not without a certain irony, for in fact it was precisely the 'discovery' of America that cancelled the ancient geographical application of the *non plus ultra*."

[3] For the *Fedeli d'Amore*, "the 'maiden,' the 'accomplished damsel,' the 'bride,' the 'widow' obviously mark as many [initiatory] degrees of Wisdom" (see A. Ricolfi, *Studi sui «Fedeli d'Amore»*, Luni Editrice, Milan, 2006).

Non-Being as Void,[1] but mainly the "one without a second," like Shekinah who is not only the Maiden but the very Widow in exile. There is something subtle here, alluding to a duality embedded in unity, that is, implying, on the one hand, a polarization in man-woman, yet reminding, on the other hand, that, in reality, there is no duality but only unity; from an initiatory perspective, to be a widow or a widower means "lacking" not only etymologically, but foremost spiritually, forcing a quest, which also aims to One, but One fulfilled by a sacred Wedding.[2]

---

[1] The word "widow," like the Sanskrit *vidhava*, the Latin *viduus*, the Gothic *viduva*, comes from a root *vidh* = "to be deprived of," but the Latin *viduus* meant also "bereft, void."

[2] The *Fedeli d'Amore* illustrated this Wedding with an "androgynous figure [*la figura 'moglier e marito' del* Tractatus amoris *di Francesco da Barberino*] with the head of a man and of a woman, signifying the spirit reunited and unified with the supreme Wisdom (*Dunque io son ella*)," suggesting the connection with the Alchemy (and its *Rebis*) (see Valli) (*ce dernier, qui porte dans ses mains la rose symbolique, a deux têtes, l'une masculine et l'autre féminine, et est manifestement identique au* Rebis *hermétique. La seule différence notable avec les figures qui se rencontrent dans les traités alchimiques est que, dans celles-ci, c'est le côté droit qui est masculin et le côté gauche féminin, tandis qu'ici nous trouvons la disposition inverse; cette particularité semble avoir échappé à M. Valli, qui pourtant en donne lui-même l'explication, sans paraître s'en apercevoir, lorsqu'il dit que "l'homme avec son intellect passif est réuni à l'Intelligence active, représentée par la femme," alors que généralement c'est le masculin qui symbolise l'élément actif et le féminin l'élément passif*, Guénon, *Aperçus sur l'Ésotérisme chrétien*, p. 76).

Dai «Documenti d'amore» del Barberino

In the Hindu tradition it is stated: "Not for love of the husband is a husband dear, but for love of *Âtmâ* a husband is dear. Not for love of the wife is a wife dear, but for love of *Âtmâ* a wife is dear" (*Bṛhadâraṇyaka Upaniṣhad*, II.4.5). This Wedding also suggests that a spiritual realization compels the neophyte to reach the status of "widow(er)" with regard to the world, that is, to have the heart void and emptied of all the mundane elements. The soul has to be prepared to receive God's presence, and, for Meister Eckhart, this was the meaning of the merchants' expulsion from the

In Masonry, even though there are only men in the lodge, the woman is raised to the *principial* level, as Widow; and it is connected to the symbolism of *Madonna Intelligenza*. Francesco da Barberino, who belonged to the *Fedeli d'Amore*,[1] mentioned a mysterious widow,

---

Temple; in his sermon, *Intravit Iesus in templum et coepit eicere vendentes et ementes*, Meister Eckhart regarded the Temple as the human soul, and God, Who created and formed the soul after His resemblance, wants this temple to be empty, that is, only when this temple is liberated of all obstacles, will God come and reside in it. The same idea is found in the *Fedeli d'Amore*'s initiatory doctrine about the *cuore gentile* (the "purified heart" that has to be void of all the external objects) (Guénon, *ibid.*, p. 58). In a religious sense, for the Christians of the Middle Ages, the widow was an image of the Church, humble, poor and merciful, yet perseverant in praying and in its pursuit of justice (see *Luke* 7:11-12, 20:45-47, 21:3-4 and *Mark* 12:41-44); this widow was seen at the same time a maiden and a bride ("In the evening, maiden/ Over night, mommy/ In the morning, little widow"). Doubtless, this is an ideal definition, together with the Knights' vow to protect the widow, a definition the human factor has increasingly corroded, as suggested by Bonichi who wrote during the time when the Order of the Temple was destroyed: "Widows and orphans are very safe/ on account of the oaths knights take,/ but everyone makes sure they lock their doors."

[1] There are strong reasons to accept that the *Fedeli d'Amore* were closely related to Dante and the Templars (Valli 274, 423-428, Guénon, *ibid.*, p. 68). Valli said, among other things: *Ho accennato qualche volta all'importanza che assumono, proprio nel momento in cui fiorisce la poesia d'amore, i Templari, e il problema dei loro rapporti con Dante non è nuovo... Il loro [Templari] centro è in Francia e verso la Francia noi sappiamo orientati parecchi di questi "Fedeli d'Amore" che vi vanno sempre per ragioni molto misteriose: Guido Cavalcanti che va a Tolosa a innamorarsi di una donna "accordellata e stretta" che somiglia a quella di Firenze; Dante che va a Parigi (e non ne parla mai e nessuno sa bene che cosa ci sia andato a fare) proprio nel momento della grande tragedia dei Templari* [Meister Eckahrt was also in Paris at that time]; *Francesco da Barberino che si trattiene lungamente in Francia e scrive là gran parte dei Documenti d'Amore, ecc., sono tanti indizi che, messi insieme, fanno pensare a un qualche rapporto tra questo movimento e i Templari.* As Guénon accepted (*D'autre part, on peut comprendre, dans ces conditions, que la destruction de l'ordre du Temple ait entraîné pour l'Occident la rupture des relations régulières avec le "Centre du Monde" et c'est bien au XIVe siècle qu'il faut faire remonter la déviation qui devait inévitablement résulter de cette rupture, et qui est allée en s'accentuant graduellement jusqu'à notre époque. Ce n'est pas à dire pourtant que tout lien ait été brisé d'un seul coup; pendant assez longtemps, des relations purent être maintenues dans une certaine mesure, mais seulement d'une façon cachée, par l'intermédiaire d'organisations comme celle de la Fede Santa ou des "Fidèles d'Amour," comme la "Massenie du Saint-Graal" et sans doute bien d'autres encore, toutes héritières de l'esprit de l'ordre du Temple, et pour la plupart rattachées à lui par une filiation plus ou moins directe, ibid.*, p. 53), the *Fedeli d'Amore* were successors of the Templars, and they bitterly lamented the destruction of the Order, describing it as the death of *Amor*, which was halved by *Mors* (Valli 245). As we have already said, on a superficial level, Death is the corrupted church, including the pope and also the

symbolizing *Sapienza*, the Wisdom.[1] Guénon, referring to Barberino's widow, added that the same symbolic widow was important for Giocchino di Fiore and Boccaccio[2]; he also underlined the similarities between the "Court of Love" (*Cour d'Amour*) and Masonry: the Court of Love and Solomon's Temple (or the Masonic Lodge) are both symbols of the Center of the World, both have the shape of a double square, both have the Northern door (or window) closed, the Court of Love's king (representing *l'Amour*) is equivalent to the Masonic "Prince king, who killed the Templars (we should remember that Dante had St. Bernard as supreme guide, above Beatrice); in a deeper sense, we see here the invasion of the profane (antitraditional) forces, slaughtering the traditional spirit with its initiatory ways; the image below shows the initiatory hierarchy of the *Fedeli d'Amore*, where we notice the androgynous "bridegroom and bride" and also the naked child (similar to Shakespeare's child from *A Midsummer Night's Dream*, see our *The Everlasting Sacred Kernel*); the halving of *Amor* is, in a sense, the halving of the androgynous unity, but also, because the *Fedeli d'Amore* spoke about the death of half of *Amor*, we could say that now *Amor* is a Widow.

[1] Valli 242.
[2] Guénon, *ibid.*, p. 75: *Chose remarquable, Joachim de Flore parle dans ses œuvres d'une "veuve" symbolique, tout comme Francesco da Barberino et Boccace, qui appartenaient l'un et l'autre aux "Fidèles d'Amour"; et nous ajouterons que, de nos jours encore, cette "veuve" est bien connue dans le symbolisme maçonnique. À ce propos, il est fâcheux que des préoccupations politiques semblent avoir empêché M. Valli de faire certains rapprochements pourtant très frappants; il a raison, sans doute, de dire que les organisations initiatiques dont il s'agit ne sont pas la Maçonnerie, mais, entre celle-ci et celles-là, le lien n'en est pas moins certain; et n'est-il pas curieux, par exemple, que le "vent" ait, dans le langage des "Fidèles d'Amour," exactement le même sens que la "pluie" dans celui de la Maçonnerie? Perseval, like Tristan, was the "widow's son."*

of Mercy," and the birds (the angelic states) populating the Court use a language known to Solomon.[1]

There are many links, visible and invisible, between Chivalry and Masonry, and especially between the Templars and the Masons: both observed the Royal Art, both were initiatory organizations, both were beyond the common "vassalage," free and directly obeying God, both constituted "brotherhoods" without women.[2] In a world where the

---

[1] *Il y a aussi des choses assez étranges dans le livre d'André, chapelain du roi de France; ...il y est dit que le palais de l'Amour s'élève "au milieu de l'Univers," que ce palais a quatre côtés et quatre portes; la porte de l'Orient est réservée au dieu, et celle du Nord demeure toujours fermée. Or il y a ceci de remarquable: le Temple de Salomon, qui symbolise le "Centre du Monde," a aussi, d'après la tradition maçonnique, la forme d'un quadrilatère ou "carré long," et des portes s'ouvrent sur trois de ses côtés, celui du Nord seul n'ayant aucune ouverture; s'il y a là une légère différence (absence de porte d'une part, porte fermée de l'autre), le symbolisme est exactement le même, le Nord étant ici le côté obscur, celui que n'éclaire pas la lumière du Soleil. De plus, l'Amour apparaît ici sous la forme d'un roi, portant sur la tête une couronne d'or; n'est-ce pas ainsi que nous le voyons également représenté, dans la Maçonnerie écossaise, au grade de "Prince de Mercy," et ne peut-on pas dire qu'il est alors le "roi pacifique," ce qui est le sens même du nom de Salomon? Il y a encore un autre rapprochement qui n'est pas moins frappant: dans divers poèmes et fabliaux, la "Cour d'Amour" est décrite comme composée entièrement d'oiseaux, qu'on y voit prendre la parole tour à tour; or nous avons dit précédemment ce qu'il fallait entendre par la "langue des oiseaux"; et serait-il admissible de ne voir qu'une pure coïncidence dans le fait que, comme nous l'avons indiqué, c'est précisément en connexion avec Salomon que, dans le* Qorân, *cette "langue des oiseaux" se trouve expressément mentionnée?* (Guénon, *ibid.*, p. 93).

[2] There are today studies giving examples of women who worked beside the medieval masons, which is something different; also, we are not saying that women did not have suitable métiers as supports for an initiation. Regarding the womanless brotherhoods, Saint Bernard admonished: "What likeness do you bear to them? Perhaps the fact that you take women not as traveling companions but as mistresses? Companionship does not lay itself open to suspicion in the same way as living together. Who would entertain dark suspicions about those who raised the dead to life? Go and do likewise, and I will suppose that a man and a woman together are merely resting. Otherwise, you are insolently abrogating to yourself the privilege of those whose sanctity you do not possess. To be always in a woman's company without having carnal knowledge of her – is this not a greater miracle than raising the dead? You cannot perform the lesser feat; do you expect me to believe that you can do the greater? Every day your side touches the girl's side at table, your bed touches hers in your room, your eyes meet hers in conversation, your hands meet hers at work – do you expect to be thought chaste? It may be that you are, but I have my suspicions. To me you are an object of scandal. Take away the cause of scandal, and prove the truth of your boast that you are a follower of the Gospel… Let us return to the question of associating and cohabiting with women, for all of

Holy Grail stories worshiped the *dame* and where troubadours sang *l'amour courtois*, the Knights of the Temple living without this love for any *dame*, the Masons working without fondness for any lady would seem strange, if we did not know that, for them, *l'amour* was the supreme love and the *dame* was the supreme *Dame*, *Notre-Dame*, Our Lady. However, to really understand this "love" we must go beyond the religious or exoteric, not to say sentimental, significance, and try to rediscover the "initiatory" mentality of these particular "lovers."[1]

---

them have some experience of this. 'Now, my good man, who is this woman, and where does she come from? Is she your wife?', 'No,' he says, 'that is forbidden by my vows.' 'Your daughter then?' 'No.' 'What then? Not a sister or niece, or at least related to you by birth or marriage?' 'No, not at all,' 'And how will you preserve your chastity with her here? You can't behave like this. Perhaps you don't know that the Church forbids cohabitation of men and women if they are vowed to celibacy. If you do not wish to cause scandal in the Church, send the woman away. Otherwise that one circumstance will give rise to other suspicions, which may not be proved but will no doubt be thought probable'" (*Sermon 65*).

[1] As Saint Bernard was saying, "The bride's form must be understood in a spiritual sense, her beauty as something that is grasped by the intellect; it is eternal because it is an image of eternity. Her gracefulness consists of love, and you have read that 'love never ends.' It consists of justice, for 'her justice endures forever'" (*Sermon 27*). We may note that the Bride (which for Saint Bernard is officially the Church) is not only *Madonna Intelligenza* (the Love) but also Astraea (the Justice).

CHAPTER V

SOLOMON
AND THE ROYAL ART OF LOVE

René Guénon, who, prompted by Luigi Valli's work about Dante and the *Fedeli d'Amore*, wrote a series of articles related to *Amor*,[1] stated *très nettement*, from the start, that "the main shortcoming of Mr. Valli ... is not to have the 'initiatory' mentality, which is appropriate for treating in depth such a subject"[2]; indeed, when Francesco da Barberino[3] mentioned a mysterious widow, symbolizing *Sapienza*, the Wisdom, we are in the realm of the initiatory love.[4] Barberino said:

> Io dico a te e chiaramente che vi fu e vi è una certa vedova che non era vedova. Era toccata eppure intatta. Era vergine e la sua verginità era ignota. Mancò di marito. Aveva marito.[5]

---

[1] Latin *amor* became Italian *amore*, French *amour*, but remained *amor* in Old Provençal, Portuguese, Spanish and Venetian.
[2] Guénon, *Aperçus sur l'Ésotérisme chrétien*, p. 56.
[3] Francesco da Barberino was contemporary with Dante.
[4] This Dame-Wisdom, sometimes Barberino calls her the Rose: *D'ogni cosa donna è rosa* [the Dame is the Rose] *(ponendo vertute lei per quella) e luce bella ed è d'ognun salute* [and the beautiful light, and she is the salvation of mankind]. And, at the question "who is this Dame?," he describes Constanza *armato al cuor che ben sai che vuol dire/ porta di donna vedova sua veste* ("armed to the heart that you know what it means/ and she wears widow's garment") (Luigi Valli, *Il linguaggio segreto di Dante e dei "Fedeli d'Amore"*, Optima, 1928, p. 242).
[5] These apparent "oppositions" to describe the Dame, also found in fairy tales, represent an initiatory description.

Per la sua prudenza eccelleva sulle donne e per la sua eloquenza su tutte le creature terrene.[1]

Alfonso Ricolfi,[2] in his *Studi sui «Fedeli d'Amore»*, also said: "the gemstone or gem symbolizes the human intelligence at its highest level; at this level, there are two widows and in opposition: one has Constanza for maid, and the one, being inconstant, has *Facometipiace* (Do-as-you-please) as servant." This partition is just one of the multiple facets of the Maiden's symbolism; Meister Eckhart said: "The Virgin Mary, before becoming Mother of God in her humanity, was Mother of God in her divinity, and the birth in heaven is illustrated by the birth of God as human being,"[3] and he said about Christ, "that his birth of Mary ghostly was more pleasing to him than his birth of Mary in the flesh."[4] In the Judaic tradition, the Pharaoh's daughter presents the same dichotomy and so does Solomon himself, as St. Bernard gracefully[5] explained.

It is well known how Solomon was criticized for falling from grace at the end of his life,[6] but we must, first and foremost, consider the

---

[1] "I say to you clearly that there was and *there is* a certain *widow* who *was not a widow*. She was touched and yet untouched (intact). She was a virgin yet her virginity was unknown. She lost her husband. She had a husband. She, for her wisdom, was the best of all women, and for her eloquence, the best of all earthly creatures." Valli commented on these lines: "Do you understand? But when we say that these people spoke in jargon, that *amore* was not *amore*, that they belonged to a sect [wrong word used by Valli], that they *mystically* celebrated these *mystical* ladies [again wrong word], that their lady was the lady of the *Song of Songs* (do you not hear the clear echo of the *Wisdom* of Solomon?), those 'positive' critics strongly say that these are fantasies, and they are capable to waste their time trying to identify from the *historical point of view* the name and origin (*la paternità*) of the widow Francesco da Barberino loved."
[2] He followed, completed and sometimes amended Valli's work in his *Studi sui 'Fedeli d'Amore"* (year 1933) (see Pierre Ponsoye, *Intelletto d'Amore*, Études Traditionnelles, no. 371, 1962).
[3] Quoted in Jean Hani, *La Vierge Noire et le mystère marial*, Guy Trédaniel, 1995, p. 112.
[4] Quoted in Ananda K. Coomaraswamy, *Spiritual Authority and Temporal Power in the Indian Theory of Government*, Munshiram Manoharlal, 1978, p. 36.
[5] That is, "full of grace."
[6] "And Solomon made affinity with Pharaoh king of Egypt, and took Pharaoh's daughter, and brought her into the city of David, until he had made an end of

symbolic and sacred significance of Solomon's tale, similar with the meaning of Samson's famous story, and, of course, with that of Adam himself: from a cosmologic viewpoint, the King will decay, eroded, and at the end of the cycle will become the Dragon[1]; consequently, there is a celestial and androgynous Solomon (*moglier e marito* of the *Fedeli d'Amore*) and an earthly, divided and multiplied one.[2] His alleged wife, the Pharaoh's daughter,[3] is very similar in this respect: on the one

---

building his own house, and the house of the Lord, and the wall of Jerusalem round about" (*1 Kings* 3:1); "But king Solomon loved many strange women, together with the daughter of Pharaoh, women of the Moabites, Ammonites, Edomites, Zidonians, and Hittites; Of the nations concerning which the Lord said unto the children of Israel, Ye shall not go in to them, neither shall they come in unto you: for surely they will turn away your heart after their gods: Solomon clave unto these in love. And he had seven hundred wives, princesses, and three hundred concubines: and his wives turned away his heart. For it came to pass, when Solomon was old, that his wives turned away his heart after other gods: and his heart was not perfect with the Lord his God, as was the heart of David his father. For Solomon went after Ashtoreth the goddess of the Zidonians, and after Milcom the abomination of the Ammonites. And Solomon did evil in the sight of the Lord, and went not fully after the Lord, as did David his father" (*1 Kings* 11:1-6).

[1] See in detail our *The Everlasting Sacred Kernel*, Rose-Cross Books, 2001. "Samson, as an archetypal solar hero, an *avatâra*, has to play all the scenarios. He has to be the divine king who reigns over a cycle of existence and changes gradually into a dragon. He has to be the dragon at the end of time. He also has to be the hero embarked on the initiatory path" (p. 29).

[2] On a historical level, Solomon's legacy was "division," considering that, after him, the kingdom was disastrously divided into two (Rehoboam – Jeroboam, who was a "widow's son"; see our *Free-Masonry: A Traditional Organization*, p. 167). Maximus the Confessor (who was in his youth an assistant to the Byzantine Emperor Heraclius), and Eriugena after him, commented on St. Paul's words, "There is neither Jew nor Greek, there is neither bond nor free, there is neither male nor female: for ye are all one in Christ Jesus" (*Galatians* 3:28), stating that the primordial man was androgynous, "neither male nor female," and the Fall produced the division of the sexes (Érigène, *De la division de la Nature, Periphyseon*, Livre I et Livre II, PUF, 1995, pp. 294, 300-1, 452; see also Henry Bett, *Johannes Scotus Erigena*, Hyperion Press, 1986, pp. 56, 67, 78).

[3] "And his house where he dwelt had another court within the porch, which was of the like work. Solomon made also a house for Pharaoh's daughter, whom he had taken to wife, like unto this porch. All these were of costly stones, according to the measures of hewed stones, sawed with saws, within and without, even from the foundation unto the coping, and so on the outside toward the great court. And the foundation was of costly stones, even great stones, stones of ten cubits, and stones

hand, she is the divine virgin-mother[1]; on the other hand, she is, like Eve or Noah's wife or Delilah, the "strange woman," whose "strangeness" has more than one symbolic aspect, related to the *prakritian* and *asurian* heritage.[2]

---

of eight cubits. And above were costly stones, after the measures of hewed stones, and cedars. And the great court round about was with three rows of hewed stones, and a row of cedar beams, both for the inner court of the house of the Lord, and for the porch of the house. And King Solomon sent and fetched Hiram out of Tyre. He was a widow's son of the tribe of Naphtali" (*1 Kings* 7:8-14); even though he built a house for Pharaoh's daughter, "Solomon brought up the daughter of Pharaoh out of the city of David unto the house that he had built for her: for he said, My wife shall not dwell in the house of David king of Israel, because the places are holy, whereunto the ark of the Lord hath come" (*2 Chronicles* 8:11). There is, we see, a connection between the Temple and the house of Pharaoh's daughter. We should not be so much concerned with the objection of the Egyptologists, who assure us that Egyptian royal women were never married to a stranger king; like in all the other cases regarding sacred writings, we should remember that the obvious meaning is the most uninteresting and superficial one (even if it has its own reality).

[1] "And Pharaoh charged all his people, saying, Every son that is born ye shall cast into the river, and every daughter ye shall save alive. And there went a man of the house of Levi, and took to wife a daughter of Levi. And the woman conceived, and bare a son: and when she saw him that he was a goodly child, she hid him three months. And when she could not longer hide him, she took for him an ark of bulrushes, and daubed it with slime and with pitch, and put the child therein; and she laid it in the flags by the river's brink. And his sister stood afar off, to wit what would be done to him. And the daughter of Pharaoh came down to wash herself at the river; and her maidens walked along by the river's side; and when she saw the ark among the flags, she sent her maid to fetch it" (*Exodus* 1:22, 2:1-5). In the Judaic tradition, Moses has three mothers: a corporeal one, an intermediary one who nurses him, and, eventually, the divine virgin, the Pharaoh's daughter. We have here a sacred scenario: for example, in the Greek mythology, Acrisius was afraid that his new-born grandson, Perseus, would kill and replace him; similarly, Laios was scared that his son, Oedipus, would kill him and take his reign. For the same reason, the Pharaoh ordered, when Moses was born, that all the new-born children be killed [implying that Pharaoh's daughter is the virgin]; the same scenario could be found in the Gospel (the "massacre of the innocents").

[2] In the Romanian traditional vestiges, Satan gives Noah's wife a jug of boiled wine and she, becoming drunk, betrays Noah's secret and confesses that he was building a boat in the woods. In *Qur'ân* (66:10), Noah's wife is an example of an unbeliever (her name was Wâila). The Gnostics also developed the theme of Noah's wife; she appears under the name of Norea, the daughter of Adam and Eve. Norea set fire to the Ark, because God (Ialdabaoth for the Sethians, an inferior and arrogant God) did not want to let her survive the flood and because Noah's God is considered the

From an initiatory perspective, the dual aspect was represented by Solomon's *Amor* for Wisdom, a woman identical to *Madonna Intelligenza*,[1] and his *Mors* for the "strange woman."[2] Wisdom is the Gate of Liberation, the *Ianua Coeli*, and she is ready to give the *Eucharist*[3]; the "strange woman" is the Jaws of Death, the Dragon's

---

evil God. In other Gnostic texts, this God, who sent the flood, is opposed by Sophia, the Wisdom that saved Noah in the Ark (See our *The Wrath of Gods*, p. 181).

[1] Wisdom, like *Shekinah*, like Astraea, is herself a "strange woman," because the decadence of the world makes her a stranger: "Wisdom crieth without; she uttereth her voice in the streets: She crieth in the chief place of concourse, in the openings of the gates: in the city she uttereth her words, saying, How long, ye simple ones, will ye love simplicity? and the scorners delight in their scorning, and fools hate knowledge? Turn you at my reproof: behold, I will pour out my spirit unto you, I will make known my words unto you. Because I have called, and ye refused; I have stretched out my hand, and no man regarded; But ye have set at nought all my counsel, and would none of my reproof: I also will laugh at your calamity; I will mock when your fear cometh; When your fear cometh as desolation, and your destruction cometh as a whirlwind; when distress and anguish cometh upon you. Then shall they call upon me, but I will not answer; they shall seek me early, but they shall not find me: For that they hated knowledge, and did not choose the fear of the Lord: They would none of my counsel: they despised all my reproof. Therefore shall they eat of the fruit of their own way, and be filled with their own devices. For the turning away of the simple shall slay them, and the prosperity of fools shall destroy them. But whoso hearkeneth unto me shall dwell safely, and shall be quiet from fear of evil" (*Proverbs* 1:20-33).

[2] The "strange woman" appears nine times in the *Proverbs*. "To deliver thee from the strange woman, even from the stranger which flattereth with her words; Which forsaketh the guide of her youth, and forgetteth the covenant of her God. For her house inclineth unto death, and her paths unto the dead" (*Proverbs* 2:16-18); "My son, attend unto my wisdom [*Amor*], and bow thine ear to my understanding: That thou mayest regard discretion, and that thy lips may keep knowledge. For the lips of a strange woman drop as a honeycomb, and her mouth is smoother than oil: But her end is bitter as wormwood, sharp as a twoedged sword. Her feet go down to death [*Mors*]; her steps take hold on hell" (*Proverbs* 5:1-5).

[3] "Wisdom hath builded her house, she hath hewn out her seven pillars: She hath killed her beasts; she hath mingled her wine; she hath also furnished her table. She hath sent forth her maidens: she crieth upon the highest places of the city, Whoso is simple, let him turn in hither: as for him that wanteth understanding, she saith to him, Come, *eat of my bread, and drink of the wine* [our *Italics*] which I have mingled" (*Proverbs* 9:1-5) ("But when thou makest a feast, call the poor, the maimed, the lame, the blind," see *Luke* 14:12-24).

jaws and the *Ianua Inferni*.¹ Solomon sacrificed himself to illustrate the two Gates, to prove that, as a projection of the Universal Man, he is complete only with both women, even though the *Bible* says that, because of this, he is *not fully*,² while Saint Bernard of Clairvaux, the Templars' mentor, illustrated from his vantage point, in almost one hundred sermons about the *Song of Songs*,³ how Solomon, Love, and Bride should be comprehended at the highest spiritual level, an illustration that we could call "initiatory," in concert with what René Guénon wrote to Ananda K. Coomaraswamy: "for me, this person [Saint Bernard] is indeed an initiate and not only a simple mystic."⁴

---

¹ "The mouth of strange women is a deep pit: he that is abhorred of the Lord shall fall therein" (*Proverbs* 22:14); "For a whore is a deep ditch; and a strange woman is a narrow pit" (*Proverbs* 23:27). Saint Bernard alluded to these two "women" in his 85th *Sermon*: "For where there is love, there is no toil, but a taste. Perhaps 'sapientia,' that is wisdom, is derived from 'sapor,' that is taste, because, when it is added to virtue, like some seasoning, it adds taste to something which by itself is tasteless and bitter. I think it would be permissible to define wisdom as a taste for goodness. We lost this taste almost from the creation of our human race. When the old serpent's poison infected the palate of our heart, because the fleshly sense prevailed, the soul began to lose its taste for goodness, and a depraved taste crept in. 'A man's imagination and thoughts are evil from his youth,' that is, as a result of the folly of the first woman. So it was folly which drove the taste for good from the woman, because the serpent's malice outwitted the woman's folly. But the reason which caused the malice to appear for a time victorious is the same reason why it suffers eternal defeat. For see! It is again the heart and body of a woman which wisdom fills and makes fruitful so that, as by a woman we were deformed into folly, so by a woman we may be reformed to wisdom."
² "And Solomon did evil in the sight of the Lord, and went *not fully* after the Lord, as did David his father. Then did Solomon build a high place for Chemosh, the abomination of Moab, in the hill that is before Jerusalem, and for Molech, the abomination of the children of Ammon. And likewise did he for all his *strange wives*, which burnt incense and sacrificed unto their gods" (*1 Kings* 11:5-7) [our *Italics*].
³ He died in 1153, without finishing his commentary on Solomon's *Song*.
⁴ Letter of November 1936. In his opuscule, *Saint Bernard*, René Guénon presents, because of the special circumstances surrounding the writing of such an essay, a view slightly adapted to the exoteric readers: "Saint Bernard's doctrine is essentially mystical; by this we mean that he envisages divine things especially from the point of view of love, something which, nonetheless, would be wrong to interpret in a merely affective sense, as modern psychologists do. Like many great mystics, he was particularly drawn to the *Song of Songs*, on which he commented in many sermons, sermons that were part of a long series that continued throughout almost all of his

For example, in *Sermon 27*, Saint Bernard said:

What does she mean then by saying: "I am beautiful like the curtains of Solomon?"[1] I feel that here we have a great and wonderful *mystery* [our *Italics*], provided that we apply the words, not to the Solomon of this Song, but to him who said of himself: "What is here is greater than Solomon." This Solomon to whom I refer is so great a Solomon that he is called not only Peaceful – which is the meaning of the word Solomon – but Peace itself; for Paul proclaims that "He is our Peace." I am certain that in this Solomon we can discover something that we may unhesitatingly compare with the beauty of the bride.

Equally, Saint Bernard interpreted the phrase "the king hath brought me into his chambers"[2] as referring to the House of Wisdom, where

---

career; this commentary, which was never completed, describes all the degrees of divine love [*Amor*], up to the supreme peace which the soul reaches in ecstasy. The ecstatic state, as he understood it, and certainly experienced it, is a sort of death [*Mors*] of the things of this world; along with sensitive images [*les images sensibles*], all natural feeling disappears; everything is pure and spiritual within the soul itself, as in its love. Naturally, this mysticism reflected itself in the dogmatic treatises that Saint Bernard wrote; the title of one of the principal ones, *De diligendo Deo* ("On Loving God"), clearly indicates the place that love held in his thought, but it would be wrong to believe that this was to the detriment of true intellectuality. If the Abbot of Clairvaux always sought to remain apart from the vain subtleties of the academics, it was because he had no need for the laborious artifices of dialectic; he resolved at a single blow the most arduous questions because his thinking did not proceed by means of a long series of discursive operations; what philosophers strove to reach by a twisty route and by fumbling, he arrived at immediately, through intellectual intuition, without which no real metaphysics is possible and someone can only grasp a shadow of the truth." We may add that, in this traditional spirit, Coomaraswamy wrote: "But there is every reason to believe that Leonardo, like so many other Renaissance scholars, was versed in the Neo-Platonic esoteric tradition, and that he may have been an initiate, familiar with the 'mysteries' of the crafts (Cf. René Guénon, *L'Esotérisme de Dante*, Paris, 1925; J. H. Probst-Biraben, "Léonardo de Vinci, Initié," *Le Voile d'Isis*, 38, 1933, pp. 260-266)" (Ananda K. Coomaraswamy, *The Iconography of Dürer's "Knots" and Leonardo's "Concatenation,"* The Art Quarterly, Detroit, VII. 2, Spring 1944, pp.109-28).

[1] *Song of Solomon*, 1:5.
[2] *Ibid.*, 1:4.

the chambers compose an initiatory (amorous) hierarchy, aiming at the same time to the Most High and to the Center:

> Let the garden, then, represent the plain, unadorned, historical sense of Scripture, the storeroom its moral sense, and the bedroom the mystery of divine contemplation. You remember that I said the bedroom of the King is to be sought in the mystery of divine contemplation[1];

and then, in the same *Sermon*:

> I feel that the King has not one bedroom only, but several. For he has more than one queen; his concubines are many, his maids beyond counting. And each has her own secret rendezvous with the Bridegroom and says: "My secret to myself, my secret to myself." All do not experience the delight of the Bridegroom's private visit in the same room; the Father has different arrangements for each,

which shows how far away (and how elevating) is Saint Bernard's exposition, in comparison to the profane one. With regard to Solomon's many concubines and his Peace, Dante also declared:

> Moreover, the Empyrean Heaven by its peace resembles the Divine Science, which is full of all peace and suffers no diversity of opinion or sophistical reasoning because of the supreme certainty of its subject, which is God. Christ says of this science to his disciples: "My peace I give to you, my peace I leave with you," giving and leaving to them his teaching, which is this science of which I speak. Solomon, speaking of this science, says: "The queens number sixty, and the concubines eighty; and of the young handmaids there is no number: one is my dove and my perfect one." He calls all sciences queens and friends and handmaids, but this one he calls perfect because it makes us see truth perfectly, in which our souls find rest.[2]

---

[1] *Sermon 23*.
[2] Dante, *The Convivio*, II, 14.

This King Solomon was praised in the Middle Ages, and *this* King Solomon was the Grand Master of the operative Masons; and Solomon became king in this way: "So Zadok the priest, and Nathan the prophet, and Benaiah the son of Jehoiada, and the Cherethites, and the Pelethites, went down, and caused Solomon to ride upon King David's mule, and brought him to Gihon. And Zadok the priest took a horn of oil out of the tabernacle, and anointed Solomon. And they blew the trumpet; and all the people said, God save King Solomon"[1]; we see this ritual act illustrated below, in the first image[2]:

---

[1] *1 Kings* 1:38-9.
[2] This picture is an original copper-plate engraving, from Pieter Mortier's so-called *Great Bible of 1700*; the artists were Jan Luyken, Picart, Elliger, and others; the legend, in Dutch, says that Nathan anointed Solomon. In our collection.

We may note that King Solomon is depicted knelt down; and so is Saint Bernard in his vision of crowned Virgin Mary, presented in the second image above,[1] which the Christian iconography adopted soon after Saint Bernard's death,[2] as illustration of the "Marian legend of Saint Bernard."[3] There are in the "legend" two similar "kneelings": the first, when a young Bernard was praying in the church Saint-Vorles of Châtillon sur Seine, at the feet of a statue of the Virgin Mary, which came to life and sprayed milk from her breast onto the parched lips of Bernard, forever proving her status as the Virgin Mother of God[4]; the second, when Saint Bernard came at Speyer to preach the Crusade, in 1146, on Christmas Eve, and the Bishop showed him into the

---

[1] The engraving is from a Flemish prayer book (the beginning of 16th century), now at the British Museum. There are other painters who endeared this subject: for instance, Filippino Lippi (*Apparition of the Virgin to Saint Bernard*), Fra Bartolommeo (*The Vision of Saint Bernard*), Perugino (*Apparition of the Virgin to Saint Bernard*), Joos van Cleve (*The Vision of Saint Bernard*), Murillo (*The Vision of Saint Bernard*), and Alonso Cano (*Miraculous Lactation of Saint Bernard*). Jean Tourniac observed: "It is strange to note that the Flemish art was often used as receptacle for many traditional details," and he gave as example Quentin Massys' *St. Anne Triptych*, illustrating "the devotion to the 'three Marys' – whose memory continues at Saintes Maries de la Mer," in accord with the legend that Anne, Virgin's mother, had three husbands: Joachim, Cleopas and Salome, who gave her three daughters (the Virgin Mary, Mary, mother of James the Minor [Mary Jacobe] and Mary, mother of John and James the Major, sons of thunder [Mary Salome] (*Principes et problémes spirituals du Rite Écossais Rectifié*, Dervy, 1969, p. 232); however, we should amend Tourniac's sayings: first, at Saintes Maries de la Mer the "three Marys" were Mary Magdalene, Mary Salome, and Mary of Cleopas; second, as showed in our text *The Three Marys*, there is a vertical initiatory hierarchy with Virgin Mary present in the Three Worlds, while in Quentin Massys' *Triptych* (Musées Royaux des Beaux-Arts) there is a "horizontal" development, rather secular than initiatory (or even religious).
[2] Saint Bernard was so on top of his contemporaries that shortly after his death, on 18 January 1174, the Pope Alexander III canonized him.
[3] We have to be cautious, because Saint Bernard regarded the Virgin Mary more from an initiatory viewpoint (like Dante did later), than a religious one, and so, even if it is said that "he fervently promulgated in his writings" the Marian cult, in fact, he scarcely wrote about the Virgin Mary, which does not mean that he was not the "knight of Virgin Mary" and that the Cistercians did not place all of their churches under the name of *Notre Dame*.
[4] This is the so-called "Lactation of Saint Bernard," which we already mentioned at the beginning of the chapter. There is a proverb that says: "If you want milk, you have to kneel" (because milking the cow requires kneeling or a prostrating position).

cathedral,¹ where Saint Bernard cried out in a transport of love, kneeling at each exclamation: "O Clement, O Loving, O Sweet Virgin Mary!"²

Kneeling and prostration is common practice in various traditions and traditional organizations, including Masonry, and well known in the rituals of the three "Abrahamic" religions, but it is also the first

---

¹ The Speyer cathedral, the largest Romanesque cathedral, the burial place of the emperors of the Holy Roman (German) Empire, was dedicated to the Blessed Virgin Mary.

[photo MAT]

² *O clemens, O pia, O dulcis Virgo Maria!* It is said that here, in the Speyer cathedral, the "lactation" occurred (sometimes the milk is directed not to Bernard's lips but to his eyes). Saint Bernard, who rejected the unorthodox idea of "Mary's Immaculate Conception," stressed though: "We cannot for a moment suppose that a privilege which has been accorded to some, though very few, mortals, was denied to that Virgin through whom all mortals have entered life. Beyond all doubt the Mother of the Lord was holy before she was born… she received a more ample blessing which not only sanctified her in the womb, but also preserved her thereafter free from sin throughout her life… she gave birth as a virgin, but not that she was born of a virgin" (*Letter to the Canons of the Church of Lyons, St. Bernard of Clairvaux, Seen through his Selected Letters*, Henry Regnery Co., 1953, pp. 204-205). Therefore, Abdul-Hâdi, in his *Pages dédiées à Mercure* (*La Gnose*, n° de janvier 1911), could describe an initiatory chain as "Marian initiation," alluding to the type of initiation Virgin Mary received (in the "Marian initiation" case, the master could be absent or dead); René Guénon wrote a note to emphasize that such an initiation, having a "within guru," is totally exceptional: *On ne saurait trop insister d'ailleurs sur le fait que ce ne sont là que des cas très exceptionnels et qu'ils ne se produisent que dans des circonstances rendant la transmission normale impossible, par exemple en l'absence de toute organisation initiatique régulièrement constituée*; Guénon added that such an initiation should not be confused with a "mystical" way (see Études Traditionnelles, no. 253, August 1946, and René Guénon, *Initiation et Réalisation Spirituelle*, Éditions Traditionnelles, 1980, p. 271).

degree of the amorous initiatory ladder, and a most favourable gesture for receiving grace and knowledge (we do not want to drastically separate *Amor* from *Gnosis*)¹.

> Lethaby says that the French labyrinths "appear to have been called *la lieue* or *Chemin de Jerusalem*; they were placed at the west end of the nave and people made a pilgrimage on their knees, following the pathway to the center, which is said to have been called *Sancta Ecclesia* or *Ciel*"... The famous medieval examples are inlaid on cathedral floors; there were examples at Amiens, St. Quentin, and Reims; and of those still existing, the most notable is that of Chartres, with a pathway some six hundred and fifty feet in length, leading round and about until the center is reached.²

There is no need to insist upon one of the most famous labyrinths, the Minotaur's maze, but we should point out that Theseus found his way using Ariadne's ball of thread,³ which, unfolded,⁴ represented symbolically the labyrinthic path itself, a path that, like the thread itself, is continuous, without interruptions,⁵ even though following the pathway on their knees, the pilgrims had to "mark" the discontinuity inherent to this earthly world,⁶ each knee breaking the path when moving forward.⁷ One way to represent this combination of

---

¹ "So that at the name of Jesus every knee should bow, in heaven and on earth and under the earth, and every tongue confess that Jesus Christ is Lord" (*Philippians* 2:10-11); "For it is written, 'As I live, says the Lord, every knee shall bow to me, and every tongue shall confess to God'" (*Romans* 14:11).
² Coomaraswamy, *ibid*.
³ It corresponds to Cusanus' "complication." "Nor must we overlook that other line of Dante's in which he speaks of God 'who draws the earth and unites it to himself' (*questi la terra in se stringe ed adune, Paradiso* I.117) or that in which he speaks of seeing all at once 'the universal form of this knot' (*nodo, Paradiso* XXXIII.91), which 'if our fingers are unable to unravel, it is from long neglect' (*ibid.*, XXVIII.58-60)" (Coomaraswamy, *ibid.*).
⁴ It corresponds to Cusanus' "explication."
⁵ It corresponds to *Qian* of *Yi:Jing*, the continuous line symbolizing the Active Perfection, Heaven and *Yang* (see our *About the Yi:Jing*, p. 5).
⁶ It corresponds to *Kun*, a discontinuous line, representing the Passive Perfection, *Yin*.
⁷ Similarly, the sound signifies the continuous line, while the words are the breaking points, because to speak man needs discontinuity. See chapter VIII of the present

continuous and discreet entities, which illustrates the fundamental metaphysical problem of One-and-multiple,[1] is to have a continuous thread provided with a multitude of knots (equalling the "words").[2]

The traditional spirit that we try, more or less maladroitly, to revive in this work guides us, almost in a natural way, to the writings of René Guénon, which explains the title we chose, but prompts us also to consider only a few other contemporary authors, one of them being Ananda K. Coomaraswamy, who was not what we could call an "initiate," but who, in the last part of his life, was a faithful, close and efficient collaborator of Guénon, much better than Schuon, who, even by the very fact that he was so warmly embraced by Westerners and

---

work. "For, in the first place, 'the cord (*tanti*, √ *tan*, extend) is his (the Breath's, Life's) word (*vâc*, here = *logos*), and the knots (*dâma* = Gk. *desmós*) are names; and so with his word as the cord and names as knots all this universe is tied-up'" (Coomaraswamy, *ibid.*).

[1] "'Continuity of the thread': in these words lies the clew to the doctrine *que s'asconde nel velame degli nodi strani* – to adapt the words of Dante that must have been familiar to Leonardo. For what our 'complex' states – and solves – is the relationship of one to many: 'one as he is there in himself, many as he is here in his children' (*Satapatha Brâhmana*); one as thread and many in the knots, for as the *Brahma Upanishad* expresses it, the solar Spider spins his web of a single thread; an omnipresent thread, immanent and transcendent, 'undivided in things divided,' 'measureless in measured things,' 'bodiless in bodies,' 'imperishable in the perishable' (*Atharva Veda*)" (Coomaraswamy, *ibid.*).

[2] "The equation of knots with names may be connected with what was once an almost worldwide (old Chinese, Sumerian, Hebrew, Mexican) method of keeping records by means of knotted string. Thus Jeremias observes that Gudea seems to speak of "knots of words," and that in Sumeria knots may have preceded writing" (Coomaraswamy, *ibid.*); the Inca *quipu* is a fine illustration (from our collection):

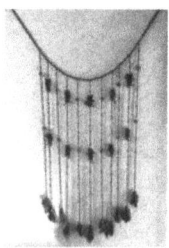
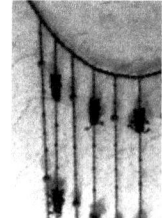

Far-Westerners, was a real disappointment and an agent of confusion for the traditional spirit.

Coomaraswamy's article about the knots, already quoted, gave Guénon the opportunity to make an essential observation:

> A. K. Coomaraswamy has studied the symbolic meaning of certain "knots" which are to be found among the engravings of Albrecht Dürer: these "knots" are very complicated tangles formed by the tracing of a single continuous line (*ces "noeuds" sont des enchevêtrements très compliqués formés par le tracé d'une ligne continue*)... Insofar as they signify the link uniting the members of an initiatic or at least esoteric organisation among themselves, these patterns (*ces traces*) obviously offer a striking similarity with the Masonic "chain of union"; and if we bear in mind the knots of the "chain," the name of "knots" (*Knoten*) given to the designs, apparently by Dürer himself, is likewise very significant. For this reason, as well as for another which we will come to later, it is also important to call attention to the fact that these lines are of unbroken continuity (*de lignes ne présentant aucune solution de continuité*) (footnote: the *pentalpha*, sign of recognition of the Pythagoreans, may be recalled here; it had to be drawn without a break in continuity). The labyrinths of churches could likewise be traversed from one end to the other without at any point encountering a break that made it necessary to stop or to turn back, so that in reality they simply constituted a very long pathway that had to be entirely completed before reaching the centre.[1]

As we said, the pathway is a continuous line; what constitute the discontinuity, the "embodiment" of the discreet quantities, are the knees "pointing" the intervals, and, in fact, there is a strong relation, more than just phonetically, between *knot* and *knee*, considering, first, the shared verbal root *gna* (*gan*), and second, their relation to the symbolism of the "vital knots."[2]

---

[1] *Symboles fondamentaux de la Science sacrée*, Gallimard, 1980, p. 391.
[2] The "vital knots" keep together the microcosmic (man, plant, cathedral) aggregate, as well as the macrocosmic one; therefore, some parts of the human body still have names related to "knot": the chin (Skr. *hanu*, Gr. *ghenos*, Got. *kinnus*, Germ. *Kinn*), the knee (Skr. *ganu*, Latin *genu*, Gr. *gonu*, Got. *kniu*, Germ. *Knie*) or the eyelid (Lat. *genae*). Especially the knee kept this significance, since the knee is a vital knot allowing the

René Guénon went on:

> We have spoken on many occasions of the symbolism of the thread, of which there are multiple aspects, though its essential and strictly metaphysical significance is always the representation of the *sûtrâtmâ* which, both from the macrocosmic and from the microcosmic point of view, links all the states of existence one to another and to their Principle. It is of little importance whether, in the different forms produced by this symbolism, it be a thread in the literal sense, a cord or a chain, or a drawn line such as those already mentioned, or a path made by architectural means as in the case of the labyrinths, a path along which the being has to go [on his knees] from one end to the other in order to reach his goal; what is essential in all the cases is that the line should be unbroken (*une ligne ne présentant aucune solution de continuité*). The path of the line may be more or less complicated, which usually corresponds to more particular modalities or applications of its general symbolism: thus the thread, or its equivalent, may double back on itself so as to form interlacing or knots; and in the structure of the whole, each of these knots represents the point of operation of the forces that determine the condensation and the cohesion of an "aggregate" corresponding to this or that state of manifestation, so that it could be said that it is

---

man to stand up (in fairy tales, the dragon steals the hero's knee ligaments); in Latin, *genu* means at the same time knee and a plant's knot (the Latin word *nodus*, knot, lost its first letter g, the same as the Latin *nosco*, to know, was primitively *gnosco*). René Guénon wrote: "The question, in its most general form, is that of what might be called the 'vital-knot,' existing in any composite, as the junction point of its elements. The cathedral, built according to the rules, constitutes a real organic assembly, and that is why it has also a 'vital-knot.' The problem that relates to this point is the same as the one expressed, in antiquity, by the famous symbol of the 'Gordian knot'; but surely, the modern Masons would be surprised if they were told that their ritual sword can play, in this regard, the same role as that of Alexander…" (*Études sur la Franc-Maçonnerie et le Compagnonnage*, Éditions Traditionnelles, 1980, I, p. 10). "There is a fairly close relationship between the last question and the one addressed in the *Grand Lodge of Iowa Bulletin* (No. May): the symbolism of the string called, in the Anglo-Saxon Masonry, *cable-tow*, expression whose origin is also not less uncertain than that of many other terms specifically Masonic. The indicated similitude with *pavitra* or the Brahmanic cord is interesting, but it seems that a relationship with the *pasha* may appear even more directly; and there are, in this regard, many things to say about the symbolism of the 'vital-knot.'" (*ibid.*, pp. 225-226).

this knot which maintains the being in the state in question, and that its "dissolution"[1] immediately brings the death to that state (*sa solution entraîne immédiatement la mort à cet état*); this is what a term such as 'vital knot' expresses very clearly.[2]

René Guénon alluded a few times to the doctrine of the "vital knots," but never really elaborated on this essential subject; nonetheless, he gave some specifics, among which we should mention one, illustrating the relation of Masonry with *Amor*:

> What makes the meaning of the symbol particularly clear is that, while the cord, as a "tool," is naturally a single line, the "chain of union," on the contrary, had knots from place to place; *in footnote*: These knots are called "lacs d'amour"; this name, as well as their particular forms, could be in a sense the brand of the 18th century, but it may also be a vestige of something that goes back much further, and may even be linked quite directly to the symbolism of "Fedeli d'Amore."[3]

We are not surprised that such a similar knot is called *Solomon's knot*, with all the implications related to its symbolism[4]; and as Solomon is

---

[1] Therefore, solving a problem means to "unknot": it is "dissolution" (from Latin *solutio* "a loosening or unfastening").
[2] *Ibid.*, p. 400. "This leads us directly to considerations of another order which relate to a more 'inward' (*un sens plus 'intérieur'*) and more profound significance of this symbolism: as the being who traverses the labyrinth or any other equivalent representation, thereby finally succeeds in finding the 'central place,' that is, from the point of view of initiatory realization, his own center, the pathway itself, with all its complications, is obviously a representation of the multiplicity of the states or of the modalities of manifested existence, throughout the indefinite series of which the being must first 'wander' before being able to establish himself in this center (*une représentation de la multiplicité des états ou des modalités de l'existence manifestée, à travers la série indéfinie desquels l'être a dû 'errer' tout d'abord avant de pouvoir s'établir dans ce centre*). The continuous line is then the image of the sûtrâtmâ which links all the states together, and moreover, in the case of 'Ariadne's thread' concerning the passage through the labyrinth, this image is so clear that it is surprising that anyone could fail to perceive it" (*ibid.*, p. 391).
[3] *Symboles fondamentaux*, p. 389.
[4] "Special senses of *nodo* include *nodo di Salomone* 'a design showing a knot without any ends in the cords being visible,' *nodo* as 'string (of pearls),' and *nodi della vita*, 'ties

associated with Wisdom, so the knot, at least from a *nirukta* viewpoint, is associated with *gnosis* and *genesis*,[1] and also with a "vital-knot" as *genu*, the knee.

The knee is directly related to *genero* ("to generate"): "And she said, Behold my maid Bilhah, go in unto her; and she shall bear upon my knees, that I may also have children by her"[2]; yet, the symbolism here signifies more than a "human" or "worldly" birth. Well known is the legend about the stork bringing the newborn to the parents, lowering

---

of the soul to the body'... 'Universal form': for, 'indeed, this All is held together by invisible powers, which the Craftsman has extended (*apáteine*) from the ends of the earth even unto the sky, taking wise forethought that the things bound (*dethénta*) and pendent, as it were, from a chain (*seirá*), should not be loosed; for the powers of the All are bonds (*desmoi*) that cannot be broken' (Philo, *Migr.* 181 with 167). Here things are thought of (in 167) as if pendent from a garland or necklace, to which they are secured, and to fall away from which would be their death. It is in this sense that in India the death of the individual is described as a being 'cut off'; and in the same way in China, 'the ancients described death as the loosening of the cord on which God suspended their life" (*Chuang Tzu* III.4) (Coomaraswamy, *ibid.*).

[1] René Guénon used to say that *connaître* (to know) means *être* (to be, to become what you know): *La conséquence immédiate de ceci, c'est que connaître et être ne sont au fond qu'une seule et même chose; ce sont, si l'on veut, deux aspects inséparables d'une réalité unique, aspects qui ne sauraient même plus être distingués vraiment là où tout est "sans dualité." ... La métaphysique affirme l'identité foncière du connaître et de l'être, qui ne peut être mise en doute que par ceux qui ignorent ses principes les plus élémentaires; et, comme cette identité est essentiellement inhérente à la nature même de l'intuition intellectuelle, elle ne l'affirme pas seulement, elle la réalise* (René Guénon, *Introduction Générale à l'étude des Doctrines Hindoues*, Les Éditions Véga, 1932, pp. 156-157); *Nous devons insister particulièrement, chaque fois que l'occasion s'en présente à nous, sur cette réalisation de l'être par la connaissance, car elle est tout à fait étrangère aux conceptions occidentales modernes, qui ne vont pas au delà de la connaissance théorique, ou plus exactement d'une faible partie de celle-ci, et qui opposent artificiellement le "connaître" à l'"être," comme si ce n'étaient pas là les deux faces inséparables d'une seule et même réalité* (*Les États multiples de l'Être*, Guy Trédaniel, 1989, p. 89). The primeval root *gnâ* has produced two series: 1. "to know": Skr. *jnâna*, Gr. *gnosis*, Lat. *(g)nosco*, Germ. *können*, Eng. *know*, Slav. *znat*; 2. "to be born": Skr. *gan* (*ganitar* = "father", *ganus* = race, lineage"); Lat. *(g)nascor* (*gigno* = "to give birth, to produce," *genitura* = "birth, seed," *genitor* = "father," *gens* = "lineage," *genero* = "to give life"); Eng. *kind, gender*; Germ. *Kind* = "child". From a metaphysical perspective, to know (spiritually, initiatory, French *connaître*) means to be born as what you know (French *naître*), and, consequently, to solve the mundane *knot* and to realize the divine *knot*. Jean Tourniac tried to connect *knot* to *gnosis* as having similar verbal roots (he specified that in the Semitic languages, *barakah* means at the same time "knee" and "blessing") (*ibid.*, p. 181).
[2] *Genesis* 30:3.

the baby through the chimney; this tale gets its reality from two sacred concepts: the "spiritual paternity" and the *avatâra*, where the stork is an emblem of the supreme Principle and the child (any child) is potentially an *avatâra*, coming down into the world along the *Axis Mundi* (the chimney). In the Hindu tradition, there are two legitimate gates: *dêva-yâna* ("the gate of gods") and *pitri-yâna* ("the gate of ancestors"), corresponding to the winter (north) and summer (south) solstices. The first one is the gate through which descend divine messengers and celestial influences, through which comes down the *avatâra*, or ascend the "liberated" ones, the "elected" beings that have achieved a complete spiritual realization, while the second one is the gate through which the beings come back into Existence, chained by their ignorance to the worldly rotations of the cycles; this gate communicates also with the domain of the ancestors, with the realm of the past cycles, with Death, that is why it is called *Ianua Inferni*. In the Western tradition, their janitor is Janus *Bifrons* ("two-faced").

The knee symbolizes such a gate, allowing birth to *avatâras* or the other beings, and therefore it is related to the solstitial gate of the Capricorn where Saturn and Janus reigned together[1]; moreover, the

---

[1] In a Medieval manuscript (year 1399), the universal man shows the sign of Capricorn corresponding to his knees; in Astrology, Saturn is presented one-footed, with a child (who is an *avatâra*), and the Capricorn nearby (the wooden leg emphasizes the knee):

 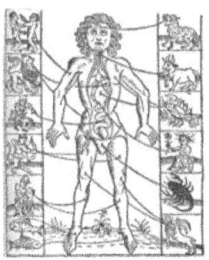

uncovered knee is a sign of the two divine attributes, Mercy and Justice,[1] and of initiation[2].

[1] René Guénon, *Le Roi du Monde*, Gallimard, 1981, pp. 25-26. Thus, the symbolism of the knee is related to the Royal Art and even to the Imperial Art.
[2] Therefore Jason was presented in the Greek mythology with one bare foot.

CHAPTER VI

THE HIERARCHY OF LOVE

We saw Solomon on his knees receiving the spiritual influence, the indispensable blessing authorizing him as king; kneeling describes not only an annihilation of the ego,[1] or a state of humility (like in the religious rites), but a "gesture" enabling "communication" with the supra-individual levels of the being.[2] Solomon is again on his knees, receiving the blessing from God[3] and transmitting it to the people:

> For Solomon had made a brasen scaffold of five cubits long, and five cubits broad, and three cubits high, and had set it in the midst of the court: and upon it he stood, and kneeled down upon his knees before all the congregation of Israel, and spread forth his hands toward heaven. And said, O Lord God of Israel, there is no God like thee in the heaven, nor in the earth; which keepest covenant, and shewest mercy unto thy servants, that walk before thee with all their hearts.[4]
>
> And it was so, that when Solomon had made an end of praying all this prayer and supplication unto the Lord, he arose from before the altar of the Lord, from kneeling on his knees with his hands spread

---

[1] We should understand "annihilation" as a state of consciousness where reality (of the Principle) and illusion (of the manifestation) are completely comprehended.
[2] The Hebrew *barak*, meaning "knee" or "kneeling," derived from a common Semitic root describing the kneeling in preparation for receiving a blessing.
[3] The symbol for the spiritual influence (blessing) is the rain: "When heaven is shut up, and there is no rain, because they have sinned against thee... give rain upon thy land, which thou hast given to thy people for an inheritance" (*1 Kings* 8:35-36).
[4] *2 Chronicles* 6:13-14.

up to heaven. And he stood, and blessed all the congregation of Israel with a loud voice, saying, Blessed be the Lord, that hath given rest unto his people Israel, according to all that he promised: there hath not failed one word of all his good promise, which he promised by the hand of Moses his servant.[1]

Similarly, Jesus Christ, on his knees, prayed in the Garden of Gethsemane: "And he went a little farther, and fell on his face, and prayed..."[2] St. Paul explained:

> Let this mind be in you, which was also in Christ Jesus: Who, being in the form of God, thought it not robbery to be equal with God: But made himself of no reputation [emptied himself – *kenosis*], and took upon him the form of a servant, and was made in the likeness of men: And being found in fashion as a man, he humbled himself, and became obedient unto death, even the death of the cross. Wherefore God also hath highly exalted him, and given him a name which is above every name: That at the name of Jesus every knee should bow, of things in heaven, and things in earth, and things under the earth.[3]

The knee plays an important role in the initiatory and all the other sacred rites: in Masonry, for example, the Entered Apprentice candidate will kneel on his naked left knee, his right foot forming the angle of a square, all these "details," unnecessary at the beginning of the cycle, unfolding the knot from complication to explication; the tribute paid to God, to the emperor and to the beloved lady, the

---

[1] *1 Kings* 8:54-56.
[2] *Matthew* 26:39.
[3] *Philippians* 2:5-10. St. Paul alludes to the Three Worlds, that is, to the entire universal manifestation that should kneel in front of the Principle; this is related to the Three Magi: "And when they were come into the house, they saw the young child with Mary his mother, and fell down, and worshipped him: and when they had opened their treasures, they presented unto him gifts; gold, and frankincense and myrrh" (*Matthew* 2:11).

knighting ritual,[1] imposed a kneeling position. The kneeling suggests obedience and humility, not in a mundane but in a metaphysical sense (if we can say so), as the pure traditional spirit entails the acceptance of a natural hierarchy, in conformity with *Dharma*, when the ego and the individuality abandon their arrogance and ignorance in favour of the spiritual influences and blessing transmitted by the hierarchical superiors; therefore, the knee symbolizes an illumination, a cognition and recognition of the true Light, in front of which the individual is a servant and pure nothingness, while the act of kneeling is a lowering leading to exaltation.[2]

The congregation kneels in front of Christ, and Christ kneels in front of God; the knights kneel in front of the emperor, and the emperor kneels in front of the *sacerdos*; also, the lover kneels in front of his beloved lady, because, as Ibn 'Arabî said, "one of the conditions of a lover is to minimize the importance of his person."[3] Even for a true "mystic,"[4] the description of "humility" and the condition of servant

---

[1] "From henceforth bear his name whose form thou bear'st: Kneel thou down Philip, but rise more great, Arise sir Richard and Plantagenet" (Shakespeare, *The Life and Death of King John*, Act I).
[2] Accordingly, St. Bernard explained how humility is the Way, because it is followed by exaltation: *persévérez dans l'enseignement que vous avez reçu: élevez-vous par l'humilité. Telle est la voie... Seul l'humilité exalte, seule elle conduit à la vie. Étant Dieu, le Christ ne pouvait grandir, car il n'y a rien au-delà de Dieu. Il a cependant trouvé le moyen de croître, et ce fut en descendant, en venant s'incarner, souffrir, mourir pour nous éviter la mort éternelle. Dieu l'a alors exalté, Jésus est ressuscité, monté, s'est assis à la droite de Dieu* (Dom Jean Leclercq, *St. Bernard et l'esprit cistercien*, Seuil, 1966, p. 171).
[3] Ibn 'Arabî, *Traité de l'Amour*, Albin Michel, 1986, p. 218. "The condition of the lover is to be a slave in all humility... the lover who reached such a state must drink the perfume of intimacy in perfect submission and humility. This type of abnegation is realized in the spiritual station of love" (*ibid.*, pp. 254-5).
[4] René Guénon made a clear distinction between a metaphysical realization and a mystical one; he said: "I don't regard the mystical 'realization' as illusory, but only as incomplete... this realization strongly differs from the metaphysical realization and this in its very principle, since it implies passivity.... also, it mixes various elements, therefore a confusion between intellectual and sentimental domain" (letter to Noële Maurice-Denis Boulet, January 3ᵈ, 1918, in René Guénon, *Fragments Doctrinaux*, Rose-Cross Books, 2013); see also *Aperçus sur l'initiation*, Éditions Traditionnelles, 1992, ch. I. However, we envisage here a special group of "mystics" like St. Bernard, Meister Eckhart, Gregory of Nyssa, Gregory of Nazianzus, Gregory Palamas and

relate only superficially to the secular world (and for "methodological" reasons mainly), because, in fact, the aim is the Principle; the true "humility" characterizes the Edenic state, when the being becomes conscious of the *principial* unity and omnipotence, of the fact that there is no comparison between universal and individual, of the fact that the only and supreme relation of master-servant vassalage is the solar Ray that connects *jîvâtmâ* to *Âtmâ* – the spiritual Sun. As the Far-Eastern tradition stated, "that nobility finds its root in humility (smallness), and what is elevated finds its stability in the lowness. Hence princes and kings call themselves 'Orphans,' 'Widowers,' and 'Destitute.' Is this not an acknowledgment that in considering the humility they see the foundation of their nobility? They do not wish to be carved in jade, but prefer to be coarse-looking as an ordinary stone."[1] We can understand better this humility if we refer to the syntagm "spiritual poverty," which in Islam is called *el-faqru*. René Guénon wrote:

> These beings, human or others, are therefore, in all that they are, in a state of complete dependence with regard to the Principle, "apart from which there is nothing, absolutely nothing that exists" (Ibn 'Arabî); it is the consciousness of this dependence which makes what several traditions call "spiritual poverty." At the same time, for the being who has acquired this consciousness, it has, as its immediate consequence, detachment with regard to all manifested things, for the being knows from then on that these things are nothing, and that they have no importance whatsoever compared with the absolute Reality... "Simplicity" and "smallness" are here equivalents, in reality, of the "poverty," which is so often mentioned also in the Gospels, and which is generally very much misunderstood: "Blessed are the poor in spirit, for theirs is the Kingdom of Heaven."[2] This "poverty" (in Arabic *El faqru*) leads, according to Islamic esotericism, to *El-Fanâ*, that is, to the extinction

---

Maximus the Confessor, for whom "mystic" meant the Greek *mystikos*, "secret, connected to mysteries, symbolical."

[1] *Lao-zi* XXXIX.
[2] *Matthew* 5:3. Here, "poor in spirit" means precisely to have a "weak mind," that is, a tamed mind, and not being "high-spirited" (with all its profane significances); see chapter VII of the present work.

of the "ego"; and, by this "extinction" the "divine station" is reached (*El-maqâmul-ilahi*), which is the central point where all the distinctions inherent in the external points of view are surpassed and where all the oppositions have disappeared and are resolved in a perfect equilibrium...[1] "Poverty," "simplicity" and "childhood," are no more than one and the same thing, and the process of being stripped [*kenosis*] which all these words express (it is the "being stripped of metals" in the Masonic symbolism) culminates in an "extinction" which is, in reality, the fullness of the being [*plerosis*], just as "inaction" (*wou-wei*) is the fullness of activity, because it is from it that all particular activities derive: "The Principle is always without acting, and yet everything is done by it" (*Tao-Te-King*, XXXVII).[2]

The knee is so symbolically important that Tacitus recorded in his writings the expression *genua advolvi*, "throwing himself at the knees [of a superior],"[3] and continued with "and weary his hand with kisses."[4] Nonetheless, what Tacitus described was just a diluted replica of an initiatory voyage in three steps, not so much "devotional" (*bhakti*) but "amorously intellectual," which Saint Bernard unveiled in his sermons on the *Song of Songs*:

> Prostrate yourself on the ground, take hold of his feet, soothe them with kisses, sprinkle them with your tears and so wash not them but yourself... Though you have made a beginning by kissing the feet,

---

[1] This equilibrium is the "true measure," that is, the "spiritual poverty" is the essence of a "measured" and balanced way of fighting the mind, which in English, curiously enough, is illustrated by expressions like: "don't mind," "it doesn't matter," "never mind."

[2] René Guénon, *Aperçus sur l'ésotérisme islamique et le Taoïsme*, Gallimard, 1978, ch. IV, *El-Faqru*. Guénon insisted that the real humility, which is "spiritual poverty," means to recognize the total dependence of the being on the Principle: the complete "normal" man has to be *yin* relative to the Principle, but only to the Principle, and, because of his "central" position, he has to be *yang* relative to the entire manifestation; on the contrary, the declined (decayed, fallen) man has a luciferian attitude, tending to be *yang* relative to the Principle and *yin* relative to manifestation (*Initiation et Réalisation Spirituelle*, pp. 127-128).

[3] Tacitus, *Annals*, book 15:71; also, for example: *Tiberii genua advolveretur*, "thrown himself at the knees of Tiberius" (1.13).

[4] *Genua ipsius advolvi et dextram osculis fatigare* (*ibid.*, 15:71).

you may not presume to rise at once by impulse to the kiss of the mouth; there is a step to be surmounted in between, an intervening kiss on the hand for which I offer the following explanation. Consider for a moment: still tarnished as you are with the dust of sin, would you dare touch those sacred lips? Yesterday you were lifted from the mud, today you wish to encounter the glory of his face? No, his hand must be your guide to that end. First it must cleanse your stains, then it must raise you up... On receiving such a grace then, you must kiss his hand, that is, you must give glory to his name, not to yourself. You have seen the way that we must follow, the order of procedure: first, we cast ourselves at his feet,[1] we weep before the Lord who made us, deploring the evil we have done. Then we reach out for the hand that will lift us up, that will steady our trembling knees. And finally, when we shall have obtained these favours through many prayers and tears, we humbly dare to raise our eyes to his mouth, so divinely beautiful, not merely to gaze upon it, but I say it with fear and trembling – to receive its kiss. 'Christ the Lord is a Spirit before our face,' and he who is joined to him in a holy kiss becomes through his good pleasure, one spirit with him.[2]

Let us note how significant the knee is: in the first degree, the neophyte's knees are completely annihilated, and the only essential and real knees are Christ's[3]; in the second degree, the knees are trembling, and only in the final degree the knees function fully.

---

[1] *Genua advolvi.*
[2] *Sermon 3.*
[3] The two feet should be compared to the Masonic columns, but also with the two sides of the Lord of the World ("According to St. Augustine and various other Fathers of the Church, the right hand, in the same way, represents Mercy or Goodness, whereas the left hand, in God especially, is the symbol of Justice," René Guénon, *Le Roi du Monde*, Gallimard, 1981, p. 26). "These signs are fear and hope, the former presenting the imprint of judgment, the latter that of mercy. Truly, the Lord takes pleasure in them that fear him, and in them that hope in his mercy, for the fear of the Lord is the beginning of wisdom, hope the growth of wisdom. Its perfection charity reserves to itself. If all this be true, then obviously this first kiss, given to the feet, brings forth no small fruit. But of one thing you must beware, that you do not neglect either of these feet. If, for instance, you feel deep sorrow for your sins along with the fear of the judgment, you have pressed your lips on the imprint of truth and of judgment. But if you temper that fear and sorrow with the thought of God's goodness and the hope of obtaining his pardon, you will realize that you have also embraced the foot of his mercy. It is clearly inexpedient to kiss

We said, as you remember, that these kisses were given to the feet, the hand and the mouth, in that order. The first is the sign of a genuine conversion of life, the second is accorded to those making progress, the third is the experience of only a few of the more perfect. The book of Scripture that we have undertaken to expound begins with this last kiss, but I have added the other two in the hope that you will attain a better understanding of the last. I leave it to you to judge whether this was necessary, but I do really think that the very nature of the discourse clearly suggests that they be included. And I should be surprised if you did not see that she who said: "Let him kiss me with the kiss of his mouth," wished to make a distinction between the kiss of the mouth and another or several other kisses.[1]

Saint Bernard,[2] like other sages, in addition to the "kiss hierarchy," regarded love itself as a ladder; here is how he, just before his death, described love and the spiritual Wedding:

---

one without the other; a man who thinks only of the judgment will fall into the pit of despair, another who deceitfully flatters God's mercy gives birth to a pernicious security (*Sermon 6*).

[1] *Sermon 4*. Obviously, the "kiss" is a seal of an "intellectual love," as Saint Bernard so infallibly explained. "I must ask you to try to give your whole attention here. The mouth that kisses signifies the Word who assumes human nature; the nature assumed receives the kiss; the kiss however, that takes its being both from the giver and the receiver, is a person that is formed by both, none other than 'the one mediator between God and mankind, himself a man, Christ Jesus.' It is for this reason that none of the saints dared say: 'let him kiss me with his mouth,' but rather, 'with the kiss of his mouth'" (*Sermon 2*). "And hence the bride, although otherwise so audacious, does not dare to say: 'Let him kiss me with his mouth,' for she knows that this is the prerogative of the Father alone. What she does ask for is something less: 'Let him kiss me with the kiss of his mouth.' Do you wish to see the newly-chosen bride receiving this unprecedented kiss, given not by the mouth but by the kiss of the mouth? Then look at Jesus in the presence of his Apostles: 'He breathed on them,' according to St. John, 'and he said: «Receive the Holy Spirit»' then it cannot be wrong to see in the kiss the Holy Spirit" (*Sermon 8*).

[2] René Guénon wrote to Ananda K. Coomaraswamy: *Puisque vous me parlez de Saint Bernard, vous ne savez sans doute pas que j'ai moi-même écrit quelque chose sur celui-ci… ce caractère, pour moi, est bien initiatique et non pas simplement mystique* [*St. Bernard, for me, is indeed an initiate and not just a mystique*] (November 5, 1936); see René Guénon, *Fragments Doctrinaux*, Rose-Cross Books, 2013.

Love is a great reality; but there are degrees to it. The bride stands at the highest. Children love their father, but they are thinking of their inheritance, and as long as they have any fear of losing it, they honour more than they love the one from whom they expect to inherit. I suspect the love which seems to be founded on some hope of gain. It is weak, for if the hope is removed it may be extinguished, or at least diminished. It is not pure, as it desires some return. Pure love has no self-interest. Pure love does not gain strength through expectation, nor is it weakened by distrust. This is the love of the bride, for this is the bride with all that means. Love is the being and the hope of a bride. She is full of it, and the bridegroom is contented with it. He asks nothing else, and she has nothing else to give. That is why he is the bridegroom and she the bride; this love is the property only of the couple. No-one else can share it, not even a son. Although she may pour out her whole self in love, what is that compared to the inexhaustible fountain of his love? The stream of love does not flow equally from her who loves and from him who is love, the soul and the Word, the Bride and the Bridegroom, the Creator and the creature – any more than a thirsty man can be compared to a fountain. Although the creature loves less, being a lesser being, yet if it loves with its whole heart nothing is lacking, for it has given all. Such love, as I have said, is marriage, for a soul cannot love like this and not be beloved; complete and perfect marriage consists in the exchange of love. No-one can doubt that the soul is first loved, and loved more intensely, by the Word; for it is anticipated and surpassed in its love. Happy the soul who is permitted to be anticipated in blessedness so sweet! Happy the soul who has been allowed to experience the embrace of such bliss! For it is nothing other than love, holy and chaste, full of sweetness and delight, love utterly serene and true, mutual and deep, which joins two beings, not in one flesh, but in one spirit, making them no longer two but one.[1]

---

[1] *Sermon 83*. This is the spiritual Wedding, the Supreme Identity realized through Knowledge and divine Love, related to gnosis and genesis. Meister Eckhart stated: "We have to understand the union between man and God with respect to the likeness of the image, because man is similar to God as image. Therefore, when it is said that man and God are one and, following this union, he is God, we have to understand man as image through which he is alike God and not as created nature... And in this way we have to understand St. Augustine's words, when he says: 'What man loves, he is. If he loves a stone, he is a stone, if he loves a human being, he is a human being; if he loves God – and I don't dare to go on, because if I had said that

For Ibn 'Arabî, Love (*Amor*) is hierarchized in relation to the constitutive triad of the human being: *Corpus*, *Anima*, and *Spiritus*:

> Love is of three kinds, not more: divine, spiritual and natural or physical. The divine love is what God has for us [it is the gracious and merciful love]. Our love for Him refers to this type of love. The spiritual love[1] is that of a lover hastened to satisfy his mistress. Nothing remains in him, no aim, no will, what might oppose her. Moreover, the lover remains fully compliant to the mistress' will. The natural love is that of a lover seeking full satisfaction of his desires, without taking into account that his zeal pleases or not his mistress. Most people today are governed by this kind of love.[2]

Similarly, Plato considers three levels in the hierarchy of love, steps that can be related to the types described by Ibn 'Arabî: the love of corporeal beauty, the love of soul's beauty and the love of beauty itself, of eternal Beauty; the first two steps refer to the individual or formal world, and only the divine Love allows the being to achieve exaltation to the universal, to the celestial spheres, but this Love is inexpressible, as well as any metaphysical notion, and therefore, Ibn 'Arabî, and

---

he is God, you would lapidate me, but I send you to the Scripture.' Thus, when man is totally united to God through love, he is free of images, formed and transformed in the divine conformity in which he and God are one" (Maître Eckhart, *Sermons*, Seuil, 1974, II, p. 64). Aristotle already underlined: *dunamei pos esti ta noêta ho nous* (*De Anima* III, 4, 429b) ("the intellect is in a sense potentially whatever is thinkable [the intelligibles]"); and: "thought and object of thought are the same" (*Metaphysics*, 1072 b, 20). St. Thomas Aquinas followed with *intellectus in actu est intellectum in actu*, and René Guénon restated: "the soul is everything he knows" ("the soul is in a way all existing things," *De Anima* III, 4, 431b). We must add what Nicolas Cusanus said about the "vision of God" (*visio sine comprehensione*), that it is an intellectual knowledge when the knower becomes identical to the object of this knowledge, but, this identification cannot be perfect without love, since *unit amor amantem cum amabili* and therefore *quanto igitur quis Deum plus amaverit, tanto plus ad divinitatem participat*; for Cusanus, intellect and love are the two facets of our "mind" ("a simple and noble power"), yet this "mind" we have to consider it like in Hesychasm, established in the heart, and representing what the Hindu tradition calls *jnâna chakshus*. Thus, Cusanus concluded, our mind cannot know God without loving Him, and there is no divine science without divine love (*ita non potest esse vera scientia Dei, ubi non est charitas*).
[1] This love is, in fact, the "psyhical love" or "the love of the soul."
[2] *Traité de l'amour*, p. 66.

others like him, are forced to resort to elements belonging to the formal or individual love to suggest, by analogy, what divine Love means.

Plato concluded Diotima's initiatory love-lesson with the words of Socrates:

> Such, Phaedrus – and I speak not only to you, but to all of you – were the words of Diotima; and I am persuaded of their truth... And therefore, also, I say that every man ought to honour Eros as I myself honour him, and walk in his ways, and exhort others to do the same, and praise the power and spirit of Eros according to the measure of my ability now and ever... Regard this speech, then, Phaedrus, if you want to, as spoken in eulogy of Eros.[1]

Some of the English translations used "love" for Eros, but, in fact, *eros* means "desire" and not the carnal but the cosmical or even metaphysical one, and in this sense we should use the equivalent word "cupidity," since the Roman god Cupid is a replica of the Greek god Eros. Plato, in *Symposium*, tried to define and describe this god, stressing, among other opinions, that Eros is the most ancient god and he is the one that guides the two hemispheres, male and female, to reunite and restore the primordial androgynous sphere. Marsilio Ficino, commenting on Plato's *Symposium*, said:

> In the *Argonautica*, when Orpheus,[2] in the presence of Chiron and the heroes, sang about the beginning of things, following theology of Hermes Trismegistus, he placed Chaos before the World, and located Eros (Love) in the bosom of that Chaos, before Saturn, Jove, and the other gods; and he praised Eros in these words: Eros (Love) is the oldest, perfect in himself, and best

---

[1] Plato, *Symposium*, 275. Diotima is, indeed, an initiatress with regard to the Art of Love.
[2] Fabre d'Olivet considered that Pythagoras and Plato received the initiatory lore from Orpheus (*The Golden Verses of Pythagoras*, Kessinger Publishing, p. 31); on the other hand, Tertullian indicated Hermes the Egyptian as source for Pythagoras and Plato (R. P. Festugière, *La révélation d'Hermès Trismégiste, I, L'Astrologie et les Sciences Occultes*, Les Belles Lettres, 1983, p. 79).

counselled. Hesiod, in his *Theogony*,[1] Parmenides the Pythagorean, in his book *On Nature*, and Acusilaus the poet agreed with Orpheus and Hermes. Plato, in the *Timaeus*, describes Chaos in a similar way, and places Eros in it. And in the *Symposium* Phaedrus recounted the same thing.[2]

Why should Eros be placed at the beginning of all things?[3] To answer this question we have to turn to the Hindu tradition, which said:

> Desire (Kâma) came upon That One (Brahma) in the beginning, that was the primal seed and germ of Spirit.[4]

Eros is therefore Kâma, the Desire; not any desire or cupidity, but the absolute Desire, the primordial Desire that activates the cosmogony and the production of the universal manifestation, an aspect of the divine Charity, of the supreme Love (*Amor*), the Love that Dante calls *L'Amor che muove il Sole e l'altre stele*. In the Hindu tradition, Kâma is, generally speaking, the god of love auto-produced from the primordial Waters as Desire. He is accompanied by the celestial maidens, the Apsaras, one Apsara carrying the god's banner, a *makara*,[5] which is

---

[1] Hesiod, in his *Theogony*, indeed said: "Verily at the first Chaos came to be, but next wide-bosomed Gaea, the ever-sure foundations of all the deathless ones who hold the peaks of snowy Olympus, and dim Tartarus in the depth of the wide-pathed Earth, and Eros, fairest among the deathless gods, who unnerves the limbs and overcomes the mind and wise counsels of all gods and all men within them."

[2] Marsilio Ficino, *Commentary on Plato's Symposium on Love*, Spring, 1994, pp. 37-38; Ficino added: "all things are preserved by the unity of their parts; with the dispersion of their parts things die. But their mutual love brings about the unity of their parts... Hence, Orpheus: 'You alone, O Love, rule the reins of all these things'" (*ibid.*, p. 65). We should think about the Masonic ritual with the answer: "Pour rechercher ce qui a été perdu. Pour rassembler ce qui est épars et répandre partout la lumière"; "to gather what is scattered" is not only a Masonic but a sacred universal objective, and beside *gnosis*, *amor* has its part in this initiatory endeavour.

[3] About Eros see also our *The Everlasting Sacred Kernel*.

[4] *Rig Vêda*; and also: "Meditating, He had the desire (*kâma*) to produce the various beings from His essence."

[5] Therefore, Kâma is called Makardhvaj.

remarkable in itself, thinking of the symbolism of *kâla-mukha*. Kâmadeva's weapon is a bow with a string of honeybees, and his arrows are decorated with five kinds of flowers.[1] Kâma, like Eros, with his functions and attributes, has a double role, Macro- and Microcosmical: Love, from a macrocosmical viewpoint, produces the universal manifestation, sustaining it as Desire, and from a microcosmical point of view, transforms – in an initiatory manner – the being, by annihilating the worldly desires and awakening a one-and-only Desire, a replica of the one born from Chaos.[2]

The divine Saint Dionysius united Eros (yearning, desire) to Love (agape) in God:

> And hence all things must desire and yearn for (*eros*) and must love (*agape*) the Beautiful and the Good. Yea, and because of It and for Its sake the inferior things yearn (*eros*) for the superior under the mode of attraction, and those of the same rank have a yearning towards their peers under the mode of mutual communion; and the superior have a yearning towards their inferiors under the mode of providential kindness; and each hath a yearning (*eros*) towards itself under the mode of cohesion, and all things are moved by a longing for the Beautiful and Good, to accomplish every outward work and form every act of will. And true reasoning will also dare to affirm that even the Creator of all things Himself yearneth after all things, createth all things, perfecteth all things, conserveth all things, attracteth all things, through nothing but excess of Goodness. Yea, and the Divine Yearning (*divine eros*) is naught else than a Good Yearning towards the Good for the mere sake of the Good. For the Yearning which createth all the goodness of the world, being pre-

---

[1] The five flowers are Ashoka tree flowers, white and blue lotus flowers, Mallika tree (Jasmine) and Mango tree flowers. They represent, among other things, the cosmogony activated by the bee's presence.

[2] The *Bhagavad-Gîtâ* explains in detail *niṣkâma karma*, the action without desire, but here this desire is the mundane one, which is also listed as an objective of the human life: *Ces buts sont au nombre de quatre, et ils sont énumérés ainsi dans un ordre hiérarchiquement ascendant:* artha, kâma, dharma, moksha… kâma *est le désir, dont la satisfaction constitue le bien de l'ordre psychique* (René Guénon, *Études sur L'Hindouisme*, Éditions Traditionnelles, 1979, p. 73). In the Islamic tradition, the desire is called *niyyah*, the intention to do an act for the love of Allah.

existent abundantly in the Good Creator, allowed Him not to remain unfruitful in Himself, but moved Him to exert the abundance of His powers in the production of the universe... But that we may not seem, in saying this, to be setting aside Holy Scripture, let those who blame the title of "Yearning" hear what the Scripture saith: Yearn for her and she shall keep thee; exalt her and she shall promote thee; she shall bring thee to honour when thou dost embrace her...[1] For, in my opinion, the Sacred Writers regard the titles Love (*agape*) and "Yearning" (*eros*) as of one meaning; but preferred, when speaking of Yearning in a heavenly sense, to qualify it with the word "real" because of the inconvenient pre-notion of such men. For whereas the title of "Real Yearning" is employed not merely by ourselves but even by the Scriptures, mankind (not grasping the unity intended when Yearning is ascribed to God) fell by their own propensity into the notion of a partial, physical and divided quality, which is not true Yearning but a vain image of Real Yearning, or rather a lapse therefrom. For mankind at large cannot grasp the simplicity of the one Divine Yearning, and hence, because of the offence it gives to most men, it is left to the Divine Wisdom to lead and raise them up to the knowledge of the Real Yearning until they are set free forth all offence thereat... To those who listen aright to Holy Scripture, the word "Love" is used by the Sacred Writers in Divine Revelation with the same meaning as the word "Yearning." It means a faculty of unifying and conjoining and of producing a special commingling together in the Beautiful and Good.[2]

This Desire or Yearning that the Sacerdotal Art elevated to the level of Absolute Wisdom is a fundamental part of the Royal Art, since kâma *ou le désir est le mobile de l'activité qui convient proprement au* Kshatriya.[3]

---

[1] *Proverbs* 4:6 and 8.
[2] Pseudo-Dionysius, *The Complete Works*, Paulist Press, 1987, pp. 79-81. Nicolaus Cusanus stated in a sermon: *Mens sine desiderio non intelligit, et sine intellectu non desiderat* ("Without desire the mind does not understand and without intellect it does not desire").
[3] Guénon, *ibid.*, p. 80.

CHAPTER VII

RENÉ GUÉNON AND *MYSTERIUM CONSCIENTIA*

Any prophet, holy interpreter, spiritual master or exponent of a sacred doctrine, imbued with the traditional spirit, had to face an apparent unsolvable problem: how to translate the divine truths into human, i.e. rational, language.[1] What words should be used to approximate as perfectly as possible the divine teachings? Mystery, secret, love, charity, metaphysics, intellect, knowledge, consciousness, and conscience, are these words apt to explain and express the unexplainable, the inexpressible and the unutterable? "Inexpressible" and "mystery," as Guénon wrote in a letter, are one and the same thing, so how can a word like "mystery" explain the Mystery?

René Guénon was criticized for his logical and rational style, for the "clear and distinct" ideas expressed in his writings, while he vehemently condemned Descartes, but these critics were blinded by their profane mentality and manipulated by their own mind and *ego*, because it is not so difficult to understand Ramana Maharshi's words:

> The mind will vanish only by pursuing the inquiry "Who am I?" Though this inquiry is a mental operation only, it destroys all mental operations including itself, just as the stick with which the funeral

---

[1] For this very reason, all the traditional doctrines used the language of symbols; for the same reason, some holy men were confused with madmen or drunkards.

pyre is kindled is itself reduced to ashes when the pyre and corpse are burnt. Then we attain knowledge or realisation of the Self.[1]

Therefore, writing about the spiritual meaning of Love we are confronted with the same danger to be misunderstood as in the case of the "intellect," which is considered by the modern man to be identical to "reason" or "rational mind," while "love" is just sentimentalism or moral charity, these types of confusions motivating Guénon's rational, in fact logical, style aimed at shaking and changing the modern mentality; yet sometimes, he, almost unwittingly, went beyond this, and unveiled a different and higher style, creator of perplexity, because, indeed, the spiritual masters wrote or spoke more or less obscurely, not on purpose but almost naturally.

Take, for example, the Roman god of desire and love, Cupid,[2] the son of Venus, with his Greek counterpart Eros: for the modern mentality it refers exclusively to erotic love, attraction and affection, yet he played a mysterious role in the ancient initiations, suggested by his young age and also by the identification, in Hellenistic times, with Horus; as an infant, Horus, called Harpocrates, was represented cross-legged[3] with a finger to his lips, imposing initiatory silence.[4] Harpocrates, like Eros (and Hermes), was sometimes represented with wings (see photo left); interesting enough, Harpocrates' "gesture of silence" (photo center) is to be found on the doors of the imperial cathedral of Speyer (photo MAT, right)[5].

---

[1] *Sri Maharshi, A Short Life Sketch*, published by Sri Ramanasramam, Tiruvanamalai, 2012, p. 13.
[2] Latin *cupido*, from *cupere*, means "desire."
[3] This is another initiatory gesture.
[4] The occultists related Harpocrates to Hermeticism and "gnosticism" and considered him as the "God of Silence," confusing, as usual, innocent minds; not to say that even the infamous Aleister Crowley used him. As Guénon said: *il y a bien peu de personnages de quelque réputation que les milieux occultistes n'aient pas prétendu accaparer ainsi à leur profit* (René Guénon, *Fragments Doctrinaux*, Rose-Cross Books, 2013, p. 339).
[5] Sédir (Yvon Le Loup) declared in his fictional book, *Initiations*: *Il m'a été permis de concevoir pour quels motifs elle* [the Holy Virgin Mary] *n'a jamais ouvert la bouche... pourquoi elle a constamment enfoui dans le silence tous les trésors...* (Éditions Albert Legrand, 1949, p. 269). He also said: *Le Christ et la Vierge sont des mystères* (*ibid.*, p. 264).

Even more recently, Cupid was included in suggested initiatory tales, like in Shakespeare's *A Midsumer Night's Dream*[1] or in *The Chymical Wedding of Christian Rosenkreutz*.[2]

---

[1] Cupid is present in Shakespeare's play, and he is as knavish as Puck: "Cupid is a knavish lad/ Thus to make poor females mad" (III.II.440-1). The magic flower used by Puck, "before milk-white, now purple," got its power from Cupid's arrow (II.I.155-167). Curiously, Shakespeare stresses that Oberon saw the flight of Cupid's arrow at the same time as he heard the celestial song of a mermaid on a dolphin's back (II.I.150-154). The dolphin bears an important spiritual meaning related to Apollo. Note that Cupid's mother, Venus, is a sea-maid. Cupid-Eros and Venus present a vast symbolism, cosmological and spiritual, closely linked to Love as Divine Madness, Creative Impulse and cosmic playful force, and used by Shakespeare in his plays. We could compare Cupid's playful role in Jason's initiation and Puck's similar function. Note that Medea is Hecate's disciple, and when Cupid shoots an arrow into her heart, she falls in love with Jason, the first man she saw; Titania falling in love with Bottom is the mockery copy. See Apollonius of Rhodes, *The Voyage of Argo*, Penguin Books, 1971, pp. 116-117, 123.

[2] "I cannot pass in silence how the little Cupid flew to and again there, but for the most part he hovered about the great crown. Sometimes he seated himself in between the two lovers, somewhat smiling upon them with his bow. Sometimes he made as if he would shoot one of us; in brief, this knave was so full of his waggery, that he would not spare even the little birds, which in multitudes flew upon, up and down the room, but tormented them all he could. The virgins seemed also to have their pastimes with him, and when they could catch him it was no easy matter for him to get from them again. Thus this little knave made all the sport and mirth... Almost all the prattle at this banquet was made by Cupid, who could not leave us, and me especially, untormented, and was perpetually producing some strange matter... 'Now, behold,' said the Page, 'when the tree shall be quite melted down, then shall Lady Venus awake, and be the mother of a King.' Whilst he was thus speaking, in flew the little Cupid, who at first was somewhat abashed at our

Harpocrates urged us, with his gesture, to be mute, but is Cupid likewise silent? In fact, the saying transmitted to the modern times is that "love is blind," which, like many other expressions, should be restored to its real spiritual value and associated with Shams-i-Tabrîzî's famous statement: "In love's country, language doesn't have its place. Love is mute."[1] These wise sayings are seemingly not very difficult to explain or to realize (*prendre conscience*) what they convey, but, again, we

---

presence, but seeing us both look more like the dead than the living, he could not refrain from laughing, and demanded what spirit had brought me thither, whom I with trembling answered, that I had lost my way in the castle, and was by chance come hither, that the Page had likewise been looking up and down for me, and at last lited upon me here, and that I hoped he would not take it amiss. 'Nay, then, 'tis well enough yet,' said Cupid, 'my old busie gransir; but you might lightly have served me a scurvy trick, had you been aware of this door. I must look better to it,' and so he put a strong lock on the copper door where we before descended. I thanked God that he lited upon us no sooner; my Page, too, was the more jocond because I had so well helped him at this pinch. 'Yet can I not,' said Cupid, 'let it pass unrevenged that you were so near stumbling upon my dear mother.' With that he put the point of his dart into one of the little tapers, and heating it somewhat, pricked me with it on the hand, which at that time I little regarded, but was glad that it went so well with us. Meantime my companions were gotten out of bed and were come into the hall, to whom I joyned myself, making as if I were then first risen. After Cupid had carefully made all fast again, he came likewise to us, and would needs have me shew him my hand, where he still found a little drop of blood, at which he heartily laughed, and bad the rest have a care of me, as I would shortly end my days... Then the wanton Cupid presented himself, and, after he had saluted us all, flew to them behind the curtain, tormenting them till they waked. This happened to them with very great amazement; for they imagined that they had slept from the hour in which they were beheaded. Cupid, after he had awaked them, and renewed their acquaintance one with another, stepped aside and permitted them to recruit their strength, meantime playing his tricks with us and at length he would needs have the music fetch to be somewhat the merrier."

[1] *Shams* means "sun" in Arabic, and Shams-i-Tabrîzî's spiritual disciple, the great Rumî, called him the "guide of Allâh's love for mankind"; Shams-i-Tabrîzî was for Rumî an initiatory Light, while his anonymous life illustrated the superior meaning of "anonymity": mystery and unexplainable. There is a well known story about Shams: "Rumî was reading next to a large pile of books when Shams Tabrîz, passing by, asked him, 'What are you doing?' Rumî scornfully replied, 'What I am doing you cannot understand.' On hearing this, Shams threw the stack of books into a nearby pool of water. Rumî hastily rescued the books and to his surprise they were all dry. Rumî, perplexed, asked Shams, 'What is this?' To which Shams replied, 'Mowlana, this is what you cannot understand.'"

have to ask: what consciousness is at work when we become aware, without much effort, that the sentiment of love is so powerful that it smothers any reason or rational judgment, or that love is proved by deeds not by words?

A Christian image, as found in a church of old Goa,[1] would help us understand the difference between a mundane consciousness and a religious one, or between a religious consciousness and a metaphysical one[2]: the naked arm (the crucified Christ's arm) represents the metaphysical domain, while the clothed one (the saint monk's arm) signifies the religious level. Such a symbolism is not uncommon in initiatory tales, where the neophyte has one foot uncovered (the axis of the universe, the naked truth – see Jason's tale) and the other one covered (the world); Titian's famous painting, "Sacred [the nude woman] and profane [the dressed woman] love," also illustrates this meaning.

There is no complicated mystery here, and the regular consciousness is enough to assimilate this significance or even to accept paradoxical descriptions, like that of an initiatory journey taking place in a "speaking silence," which could be easily explained by considering that the initiate becomes mute, closing the mouth as far as the world is concerned, annihilating the multiplicity of words, and regaining the lost Word. In the same way, the initiate becomes blind with regard to the world, opening the "eye of the heart" in exchange; but we could say that through initiation the neophyte enters the

---

[1]

[photo MAT]

[2] We note that here consciousness must be understood only analogical, and the "consciousness" beyond the individual domain remains essentially mysterious.

darkness of non-manifestation, and also the darkness inside the veil. Various reliefs show the initiate of the Dionysian Mysteries covered with a veil; similarly, Heracles, when he was initiated into the *Mysteries*, had his head covered with a veil, this veil parting the esoteric and exoteric domains; we could add Plato's sayings, who, in *Symposium* (218 b), asks the uninitiated to close their ears.

Therefore, expressions like "love is mute" or "love is blind" are not difficult to accept and the modern mentality is satisfied with rational descriptions, all of them (religious, philosophical, moral, sentimental, or biological) being recognized as part of the normal human thinking process. Similarly, there is no mystery about "mystery": there are "mystery novels" and the public at large understands their meaning; there are the "unsolved mysteries," from Atlantis to the Bermuda Triangle, from Eldorado to UFO, etc. all presented and understood in accord with the profane thinking and following a dubious inspiration; and there is no mystery about the "secret": the "secret of the Templars," the "secret of the Masons," the "secret of the Holy Grail," the "secret of Jesus," all are now revealed.

Even traditionalist seekers do not need to make a special effort to understand the meaning of "mystery" and "secret" for initiatory organizations and for traditional civilizations; a simple etymological study will allow comprehending their operative significance.[1]

In Greek, μυεἰσθαι τὰ μεγάλα means "to be initiated into the Greater Mysteries," the verb *mueo* being translated as "to be initiated into mysteries" or "to instruct." In the Eleusinian *Mysteries*, *muesis* was the initiation preceding that of the *Greater Mysteries* (called *telete*, Gr. *teleo* meaning "to initiate"). Both the words "mysteries" and *mueo* (and also *mystai*, "initiate") derive from a common radical *mu*, signifying a closed

---

[1] The English "mystery" comes from Old French *mistere* ("secret, mystery, hidden meaning"), which comes from Latin *mysterium* ("secret rite, secret worship, secret thing"), which comes from Greek *mysterion* (pl. *mysteria*, "secret rite, secret doctrine"), which comes from *mystes* ("one who has been initiated"), which comes from *myein* ("to close, shut," referring to the lips or to the eyes); from the same root comes the English "mute" and "myopia" (closing the eyes).

mouth, that is, silence,[1] but also with the eyes closed. Guénon stressed that *mueo*, "to initiate," indicates also "to consecrate," namely, to transmit spiritual influence, which actually is the essence of initiation.[2] It is very important that the Greeks correlated "the initiation into mysteries" with silence and with darkness (closing of the eyes).

Since Western society was built on Greco-Roman heritage, it is no surprise that the Christian esoteric domain took over the two terms "initiation" and "mysteries" in a spiritual sense, yet from the beginning of Christianity we see the Fathers of the Church using the word "mysteries" with the same significance, following Jesus' example. "He said, 'The knowledge of the secrets [*mysteria*] of the kingdom of God has been given to you, but to others I speak in parables, so that, though seeing, they may not see; though hearing, they may not understand'".[3] Or: "He told them, 'The secret [*mysterion*] of the kingdom of God has been given to you. But to those on the outside [the outsiders, the exoteric people] everything is said in parables so that, they may be ever seeing but never perceiving, and ever hearing but never understanding; otherwise they might turn and be forgiven!'".[4]

There is, however, an aspect that incommensurably surpasses all the explanations and rationalizations mentioned above: the invisible or inexpressible essence of the mystery; as Guénon said, "The idea of

---

[1] Eustathius affirmed that the initiates had "to shut their mouths, and not reveal what they were taught in the mysteries" (μυειν το στομα, και μη εκφαινειν ἁ μεμυηνται).
[2] René Guénon, *Aperçus sur l'Initiation*, Éditions Traditionnelles, 1992, p. 123.
[3] *Luke* 8:10.
[4] *Mark* 4:11-12. René Guénon tried to recover the meaning of the words "myth," "mythology" and "mystery," in accord with the traditional spirit (*si l'on peut parler de "myths" en ce qui concerne cette tradition même, à la condition de rétablir le vrai sens du mot et d'écarter tout ce qui s'y attache trop souvent de "pejorative" dans le langage courant, il n'y avait pas alors, en tout cas, de "mythologie," celle-ci, telle que l'entendent les modernes, n'étant rien de plus qu'une étude entreprise "de l'extérieur," et impliquant par conséquent, pourrait-on dire, une incompréhension au second degré* – Guénon, *ibid.*, p. 120); he added: *Il n'est pas sans intérêt de remarquer que ce qu'on appelle dans la Maçonnerie les "legends" des différents grades rentre dans cette définition des mythes, et que la "mise en action" de ces "legends" montre bien qu'elles sont véritablement incorporées aux rites mêmes, dont il est absolument impossible de les séparer; ce que nous avons dit de l'identité essentielle du rite et du symbole s'applique donc encore très nettement en pareil cas* – *ibid.*, p. 121.

'silence' must be related to things that by their very nature are inexpressible,"[1] and this is a "secret" that should be continuously contemplated and conquered.[2] Yet these are also just words, because how can we know for sure that we have conquered such a "secret"? And what is the secret of actually contemplating the "secret" and the "mystery"? Following what René Guénon suggested a couple of times, it means that we have to *prendre conscience* ("become aware") of the inner most truth or of the most high truth, that is, to contemplate the inexpressible secret and the invisible mystery we have to realize them and to acquire the "consciousness" of their reality.

---

[1] *Ibid.*, p. 124.
[2] *Revenons maintenant aux divers sens du mot "mystère": au sens le plus immédiat, nous dirions volontiers le plus grossier ou tout au moins le plus extérieur, le mystère est ce dont on ne doit pas parler, ce sur quoi il convient de garder le silence, ou ce qu'il est interdit de faire connaître au dehors; c'est ainsi qu'on l'entend le plus communément, même lorsqu'il s'agit des mystères antiques... Comme nous l'avons dit à ce propos, ce qu'on a appelé la "discipline du secret"... est fort loin de nous apparaître uniquement comme une simple précaution contre l'hostilité, du reste très réelle et souvent dangereuse, due à l'incompréhension du monde profane; nous y voyons d'autres raisons d'un ordre beaucoup plus profond, et qui peuvent être indiquées par les autres sens contenus dans le mot "mystère." Nous pouvons d'ailleurs ajouter que ce n'est pas par une simple coïncidence qu'il y a une étroite similitude entre les mots "sacré" (*sacratum*) et "secret" (*secretum*): il s'agit, dans l'un et l'autre cas, de ce qui est mis à part (*secernere*, *mettre à part*, *d'où le participe* secretum), réservé, séparé du domaine profane... Suivant le second sens du mot "mystère," qui est déjà moins extérieur, il désigne ce qu'on doit recevoir en silence, ce sur quoi il ne convient pas de discuter; à ce point de vue, toutes les doctrines traditionnelles, y compris les dogmes religieux qui en constituent un cas particulier, peuvent être appelées mystères (l'acception de ce mot s'étendant alors à des domaines autres que le domaine initiatique, mais où s'exerce également une influence "non-humaine"), parce que ce sont des vérités qui, par leur nature essentiellement supra-individuelle et supra-rationnelle, sont au-dessus de toute discussion. Or on peut dire, pour relier ce sens au premier, que répandre inconsidérément parmi les profanes les mystères ainsi entendus, c'est inévitablement les livrer à la discussion, procédé profane par excellence, avec tous les inconvénients qui peuvent en résulter et que résume parfaitement ce mot de "profanation" que nous employions déjà précédemment à un autre propos, et qui doit être pris ici dans son acception à la fois la plus littérale et la plus complète; le travail destructif de la "critique" moderne à l'égard de toute tradition est un exemple trop éloquent de ce que nous voulons dire pour qu'il soit nécessaire d'y insister davantage. Enfin, il est un troisième sens, le plus profond de tous, suivant lequel le mystère est proprement l'inexprimable, qu'on ne peut que contempler en silence; et, comme l'inexprimable est en même temps et par là l'incommunicable, l'interdiction de révéler l'enseignement sacré symbolise, à ce nouveau point de vue, l'impossibilité d'exprimer par des paroles le véritable mystère dont cet enseignement n'est pour ainsi dire que le vêtement, le manifestant et le voilant tout ensemble* (*ibid.*, pp. 125-127).

Nonetheless, is it correct to use the term "consciousness" or we should say "knowledge"? And when Guénon appeals to the syntagm *prendre conscience*,[1] what "consciousness" can we expect: our common, individual consciousness, our consciousness related to us as human beings?[2] Nobody can deny that the "greater" cannot emerge from the "lesser," and therefore the elements belonging to the inferior order symbolize those of the superior orders and not the other way around[3];

---

[1] He used this expression many times: *L'initiation véritable étant une prise de possession consciente des états supérieurs* (*L'ésotérisme de Dante*, Gallimard, 1981, p. 46); *Contrairement à ce qui a lieu pour les états relatifs et conditionnés, l'état suprême n'est pas quelque chose à obtenir par une "effectuation" quelconque; il s'agit uniquement de prendre conscience de ce qui est. Mais alors il ne peut plus être question d'individualité* (letter to Louis Caudron, 29 Janvier 1933) [since it is no more about the individuality, we should understand the consciousness only analogically]; *il s'agit donc seulement, pour l'être individuel (car ce n'est que par rapport à celui-ci qu'on peut parler de "réalisation"), de prendre effectivement conscience de ce qui est réellement et de toute éternité, mais cette prise de conscience implique l'affranchissement des limitations qui constituent l'individualité comme telle, et qui, plus généralement, conditionnent toute manifestation* (*L'Homme et son Devenir selon le Védânta*, Éditions Traditionnelles, 1991, pp. 42, 45); *c'est par la conscience de l'Identité de l'Être, permanente à travers toutes les modifications indéfiniment multiples de l'Existence unique, que se manifeste, au centre même de notre état humain aussi bien que de tous les autres états, cet élément transcendant et informel, donc non-incarné et non-individualisé, qui est appelé le "Rayon Céleste"; et c'est cette conscience, supérieure par là même à toute faculté de l'ordre formel, donc essentiellement supra-rationnelle, et impliquant l'assentiment de la loi d'harmonie qui relie et unit toutes choses dans l'Univers, c'est, disons-nous, cette conscience qui, pour notre être individuel, mais indépendamment de lui et des conditions auxquelles il est soumis, constitue véritablement la "sensation de l'éternité"* (*Le Symbolisme de la Croix*, Guy Trédaniel, 1989, p. 155).

[2] The individual consciousness is a "reflected consciousness" (reflecting the Intellect, *Buddhi*): *La distinction entre* shruti *et* smriti *équivaut, au fond, à celle de l'intuition intellectuelle pure et immédiate, qui s'applique exclusivement au domaine des principes métaphysiques, et de la conscience réfléchie, de nature rationnelle* (René Guénon, *Introduction générale à l'Étude des Doctrines hindoues*, Guy Trédaniel, 1987, p. 190); *Ce passage [de l'initiation virtuelle à l'initiation effective] implique la renonciation au mental... On peut, en employant le symbolisme traditionnel fondé sur les correspondances organiques, dire que le centre de la conscience doit être alors transféré du "cerveau" au "cœur"; pour ce transfert, toute "speculation" et toute dialectique ne sauraient évidemment plus être d'aucun usage (Il est à peine besoin de rappeler que le "cœur," pris symboliquement pour représenter le centre de l'individualité humaine envisagée dans son intégralité, est toujours mis en correspondance, par toutes les traditions, avec l'intellect pur)* (Guénon, *Aperçus sur l'Initiation*, p. 213).

[3] *Il est évident que le "plus" ne peut pas sortir du "moins"* (René Guénon, *Introduction générale*, p. 18; *Le Symbolisme de la Croix*, p. 154); *il ne l'est pas que quiconque a des prétentions à l'ésotérisme veuille ignorer l'exotérisme, ne fût-ce que pratiquement, car le "plus" doit forcément*

similarly, the superior "consciousness" cannot come out of the inferior one, that is, our common consciousness, like our mind is not enough to realize the supra-individual realities and we need to travel beyond it. This, in fact, defines the traditional spirit: the traditional spirit means to *prendre conscience* of the secret, that is, of the sacred, which means to effectively realize this secret beyond the common consciousness, and therefore what we have to consider here is not so much the "consciousness" but the Knowledge. Indeed, as we shall see, René Guénon preferred, when describing the supreme spiritual realization, the Liberation and the taking in possession of the supra-individual states, to use the term "knowledge" and not "consciousness" that only analogically could be extended to the whole realm of the Being.[1] Guénon wrote: "Knowledge, on the contrary, considered in itself and independently of the conditions attaching to any particular state, can admit of no restriction, and to be adequate to total truth must be coextensive not only with Being but also with universal Possibility itself, and therefore it must be infinite, as the latter necessarily is. This amounts to saying that knowledge and truth, envisaged thus metaphysically, are basically nothing other than what we have called rather inadequately 'aspects of the Infinite'; this is something clearly expressed in one of the fundamental formulations of the *Vêdânta*:

---

comprendre le "moins" … Le "moins" ne peut pas contenir le "plus," pas plus qu'il ne peut le produire; ceci est d'ailleurs applicable à différents niveaux, ainsi que nous le verrons par la suite; mais, pour le moment, nous envisageons le cas le plus extrême, celui qui concerne le rapport entre le principe même de l'être et la modalité la plus restreinte de sa manifestation individuelle humaine (René Guénon, *Initiation et Réalisation spirituelle*, Éditions Traditionnelles, 1980, pp. 71, 229).

[1] Nonetheless, even the "knowledge" should be considered analogical to and not identical with the individual act of knowing: *Il me semble qu'il y a une équivoque sur les termes "conscience," "connaissance," etc.; ils doivent tous être transposés analogiquement pour s'appliquer à l'état suprême, et ainsi ce qu'ils désignent n'a plus aucune commune mesure avec les modalités limitées qui, en ce qui concerne les états conditionnés, sont désignés par les même mots pour exprimer une certaine correspondance, qui ne saurait en aucune façon être regardée comme une identité, ni même comme une similitude; cette question de l'application du sens analogique est extrêmement importante* (letter of Guénon, December 3, 1932).

'*Brahma* is Truth, Knowledge, Infinity' (*Satyam Jnânam Anantam Brahma*).[1]

Beyond the common consciousness, which is related to the individual human state, the Hindu tradition mentions *Chit*, a "supra-consciousness" translated into English as "the Consciousness."[2] The English words "conscience" and "consciousness" both came from the Latin *conscientia*,[3] where the first now signifies "an individual's inner awareness of right and wrong" and therefore we preferred the Latin word for this chapter's title, keeping in mind that *conscientia* (like the word "notion") is related to "co-knowledge" as some authors of the Greco-Roman world indicated.[4] Various translations of the Hindu

---

[1] *Au contraire, la connaissance, considérée en soi et indépendamment des conditions afférentes à quelque état particulier, ne peut admettre aucune restriction, et, pour être adéquate à la vérité totale, elle doit être coextensive, non pas seulement à l'Être, mais à la Possibilité universelle elle-même, donc être infinie comme celle-ci l'est nécessairement. Ceci revient à dire que connaissance et vérité, ainsi envisagées métaphysiquement, ne sont pas autre chose au fond que ce que nous avons appelé, d'une expression d'ailleurs fort imparfaite, des 'aspects de l'Infini'; et c'est ce qu'affirme avec une particulière netteté cette formule qui est une des énonciations fondamentales du Védânta:* 'Brahma est la Vérité, la Connaissance, l'Infini' *(*Satyam Jnânam Anantam Brahma*) (Les États multiples de l'Être*, Guy Trédaniel, 1989, p. 91).

[2] The Consciousness (with capital *c*) is a mysterious notion, because it is inexpressible, but today we see some traditionalists (not to mention the pseudo-traditional and the profane ones) using it facetiously, confusing the various levels and projections of the supreme Consciousness, and degrading the primary sense of the word "notion." The English word "notion" comes from the Latin *noscere* "come to know," translating the Greek *ennoia*, "the act of thinking, meditation, understanding"; *ennoia* was used by St. Paul: "For the word of God is living and active and sharper than any two-edged sword, and piercing as far as the division of soul and spirit, of both joints and marrow, and able to judge the thoughts and intentions of the heart" (*Hebrews* 4:12), where "intentions" (*ennoia*) should be compared to the Islamic *niyyah*.

[3] The English "consciousness" comes, through Old French *conscience*, from Latin *conscientia* "knowledge within oneself, sense of right, a moral sense," from *conscientem* (nominative *consciens*), present participle of *conscire* "be (mutually) aware," from *com-* ("with") + *scire* ("to know"). Let us compare it to Greek *syneidesis*, "with-knowledge" and to Russian совесть (*сознание*), "conscience," literally "with-knowledge."

[4] See for example Cicero. There is also a connection with the idea of "secrecy": "conscience is a specific sort of knowledge possessed by a group that separates the members of the group from other people [the etymological sense of the word 'secret'], and the smaller the number is of those who are in the know, the more likely it is that what they share is a secret (*maxima beneficia...saepe intra tacitam duorum*

sacred texts use either "consciousness" or "knowledge" to describe Brahma, but should we accept them without any discrimination (*viveka*)?

René Guénon wrote about "knowledge and consciousness," which became the title of the 16th chapter (*Connaissance et Conscience*) in his book *Les États multiples de l'Être*, where he stressed:

> Une conséquence très importante de ce qui a été dit jusqu'ici, c'est que la connaissance, entendue absolument et dans toute son universalité, n'a aucunement pour synonyme ou pour équivalent la conscience, dont le domaine est seulement coextensif à celui de certains états d'être déterminés, de sorte que ce n'est que dans ces états, à l'exclusion de tous les autres, que la connaissance se réalise par le moyen de ce qu'on peut appeler proprement une "prise de conscience."[1]

We observe at once how prudent Guénon is concerning the meaning of "consciousness" and of the syntagm *prise de conscience*. In a letter of 1919, he wrote:

> Seulement, l'être individuel, pour "réaliser," n'a pas à "se faire infini," ce qui serait contradictoire; il a à prendre effectivement conscience (si toutefois ce mot de conscience peut s'appliquer ici), qu'il n'est pas seulement l'être individuel, ou plutôt que l'être qu'il est dans un certain état est aussi autre chose dans d'autres états[2];

---

conscientiam latent – 'the greatest benefits often lie hidden within the silent co-knowledge of two people,' Seneca, *De Beneficiis*, 3.10.2), and the more likely they are to be leagued in a conspiracy (*in conscientiam facinoris pauci adsciti* – 'few were admitted into co-knowledge of the crime,' Tacitus, *Histories*, 1.25)" (see the article *Conscience and Co-Knowledge in Hamlet and Classical Antiquity*, Vancouver, 2005). In the Christian tradition, the above connection is suggested by St. Paul: "Holding the mystery of the faith in a pure conscience" (*1 Timothy* 3:9).

[1] "A very important consequence of the foregoing is that knowledge, understood absolutely and in all its universality, is in no way synonymous with or equivalent to consciousness, whose domain is coextensive only with that of certain determined states of the being, so that it is only in those states to the exclusion of all others, that knowledge is realized by means of what can properly be called 'to become aware.'"

[2] René Guénon, *Fragments Doctrinaux*, Rose-Cross Books, 2013, pp. 56-57.

it is suggested that this *prise de conscience* is difficult to define, like the "consciousness" itself, and that words hardly can express the inexpressible.

For René Guénon, the consciousness "does not constitute a particular state of the being" but "more a condition of existence in certain states, but not strictly in the sense in which we speak of the conditions of corporeal existence, for example. It would be more accurate to say that consciousness is a *raison d'être* for the states in question"[1]; and he insisted that consciousness is "something particular, whether in the human state or in other individual states more or less analogous to it, and consequently is in no way a universal principle; if it nevertheless constitutes an integral part and a necessary element of universal Existence, it does so only by exactly the same right as do all conditions proper to any states of the being whatsoever, and it possesses no more privilege in this respect than do the states to which it refers with respect to other states."[2]

However, as always, we have to search for the *spirit* and not for the *letter* of Guénon's sayings, and the last text was specially written to combat various aberrant modern theories (referring to transformism, reincarnation, the Cartesian "animal-machines," and to psychoanalysis), for which reason Guénon considered here the consciousness in relation to the individual human state with its indefinite extensions (hence the "subconscious" and the "supraconscious"), without excluding other forms of consciousness applied to various beings of the corporeal world. There is, among these forms, one that is properly

---

[1] *Pour nous, la conscience… ne constitue pas un état d'être particulier… La conscience serait plutôt une condition de l'existence dans certains états, mais non pas strictement dans le sens où nous parlons, par exemple, des conditions de l'existence corporelle; on pourrait dire, d'une façon plus exacte, quoique pouvant paraître quelque peu étrange à première vue, qu'elle est une 'raison d'être' pour les états dont il s'agit* (Les États multiples de l'Être, p. 48).

[2] *La conscience… est donc quelque chose de spécial, soit à l'état humain, soit à d'autres états individuels plus ou moins analogues à celui-là; par suite, elle n'est aucunement un principe universel, et, si elle constitue cependant une partie intégrante et un élément nécessaire de l'existence universelle, ce n'est qu'exactement au même titre que toutes les conditions propres à n'importe quels états d'être, sans qu'elle possède à cet égard le moindre privilège, non plus que les états auxquels elle se réfère n'en possèdent eux-mêmes par rapport aux autres états* (ibid.).

human, called in the Hindu tradition *ahankâra*, and this consciousness, as a *raison d'être* for the individual human state, is "that by which the individual being participates to the universal Intelligence (*Buddhi*)[1]; but naturally in its determined form (as *ahankâra*) it belongs to the individual mental faculty (*manas*), so that in other states the same participation of the being to the universal Intelligence may express itself in an entirely different mode."[2]

Certainly, René Guénon is perfectly aware of the Sanskrit term *Chit*, which he described in a previous work, published 7 years earlier (*L'Homme et son Devenir selon le Vêdânta*, chapter XV), and therefore he wrote: "like the word 'reason,' the word 'consciousness' can sometimes be universalized by a purely analogical transposition,[3] something we ourselves have done elsewhere to render the meaning of the Sanskrit word *Chit*; but such a transposition is only possible when one restricts oneself to the Being, as was done when the ternary *Satchidânanda* was

---

[1] *Pour ce qui est de la distinction essentielle du "mental" d'avec l'intellect pur, nous rappellerons seulement ceci: l'intellect, dans le passage de l'universel à l'individuel, produit la conscience, mais celle-ci, étant de l'ordre individuel, n'est aucunement identique au principe intellectuel lui-même* ("As for the essential distinction of the "mental" from pure intellect, we will only recall the following: in the passage from universal to individual, the intellect produces the consciousness, but the consciousness, being of the individual order, is in no way identical with the intellectual principle itself," *ibid*., p. 57).

[2] *Ce par quoi l'être individuel participe de l'Intelligence universelle* (Buddhi *de la doctrine hindoue*); *mais, naturellement, c'est à la faculté mentale individuelle* (manas) *qu'elle est inhérente sous sa forme déterminée (comme* ahankâra*), et, par suite, dans d'autres états, la même participation de l'être à l'Intelligence universelle peut se traduire en un tout autre mode* (*ibid*., p. 48); Guénon defined ahankâra *ou la conscience individuelle* [*la "conscience du moi," Les États multiples de l'Être*, p. 54], *qui engendre la notion de "moi": il* [Buddhi] *produit alors, comme résultante de cette intersection, la conscience individuelle* (ahankâra), *impliquée dans l'"âme vivante"* (jîvâtmâ) *à laquelle elle est inhérente... cette conscience... donne naissance à la notion du "moi"* (aham, *d'où le nom d'*ahankâra, *littéralement "ce qui fait le moi"*) (Guénon, *L'Homme*, pp. 63, 85). On the contrary, passing from the virtual initiation to the effective or actual one means to leap from *ahankâra* to *Buddhi* and transfer the center of consciousness from "mind" to "heart."

[3] As Guénon said, *Chit* is not the psychological consciousness: *Ce que vous dites au sujet de Sat-Chit-Ânanda est sûrement juste, mais il est bien entendu que ce dont il s'agit en pareil cas (en ce qui concerne* Chit*) est tout autre chose que la conscience psychologique, qui ne peut être considérée tout au plus que comme un simple reflet extérieur et superficiel* (letter to Guido di Giorgio, November 15, 1947).

under consideration. Nonetheless, it should be well comprehended that, even with this restriction, consciousness thus transposed is no longer understood in its proper sense, such as we have defined it above."[1]

The word "consciousness" was used and abused in so many ways that much too often, in modern times, traditional texts containing this term are misunderstood and reduced to the human individuality and this world.[2] A similar mistake has produced the absurd and modern

---

[1] *Comme le mot "raison," le mot "conscience" peut être parfois universalisé, par une transposition purement analogique, et nous l'avons fait nous même ailleurs pour rendre la signification du terme sanscrit* Chit; *mais une telle transposition n'est possible que lorsqu'on se limite à l'Être, comme c'était le cas alors pour la considération du ternaire Sachchidânanda. Cependant, on doit bien comprendre que, même avec cette restriction, la conscience ainsi transposée n'est plus aucunement entendue dans son sens propre, tel que nous l'avons précédemment défini* (Les États multiples de l'Être, p. 94). And Guénon, once more, defines the consciousness: "In this sense, let us repeat, consciousness is only the special mode of a contingent and relative knowledge, as relative and contingent as it is the conditioned state of the being to which it essentially belongs; and, if one can say that it is a 'raison d'être' for such a state, it is so only insofar as it is a participation, by refraction, to the nature of that universal and transcendent intellect that is itself, finally and eminently, the supreme 'raison d'être' of all things, the true metaphysical 'sufficient reason' that determines itself in all the orders of possibilities."

[2] In the modern world, where nothing is "in accordance with the order" (which implies hierarchy, justice and a traditional spirit) the effective consciousness of this accord was lost and replaced with a sentimental "moral consciousness": *L'action rituelle, ainsi que nous l'avons expliqué ailleurs, est, suivant le sens originel du mot lui-même, celle qui est accomplie "conformément à l'ordre," et qui par conséquent implique, au moins à quelque degré, la conscience effective de cette conformité; et, là où la tradition n'a subi aucun amoindrissement, toute action, quelle qu'elle soit, a un caractère proprement rituel... Pour quiconque n'est pas aveuglé par certains préjugés, il est facile de voir quelle distance sépare la conscience de la conformité à l'ordre universel, et de la participation de l'individu à cet ordre en vertu de cette conformité même, de la simple "conscience morale," qui ne requiert aucune compréhension intellectuelle et n'est plus guidée que par des aspirations et des tendances purement sentimentales, et quelle profonde dégénérescence implique, dans la mentalité humaine en général, le passage de l'une à l'autr*e (Guénon, *Initiation et Réalisation spirituelle*, pp. 85-86). Even worse, modern theories, pseudo-spiritual or scientific, belonging to this last phase of *Kali-Yuga*, try to suggest that everything takes place in the human consciousness, which would mean that the counter-initiatory forces don't have an objective existence and are part of this consciousness ("As for the 'counter-initiation,' it is certainly not a mere illusory counterfeit, but on the contrary something very real in its own order," Guénon, *Le règne de la quantité et les signes des temps*, Gallimard, 1970, p. 323); let us mention Jean Gebser's theory about the evolution and progress of the

theory of reincarnation, where the meaning of some texts of the Hindu tradition were applied to the (terrestrial) present world exclusively, when, in fact, they should have been understood as analogies; not to say that the description of Paradise, with its trees and fountains and rivers and virgins, etc. is just an analogy and has actually nothing to do with our corporeal state. Therefore, to grasp the *mysterium conscientia* we must keep in mind the "purely analogical transposition" for the word consciousness and finally accept the impossibility to define or describe it for the supra-individual states; moreover, we should ponder Guénon's words: "such a transposition is only possible when one restricts oneself to the Being, as was done when the ternary *Satchidânanda* was under consideration."

About the same time René Guénon was finalizing his metaphysical writings that became later *Le Symbolisme de la Croix* and *Les États multiples de l'Être*, Sir John Woodroffe (Arthur Avalon), in his articles about Tantra (published in 1918 as *Shakti and Shakta*), insisted on explaining this mysterious notion of "consciousness."

Striving to define *Chit*, Avalon admitted: "But what is *Chit*? There is no word in the English language which adequately describes it," and using the traditional method he indicated what *Chit* is not:

> It is not mind: for mind is a limited instrument through which *Chit* is manifested... If then we use (as for convenience we do) the term "Consciousness" for *Chit*, we must give it a content different from that which is attributed to the terms in ordinary English parlance... *Chit* in itself (*Svarûpa*) is not particular, nor conditioned and concrete.

And then Avalon related *Chit* to Knowledge:

---

consciousness, with the phases: archaic, magic, mythical, and mental-rational, while now the consciousness is in transition striving to obtain liberation from the ego and time (this theory was taken over by a recent sinister author who babbled about how the human consciousness will develop).

Though *Chit-Svarūpa* is not knowledge of objects in the phenomenal sense, it is not, according to Shaiva-Shâkta views, a mere abstract knowing (*Jnâna*) wholly devoid of content. It contains within itself the Vimarsha-Shakti which is the cause of phenomenal objects, then existing in the form of *Chit* (*Chidrûpinî*). The Self then knows the Self. Still less can we speak of mere "awareness" as the equivalent of *Chit*. And in Vêdânta, *Chit* and *Ânanda* or Bliss or Love are one. For Consciousnes then is not consciousness *of* being (*Sat*) but Being-consciousness (*Sat-Chit*): nor a Being which is conscious *of* Bliss (*Ânanda*) but Being-Consciousness-Bliss (*Saccidânanda*).

Consequently, Avalon defined *Chit* as the "eternal, changeless substratum, which may thus be defined as the *changeless principle of all our changing experience... Chit* is Being or Reality itself. *Chit* as such is identical with Being as such. The Brahma is both *Chit* and *Sat*."[1]

This *plenum* or *continuum* is as such all-pervading, eternal, unproduced, and indestructible: for production and destruction involve the existence and bringing together and separation of parts which in an absolute partless *continuum* is impossible. It is necessarily in itself, that is, as *Chit*, motionless, for no parts of an all-filling *continuum* can move from one place to another. *Chit* is one undifferentiated, partless, allpervading, eternal, spiritual substance. In Sanskrit, this *plenum* is called *Chidâkâsha*; that is, just as all material things exist in the all-pervading physical Ether, so do they and the latter exist in the infinitely extending Spiritual "Ether" which is *Chit*. The Supreme Consciousness is thought of as a kind of permanent spiritual "Space" (*Chidâkâsha*) which makes room for and contains all varieties and forms appearing and disappearing.

Arthur Avalon peremptorily declared: "That which is the general characteristic of the Indian systems, and that which constitutes their real profundity, is the paramount importance attached to Consciousness."[2]

---

[1] But only as *saguna* Brahma.
[2] Arthur Avalon, *La puissance du serpent*, Dervy, 1981, p. 27; *The Serpent Power*, Ganesh & Co. (Madras), 1950, p. 19; two of the seven chapters of this work are dedicated to the Consciousness: *Bodiless Consciousness* and *Embodied Consciousness*.

CHAPTER VIII

MYSTERIUM CONSCIENTIA AND *KALI-YUGA*

There is a significant difference from the spiritual viewpoint between *Satya-Yuga* and *Kali-Yuga*, and we chose in this work to restore (in fact, attempting to restore) the traditional spirit with regard to notions like "love," "consciousness" and "money." René Guénon rightfully underlined, for example, that "initiation" was completely futile in *Satya-Yuga*, but today, in *Kali-Yuga*, it became indispensable for those engaged on a spiritual path.[1] Similarly, the Tantrism became preponderant as an assembly of teachings and ways of "realization" favourable to the conditions of *Kali-Yuga*[2]; the Tantrism, an orthodox doctrine ("the fifth Vêda"), was originally concealed in the

---

[1] *Pour les hommes des temps primordiaux, l'initiation aurait été inutile et même inconcevable, puisque le développement spirituel, à tous ses degrés, s'accomplissait chez eux d'une façon toute naturelle et spontanée, en raison de la proximité où ils étaient à l'égard du Principe; mais, par suite de la "descente" qui s'est effectuée depuis lors, conformément au processus inévitable de toute manifestation cosmique, les conditions de la période cyclique où nous nous trouvons actuellement sont tout autres que celles-là, et c'est pourquoi la restauration des possibilités de l'état primordial est le premier des buts que se propose l'initiation* (Initiation et Réalisation spirituelle, Éditions Traditionnelles, 1980, p. 52).

[2] *C'est par ces considérations qu'on peut vraiment comprendre la place qu'occupe, dans la tradition hindoue ce qui est habituellement désigné par le nom de "Tantrisme," en tant qu'il représente l'ensemble des enseignements et des moyens de "réalisation" plus spécialement appropriés aux conditions du* Kali-Yuga (Études sur l'Hindouisme, Éditions Traditionnelles, 1979, pp. 89-90).

Vêda, becoming "explicit" only in *Kali-Yuga*,¹ and it is important to add that, to adjust to the mentality of the "dark-age," the Tantrism had to promote the aspect of "power" (*shakti*) rather than the aspect of "contemplation,"² and likewise the notion of "consciousness" rather than the notion of "knowledge."³

Jnâna-mârga, considered by Shankarâchârya and René Guénon the supreme way leading to the Principle, became so difficult, so impossible, so incomprehensible in *Kali-Yuga* that for many the Tantric way emphasizing the "consciousness" and the "power" seemed much more accessible, and, in any case, closer to the Hindu traditional spirit than Buddhism, where the "sentimentalism" developed by the various schools appeared too impure and "human," compelling Shankarâchârya to victoriously annihilate it by proclaiming the supremacy of the *Jnâna-mârga*.

In *Kali-Yuga*, and especially at the end of it, various sacred notions like Consciousness, Bliss or Intellect were inevitable degraded,⁴ their content limited and impoverished, and any attempt to define or translate them in a different language is hazardous and jeopardized by the mentality to which that language belongs.⁵

---

¹ *Ces* Tantras *sont souvent regardés comme formant un "cinquième Vêda," spécialement destiné aux hommes du* Kali-Yuga (*ibid.*, p. 91).
² *Ce que nous venons d'indiquer en dernier lieu s'applique exactement au Tantrisme, dont la "voie," d'une façon générale, apparaît comme plus "active" que "contemplative," ou, en d'autres termes, comme se situant plutôt du côté de la "puissance" que de celui de la connaissance* (*ibid.*, p. 93).
³ *Les aptitudes à parvenir directement à la pure connaissance devenant toujours plus rares, il fallut ouvrir d'autres "voies" mettant en oeuvre des moyens de plus en plus contingents, suivant en quelque sorte, pour y remédier dans la mesure du possible, la "descente" qui s'effectuait d'âge en âge dans le parcours du cycle de l'humanité terrestre* (Guénon, *ibid.*, p. 89).
⁴ Today, for example, people talk about how "emotional" is a trial, but a trial must provide justice and not emotions, which is impossible now when the goddess of Justice is no longer in this world.
⁵ *D'ailleurs, toute exposition possible est ici nécessairement défectueuse, parce que les conceptions métaphysiques, par leur nature universelle, ne sont jamais totalement exprimables, ni même imaginables, ne pouvant être atteintes dans leur essence que par l'intelligence pure et "informelle"; elles dépassent immensément toutes les formes possibles, et spécialement les formules où le langage voudrait les enfermer, formules toujours inadéquates qui tendent à les restreindre, et par là à les*

Arthur Avalon declared:

> The One is said to be Being (*Sat*), Bliss (*Ananda*) and *Chit* – an untranslatable term[1] which has been most accurately defined as the Changeless Principle of all changing experience, a Principle of which sensation, perception, conception, self-consciousness, feeling, memory, will and all other psychic states are limited *modes*. It is not therefore Consciousness or Feeling as we understand these words, for these are directed and limited. But Consciousness and possibly (according to the more ancient views) Feeling [we notice the "sentimental" element] approach the most nearly to a definition, provided that we do not understand thereby Consciousness and Feeling in man's sense. We may thus (to distinguish it) call *Chit*, Pure Consciousness or Pure Feeling as Bliss (*Ananda*) knowing and enjoying its own full Reality. This, as such Pure Consciousness or Feeling, endures even when finite centres of Consciousness or Feeling arise in It.[2]

Similarly, *Shakti* received considerably more attention as part of the "explication" process specifically occurring in *Kali-Yuga*,[3] but, like *Chit*, *Shakti* did not allow a precise translation, so she was referred to as "power," "energy" or "mother"; however, Guénon preferred to describe the manifestation of *Shakti* as Will, Action and Knowledge (not Consciousness).[4]

---

dénaturer (René Guénon, *Introduction générale à l'étude des doctrines hindoues*, Guy Trédaniel, 1987, pp. 92-93).
[1] Our *Italics*.
[2] Sir John Woodroffe, *Shakti and Shakta*, Celphaïs Press, 2009, pp. 38-39.
[3] It is the "tautological" process applied to the various symbols: a symbol became more and more explicit and we can see today strange tautologies (the symbol being doubled by more evident explanations).
[4] *Chacun des "aspects divins" est regardé comme doué d'une puissance ou énergie propre, qui est appelée* shakti, *et qui est représentée symboliquement sous une forme feminine* (Guénon, *Introduction générale*, p. 202); *C'est pourquoi* Brahma *même est* Purushottama, *tandis que* Prakriti *représente seulement, par rapport à la manifestation, Sa* Shakti, *c'est-à-dire Sa "Volonté productrice," qui est proprement la "toute-puissance" (activité "non-agissante" quant au Principe, devenant passivité quant à la manifestation)* (René Guénon, *L'Homme et son Devenir selon le Védânta*, Éditions Traditionnelles, 1991, p. 92); *Cette surface, c'est également* Mâyâ *envisagée dans son sens le plus élevé, comme la* Shakti de Brahma, *c'est-à-dire la "toute-puissance" du Principe Suprême* (ibid., p. 93); …*la Volonté productrice* (Shakti) (*ibid.*, p. 177);

There is no doubt that *Sachchidânanda*, which was a primeval explication of the Principle as pure Being (or as Brahma *saguna*) made the use of "consciousness" more than legitimate, and Shankarâchârya himself did not avoid the principial ternary, but it was in the times of Tantra when *shakti* and "consciousness" propagated with escalating speed,[1] and the controversial Sri Aurobindo (or *Aravinda* as Tilak called him) is another notable example of this increasing interest in describing the spiritual path by employing the notion of "consciousness."[2] Before studying deeper the Tantras, Sri Aurobindo made a logical assertion: "Consciousness in its very nature could not be limited by the ordinary physical human-animal consciousness, it must have other ranges."[3]

When explaining the Tantras, Arthur Avalon described a ladder with various steps of consciousness; akin to him, Sri Aurobindo introduced various levels of consciousness on which he based "his

---

Kundalinî *est un aspect de la* Shakti *considérée comme force cosmique* (Guénon, *Études sur l'Hindouisme*, p. 35); *Une des raisons pour lesquelles la* Shakti *est symbolisée par le triangle est la triplicité de sa manifestation comme Volonté* (Ichchhâ), *Action* (Kriyâ) *et Connaissance* (Jnâna) (*ibid.*, p. 40).
[1] We should be aware though that the traditional duration of *Kali-Yuga* is of the order of thousands not hundreds of years (6,480 years) and the escalation became plainly visible at the end of the "dark-age"; as René Guénon wrote: *si l'on songe d'ailleurs que le début de* Kali-Yuga *remonte fort au delà des temps dits "historiques" on devra reconnaître que l'origine même du Tantrisme, loin d'être si "tardive" que certains le prétendent* (*Études sur l'Hindouisme*, p. 90).
[2] It is instructive to quote from a letter of Mirra Alfassa (the "Mother") to Sri Aurobindo, year 1915: "The entire consciousness immersed in divine contemplation, the whole being enjoyed a supreme and vast felicity... the body of the awakened consciousness was the terrestrial globe... And the consciousness knew that its global body was thus moving in the arms of the universal Personality... The consciousness of the universe sprang towards the Divine in an ardent aspiration" (Rishabhchand, *Sri Aurobindo. His Life Unique*, Sri Aurobindo Ashram, Pudducherry, 2007, p. 403); visiting the utopian city Auroville, near Pondicherry, a creation of Mirra Alfassa, one will better understand the deviations and confusion that developed and encircled Sri Aurobindo. Rishabhchand said about Auroville: "Auroville belongs to humanity as a whole. But to live in Auroville one must be the willing servitor of the Divine's Consciousness" (p. 368) – such a unfortunate statement.
[3] Rishabhchand 136.

yoga."[1] It is so impossible to explicate the spiritual realization that Sri Aurobindo's answers regarding this topic should be accepted with prudence.[2] When, for instance, he introduces a "cosmic consciousness" as an intermediary between the individual consciousness and the divine one, we should keep in mind Guénon's warning to his coevals about the abuse of such expressions:

> There is therefore all the more reason to exercise extreme vigilance (for the enemy knows only too well how to take on the most insidious disguises) against anything that may lead the being to become "fused" or preferably and more accurately "confused" or even "dissolved" in a sort of "cosmic consciousness" that shuts out all "transcendence" and so also shuts out all effective spirituality[3]... but what is to be said of someone who flings himself into the ocean and has no aspiration but to drown himself in it? This is very precisely the significance of so-called "fusion" with a "cosmic consciousness" that is really nothing but the confused and indistinct assemblage of all the psychic influences; and, whatever some people may imagine, these influences have absolutely nothing in common

---

[1] Following the Tantric way, Sri Aurobindo considered that the *mûlâdhâra* is the center of the physical consciousness (Shrî Aurobindo, *Le guide du Yoga*, Albin Michel, 1970, p. 108); that the light of the "divine consciousness" would descend in man during "his (Aurobindo's) yoga" (*ibid.*, pp. 114, 139), or that the force of divine Shakti descends and takes control, organizing the consciousness (*ibid.*, p. 167); that "concentration" means concentrating the dispersed consciousness (*ibid.*, p. 170).

[2] Therefore Sri Ramana Maharshi and René Guénon answered to various questions without describing any specific steps regarding the spiritual process; Guénon wrote in a letter: *Il n'entre pas dans mon rôle d'indiquer les moyens "pratiques" de réalisation, ce serait d'ailleurs tout à fait inutile, non pas seulement à cause de l'incompréhension occidentale, mais parce que, sans transmission initiatique régulière, ces moyens sont inopérants ; ce qui peut en être appris par les livres ne sert donc absolument à rien* (Fragments Doctrinaux, Rose-Cross Books, 2013, p. 249).

[3] *À plus forte raison doit-on se garder avec une extrême vigilance (car ce dont il s'agit ne sait que trop bien prendre les déguisements les plus insidieux) de tout ce qui induit l'être à "se fondre," nous dirions plus volontiers et plus exactement à "se confondre" ou même à "se dissoudre" dans une sorte de "conscience cosmique" exclusive de toute "transcendance," donc de toute spiritualité effective* (*Le règne de la quantité et les signes des temps*, Gallimard, 1970, p. 319).

with spiritual influences, even if they may happen to imitate them to a certain extent in some of their outward manifestations.[1]

Also, Sri Aurobindo gave a bizarre answer when he described the goal of Yoga as making the supramental consciousness to descend on earth, to fix it there, to create a new race with the supramental consciousness governing the inner and outer life, the individual and collective life.[2]

Indubitably, some traditionalists (not to mention others) will be unhappy with any criticism addressed to this almost "taboo" notion of "consciousness" (even if accepting Guénon's work), and Sri Aurobindo sure did not help with his answers, like the one where he described how, through "his yoga," someone could reach a "state of consciousness" no longer limited by the ego, by his own mental and vital levels, by his body, a state of union with the supreme Self or the universal (or cosmic) consciousness, or with a more profound internal consciousness,[3] and beyond that he should become aware (*prendre conscience*) of a vast Force in which everything is power, a vast Light in which everything is knowledge, a vast Ananda in which everything is bliss, and all this constitutes what Sri Aurobindo called the "spiritual superior consciousness" or the "divine consciousness."[4] As we said,

---

[1] *Mais que dire de celui qui se jetterait en plein milieu de cet Océan et n'aurait d'autre aspiration que de s'y noyer? C'est là, très exactement, ce que signifie cette soi-disant "fusion" avec une "conscience cosmique" qui n'est en réalité rien d'autre que l'ensemble confus et indistinct de toutes les influences psychiques, lesquelles, quoi que certains puissent s'imaginer, n'ont certes absolument rien de commun avec les influences spirituelles, même s'il arrive qu'elles les imitent plus ou moins dans quelques-unes de leurs manifestations extérieures* (*ibid.*, p. 320).

[2] *Le guide du Yoga*, p. 190. We almost could hear the Mother talking. This answer was, it seems to us, consequential to Sri Aurobindo's political activities (he said once: "I say that it is the Sanatana Dharma which for us is nationalism," Rishabhchand 168).

[3] Aurobindo, *ibid.*, pp. 140, 164. For Sri Aurobindo, the cosmic consciousness is that of the universe, of the cosmic spirit and of the cosmic nature (*ibid.*, p. 149).

[4] *Ibid.*, p. 165. Indeed, the "cosmic consciousness" is only an intermediary: "But the cosmic consciousness too is not sufficient; for it is not all the Divine Reality, not integral. There is a divine secret behind personality that he must discover; there, waiting in it to be delivered here into Time, stands the mystery of the embodiment of the Transcendence. In the cosmic consciousness there remains at the end a hiatus, an unequal equation of a highest Knowledge that can liberate but not

the ternary *Sachchidânanda*, even though a notion that we cannot explain but realize, incited people to approach it discursively, and so Sri Aurobindo introduced appellations like "Overmind" and, over it, the "Supermind," which is between *Sachchidânanda* and the inferior manifestation, and contains the truth of the divine consciousness[1]; yet for him, the "ancient yogas" attained only the static *Sachchidânanda*, while "his yoga" allowed to realize the dynamic *Sachchidânanda* in the supramental plane, when the supramental consciousness enters the supreme consciousness of the *Sachchidânanda*, and Sri Aurobindo explained that the Supermind is a totally different consciousness from all the other inferior planes, that passing beyond the Overmind to the Supermind someone enters in a consciousness governed by different norms and where even the same Truth like *Sachchidânanda* is regarded in a different way,[2] but saying this is like saying that the realization of *Sachchidânanda* is ineffable.

However, Sri Aurobindo, in one of his answers, conceded that the Supermind is the Knower who possesses the Knowledge, being one with it and with what is known[3]; indeed, this is the only way the

---

effectuate with a Power seeming to use a limited Knowledge or masking itself with a surface Ignorance that can create but creates imperfection or a perfection transient, limited and in fetters... What will be the relation of our individual existence to this cosmic consciousness to which we have attained? For since we have still a mind and body and human life, our individual existence persists even though our separate individual consciousness has been transcended. It is quite possible to realise the cosmic consciousness without becoming that; we can see it, that is to say, with the soul, feel it and dwell in it; we can even be united with it without becoming wholly one with it; in a word, we may preserve the individual consciousness of the Jivâtman within the cosmic consciousness of the universal Self (*The Synthesis of Yoga*, Sri Aurobindo Ashram, 1999, pp. 259, 411).

[1] *Le guide du Yoga*, p. 151. Sri Aurobindo calls this a dynamic "Truth-Consciousness," in which there are many degrees, with the supermind as summit or source (*ibid.*, pp. 186-188).

[2] Shri Aurobindo, *Réponses*, Albin Michel, 1978, pp. 186-187.

[3] As Guénon wrote in a perfect traditional utterance: *Ainsi ces trois*, Sat, Chit et Ânanda (*généralement réunis en* Sachchidânanda) *ne sont absolument qu'un seul et même être, et cet "un" est* Âtmâ (*En arabe, on a, comme équivalent de ces trois termes, l'Intelligence* (El-Aqlu) [Guénon said: chit, *qu'on peut sans doute traduire par* intelligence, *mais qu'il faudrait cependant distinguer de* buddhi], *l'Intelligent* (El-Âqil) *et l'Intelligible* (El-Maqûl): *la*

expression *prendre conscience* could be extrapolated and the notion of "consciousness" understood beyond the individual domain. As Coomaraswamy wrote, "the distinction of subject and object is the primary condition of ignorance, or imperfect knowledge, for nothing is known essentially except as it exists in consciousness; everything else is supposition."[1]

In *Satya-Yuga*, *Sachchidânanda* was at hand and was reached spontaneously, while in *Kali-Yuga*, and especially at the end of it, tremendous efforts are to be made, and, even if the goal is to realize the supreme Consciousness (or Aurobindo's Supermind), the Tantric methods have focused on the individual being, with the two components: corporeal and subtle.[2] For that reason Arthur Avalon could call the *chakras* of the *Kundalinî-Yoga* "centres of consciousness," belonging to the subtle (but still individual) domain,[3] but in accord with the Tantras these are centers where the universal Consciousness acts,[4] because the conscious *Shakti*[5] is veiling herself and so appearing as

---

première est la Conscience universelle (Chit), *le second est son sujet* (Sat), *et le troisième est son objet* (Ânanda), *les trois n'étant qu'un dans l'Être "qui Se connaît Soi-même par Soi-même"*) (*L'Homme*, p. 119). Sri Aurobindo, like Arthur Avalon, influenced by the Tantras, was reticent in accepting Shankarâchârya with the *Jnâna-mârga* as the supreme way.

[1] Ananda K. Coomaraswamy, *Traditional Art and Symbolism*, Princeton University Press, 1977, p. 141.

[2] In the Hindu tradition, the individual consciousness is the "body with consciousness": "It is to this 'spirit' (Gk. *pneuma*, Skr. *âtman*, Arabi *rûh*) as distinguished from body and soul – i.e., whatever is phenomenal and formal (Gk. *soma* and *psyche*, Skr. *nâma-rûpa*, and *savijnana-kâya*, 'name and appearance,' the 'body with consciousness') – that tradition attributes with perfect consistency an absolute liberty" (Ananda K. Coomaraswamy, *Metaphysics*, Princeton University Press, 1977, p. 91).

[3] Arthur Avalon, *La puissance du serpent*, Dervy, 1981, p. 15; *The Serpent Power*, Ganesh & Co. (Madras), 1950, p. 16.

[4] *The Serpent Power*, p. 15. *Kundalinî* in herself is pure Consciousness. When she sleeps in the *mûlâdhâra*, the men's consciousness is awake to the world; when she awakes and Yoga is completed man sleeps to the world (*La puissance*, p. 18, *The Serpent Power*, p. 9).

[5] From a Tantric viewpoint, *Shakti* is consciousness (*Chidrûpâ*) (Avalon, *Shakti and Shakta*, p. 184).

limited consciousness[1]; since everything originates in the Principle, there is no essential contradiction between Tantra and other traditions (or in respect to Vedânta).[2]

René Guénon, commenting on Avalon's *The Serpent Power*, pointed out, in an article called *Kundalinî-Yoga*, the *chakras* as "centers of consciousness" of the human individuality (with its two modalities, subtle and corporeal), each *chakra* having its presiding deity (*dêvatâ*), where the deities are "forms of consciousness"[3]; these deities reside in fact in the various "worlds" (*lokas*) hierarchically superposed, but these *lokas* have exact correspondences in the human being in accord with the law of analogy.[4] Therefore, even though the forms and centers of

---

[1] Avalon, *Shakti and Shakta*, p. 312. Avalon tried to oppose Tantra to Shankarâchârya: for the latter, Avalon said, "mind and matter are in themselves unconscious but appear to be conscious through *Chidâbhâsa*, that is, the appearance of something as *Chit* (Consciousness), which is not really *Chit*. This appearance of Consciousness is due to the reflection of *Chit* upon it. Mind as one such unconscious forces takes on the semblance of Consciousness, though this is borrowed from *Chit* and is not its own natural quality" (*ibid.*, pp. 288-292); "the *Shâkta Âgama* [the Tantra] reverses the position, and says that they are in themselves, that is, in their ground, conscious, for they are at base *Chit*; but they yet appear to be unconscious, or more strictly limited consciousness, by the veiling power of Consciousness Itself as *Mâyâ-Shakti*... it is not unconscious *Mâyâ* in Shankarâchârya's sense which veils consciousness, but Consciousness as *Shakti* veils Itself, and, as so functioning, it is called *Mâyâshaktî*"; but, in the end, Avalon conceded that "as with so many other matters, these apparent differences are to some extent a matter of words" (*ibid.*, pp. 319, 336-337).

[2] "By this Prajâpati this body of ours is set up in possession of consciousness (*cetanâvat*)" (Coomaraswamy, *Metaphysics*, p. 72); evidently, *manas* and *ahankâra* are born from a superior principle (*Buddhi*).

[3] "That Essence is in itself one and changeless, but as related to a particular psycho-physical form as its cause and Director of its functions it is its Presiding Consciousness. Mind and Matter are not, as such, self-guiding. They are evolved and directed by Consciousness. The presiding consciousness of the Form and its functions is its presiding *Devatā*. A *Deva* is thus the consciousness aspect of the psycho-physical form. So the *Deva* Agni is the one Consciousness in its aspect as the Lord of Fire" (Avalon, *Shakti and Shakta*, p. 401; *La puissance du serpent*, p. 22).

[4] Guénon, *Études sur l'Hindouisme*, p. 34. In this sense we should understand the words of Guillaume de St. Thierry, the friend of St. Bernard de Clairvaux, in his famous *Golden Epistle*: "Thou hast one cell without, another within. The outward cell is the house wherein thy soul and thy body dwell together; the inward is thy

consciousness refer to the human individuality in its integrality, it must be acknowledged the reality of the multiple states of the being and the continuity of the human state upwards and downwards, which allows the use of expressions like "subconscious" and "supraconscious," the former being the door open to the influences of the inferior states [the most maleficent influences of the subtle world][1] and the latter the door open to the influences of the superior states, relative to the human state[2]; accordingly, the seventh *chakra*, *sahasrâra*, corresponds to this

---

conscience (*conscientia*, 'inward controller') which ought to be dwelt in by God" (Coomaraswamy, *Traditional Art*, p. 425).

[1] *Parmi des éléments assez divers, le "subconscient" contient incontestablement tout ce qui, dans l'individualité humaine, constitue des traces ou des vestiges des états inférieurs de l'être, et ce avec quoi il met le plus sûrement l'homme en communication, c'est tout ce qui, dans notre monde, représente ces mêmes états inférieurs. Ainsi, prétendre que c'est là une communication avec le Divin, c'est véritablement placer Dieu dans les états inférieurs de l'être*, in inferis *au sens littéral de cette expression; c'est donc là une doctrine proprement "infernale," un renversement de l'ordre universel, et c'est précisément ce que nous appelons "satanisme"* (René Guénon, L'Erreur spirite, Éditions Traditionnelles, 1984, p. 307).

[2] *La conscience organique dont il vient d'être question rentre naturellement dans ce que les psychologues appellent la "subconscience"; mais leur grand tort est de croire qu'ils ont suffisamment expliqué ce à quoi ils se sont bornés en réalité à donner une simple dénomination, sous laquelle ils rangent d'ailleurs les éléments les plus disparates, sans pouvoir même faire la distinction entre ce qui est vraiment conscient à quelque degré et ce qui n'en a que l'apparence, non plus qu'entre le "subconscient" véritable et le "superconscient," nous voulons dire entre ce qui procède d'états respectivement inférieurs et supérieurs par rapport à l'état humain* (Guénon, L'Homme, p. 146); *C'est précisément cette confusion que nous retrouvons encore ici: que les productions des malades observés par les psychiatres procèdent du "subconscient," c'est là une chose qui assurément n'est pas douteuse; mais, par contre, tout ce qui est d'ordre traditionnel, et notamment le symbolisme, ne peut être rapporté qu'au "superconscient," c'est-à-dire à ce par quoi s'établit une communication avec le supra-humain, tandis que le "subconscient" tend au contraire vers l'infra-humain* (René Guénon, Symboles fondamentaux de la Science sacrée, Gallimard, 1980, pp. 64, 67); *Dans le domaine philosophique et psychologique, les tendances correspondant à la seconde phase de l'action antitraditionnelle se traduisent naturellement par l'appel au "subconscient" sous toutes ses formes, c'est-à-dire aux éléments psychiques les plus inférieurs de l'être humain* (Guénon, Le règne, p. 294); *Il y a certainement bien plus qu'une simple question de vocabulaire dans le fait, très significatif en lui-même, que la psychologie actuelle n'envisage jamais que le "subconscient" et non le "superconscient" qui devrait logiquement en être le corrélatif; c'est bien là, à n'en pas douter, l'expression d'une extension qui s'opère uniquement par le bas, c'est-à-dire du côté qui correspond, ici dans l'être humain comme ailleurs dans le milieu cosmique, aux "fissures" par lesquelles pénètrent les influences les plus "maléfiques" du monde subtil, nous pourrions même dire celles qui ont un caractère véritablement et littéralement "infernal"* (ibid., p. 304).

"supraconscious" or "superconscious."[1] Arthur Avalon peremptorily stated: "That which is the general characteristic of the Indian systems, and that which constitutes their real profundity, is the paramount importance attached to Consciousness[2] and its states. It is these states which create, sustain and destroy the worlds. Brahmâ, Vishnu and Shiva are the names for functions of the one Universal Consciousness operating in ourselves."[3]

The recognition of the Principle (in truth the pure Being) as the universal Consciousness, and closing the eyes to the other aspects, makes it possible to rephrase the sacred texts and to even say: "in the beginning was consciousness,"[4] but such a strict statement could be confusing, and so could this description: "Consciousness at its elevated

---

[1] *Au sommet de la tête, autour du* Brahma-randhra, *est un septième "lotus,"* sahasrâra *ou le "lotus à mille pétales," qui n'est pas compté au nombre des* chakras, *parce que, comme nous le verrons par la suite, il se rapporte, en tant que "centre de conscience," à un état qui est au delà des limites de l'individualité* (Guénon, *Études sur l'Hindouisme,* p. 34). *Par ce passage (la* sushumnâ *et la couronne de la tête où elle aboutit), en vertu de la Connaissance acquise et de la conscience de la Voie méditée (conscience qui est essentiellement d'ordre extra-temporel, puisqu'elle est, même en tant qu'on l'envisage dans l'état humain, un reflet des états supérieurs)* (Guénon commenting on the Hindu tradition, *L'Homme,* p. 162).

[2] As in the Tantras and as a teaching not for an elite but for everybody. "Supreme Consciousness is the Supreme Shiva-Shakti (Parashiva-Parashakti) which never changes" (*The Serpent Power,* p. 29, *La puissance du serpent,* p. 37).

[3] *The Serpent Power,* p. 19, *La puissance du serpent,* p. 27.

[4] See Seyyed Hossein Nasr, *In the Beginning of Creation was Consciousness,* The Dudleian Lecture, 2003. "Before the manifestation of the universe, infinite Being-Consciousness-Bliss alone was – that is, *Shiva-Shakti* as *Chit* and *Chidrûpinî* respectively (*Aham prakritirûpâ chet chidânanda-parâyanâ*)" (*The Serpent Power,* p. 32, *La puissance du serpent,* p. 39); "At the time of Dissolution (*Pralaya*) there is in Consciousness as *Mahâkundalî*, though undistinguishable from its general mass, the potentiality or seed of the universe to be... At the end of the period of rest, which is Dissolution, this seed ripens in Consciousness" (*The Serpent Power,* p. 37, *La puissance du serpent,* p. 44); "It is *Chidghana* or massive consciousness – that is, *Chit* associated with undifferentiated (that is, *Chidrûpinî*) *Shakti*, in which lie potentially in a mass (*Ghana*), though undistinguishable the one from the other, all the worlds and beings to be created" (*The Serpent Power,* p. 42, *La puissance du serpent,* p. 49); "*Prakriti Shakti*, like all else, is Consciousness, for Consciousness as Power and static Consciousness are one. Consciousness, however, assumes the role of *Prakriti* – that is, creative power – when evolving the universe" (*The Serpent Power,* p. 52, *La puissance du serpent,* p. 58).

levels is at once knowing and knowing that it knows, knowledgeable of its own knowledge,"[1] if there is no clear avowal that between the individual consciousness and all the other levels of consciousness there is analogy and we cannot (and better not) define them,[2] and in the infinite Consciousness (which is the Unconsciousness) there is no subject and object of knowledge.[3]

It is also recomanded to be less exclusive and if "*in principio* was *Chit*," so it was *Sat* and *Ananda*, and the source of this expression, St. John, in fact said: "In the beginning was the Word, and the Word was with God, and the Word was God," not rigidly "in the beginning was the Word"; therefore, we must say: *in Principio* was *Sat-Chit-Ananda*.[4]

---

[1] Or, "There is no religion whose traditional universe is not filled with consciousness"; "They lived in a universe in which God could speak to the trees as well as to us. Angelic beings could manifest themselves and they could even transmit knowledge. Knowledge and consciousness were not limited to the human order"; "Finally, if you take seriously the rejection of the idea of consciousness being the beginning not only of time but also, in principal, of the universe, it really shatters all the deepest hopes of human beings" (Nasr, *ibid*.).

[2] Even the arrogant profane world admitted the difficulty in defining "consciousness": "We have no idea how consciousness emerges from the physical activity of the brain and we do not know whether consciousness can emerge from non-biological systems, such as computers... At this point the reader will expect to find a careful and precise definition of consciousness. You will be disappointed. Consciousness has not yet become a scientific term that can be defined in this way. Currently we all use the term *consciousness* in many different and often ambiguous ways. Precise definitions of different aspects of consciousness will emerge ... but to make precise definitions at this stage is premature" (*Human Brain Function*, 2004).

[3] "'The dead know not anything' (Eccl 9:5). *Na pretya samjnâsti* (BU II.4.12)... The Self is indestructible (BU IV.5.14; BG IV.13), but 'consciousness' in terms of subject and object is a contingency and loses its meaning 'where everything has become just the Self' (BU II.4.14), 'actively Itself when it is not intelligizing (Plotin IV.4.2)" (Coomaraswamy, *Metaphysics*, p. 68). "After death is no consciousness" (*ibid*., p. 137). However, if the being after death has reached a high level of "knowledge" he could remain in the invidual condition (the subtle form) till the dissolution of the cycle (*pralaya*): *Cette forme subtile (où réside après la mort l'être qui demeure ainsi dans l'état individuel humain) est (par comparaison avec la forme corporelle ou grossière) imperceptible aux sens... la conscience individuelle qui, demeurant liée à celle-ci, n'a plus de relation avec le corps* (Guénon commenting on the Hindu tradition, *L'Homme*, pp. 153-155).

[4] Guénon expressed Ramana Maharshi's thoughts, when reviewing his works: *Il ne peut donc être identifié qu'avec ce qui subsiste après que tous ces éléments adventices ont été éliminés, c'est-à-dire la pure conscience qui est* Sat-Chit-Ananda. *C'est le "Soi"* (Âtmâ), *qui réside dans le*

This ternary is God and *Âtmâ* and pure Consciousness and pure Knowledge,[1] and supreme Reality,[2] though still *intelligible*, and accepting to be symbolized as a visible unique Mountain.[3] Beyond God there is the Supraluminous Darkness where reigns no consciousness, no intelligence, no ternary, no nothing.[4]

---

cœur (hridaya) *et qui est l'unique source de toutes les manifestations mentales, vitales, psychiques et corporelles* (*Études sur l'Hindouisme*, p. 169) (*The Collected Works of Ramana Maharshi*, Sri Ramanasramam, 1979, p. 37). The perfect union in the pure Consciousness, either the union *Shiva-Shakti*, or *jivâtmâ-Âtmâ*, or *Sachchidânanda*, is illustrated by the well-known gesture *chinmudra*, the "gesture of pure Consciousness."
[1] *Enfin, le caractère de l'état de celui qui demeure fermement établi dans la Connaissance* (ârûdhasthiti), *état immuable qui est celui de complète identité ou d'absorption dans le "Soi"* (Guénon, *ibid.*, p. 178). "This inherence in the central consciousness is accordingly the means of a 'unified density of cognition' (*ekîbhûta prajnâna-ghana*, Mand. Up. 5), a 'cognitive pleroma' (*krtsnah prajnâna-ghana*, BU IV.5.13)"; "Veda is the body of Truth in which is set forth the way of life; and this Truth, eternal in the consciousness of the Self *(without distinction of 'knowledge' from 'being'* [*our Italics*]), is transmitted as it has been 'heard,' by a succession of Prophets (*rsayah*) from *manvantara* to *manvantara*" (Coomaraswamy, *Metaphysics*, pp. 180, 404). "The self-effulgent *Âtmâ*, which is Pure Knowledge"; "Thy own Self, which is Knowledge Absolute" (*Vivekachûdâmani of Shri Shankaracharya*, English translation Swami Madhavananda, Advaita Ashrama, Calcutta, 1974, pp. 73, 113).
[2] *L'enseignement essentiel concernant la "Réalité Suprême," ou la "Conscience Absolue" qui doit être réalisée comme le "Soi,"* wrote Guénon reviewing Maharshi (*ibid.*, p. 134).
[3] Arunachala *est le nom d'une montagne considérée comme lieu sacré et symbole du "Cœur du Monde"; il représente l'immanence de la "Conscience Suprême" dans tous les êtres. Ces hymnes respirent une incontestable spiritualité*, Guénon commented on one of Maharshi's hymns (*ibid.*, p. 131). "Each radius, spoke, or ray represents the whole being of an individual consciousness, its intersection with any circumference the operation of this consciousness... the unique point from which all radii proceed and to which all converge represents an omniscient, supra-individual consciousness, metaphysically the First Principle, theologically God in his *intelligible* [our *Italics*] aspect, that of the Supernal Sun, or Light [beyond which is the Godhead or Divine Darkness]" (Coomaraswamy, *Metaphysics*, pp. 178-179).
[4] "For a further analysis of what is meant by 'unconsciousness' (*asamjnâna*) post mortem and in 'deep sleep' see SB X.5.2.11-15 and BU II.1.19, II.4.12-14, and IV.5.13-15. It is an unconsciousness because it is not a consciousness of anything, which would be impossible where there is no duality, but so far from being an absence or privation of consciousness, it is a consciousness as all that might otherwise be known only conceptually, and hence it is described by such expressions as 'condensation of discrimination' (*vijnâna-ghana*) and 'cognoscent' (*samvit*)" (*ibid.*, p. 212).

At the end of *Kali-Yuga*, the notion of "consciousness" became so overwhelming that the essential meaning of "knowledge" was almost forgotten, the public at large, as expected, foolishly preferring the first and rejecting anything that even by far was connected to the intellect, for the modern mentality knowledge representing the quantity of data acquired through the super- hyper- devices of media communication; "consciousness" was better (but wrongly) understood since it implied something sentimental and infra-psychological; therefore even the translations of the Hindu sacred texts favoured the term "consciousness" to that of "knowledge" reinterpreting the Sanskrit word *jnâna* ("knowledge") and its derivatives (*prajnâna, prâjna*).[1]

The Latin *conscientia* (*com* – "with" + *scire* – "to know"), like the Greek *syneidesis*, means "with knowledge," and we should mention again what René Guénon wrote about knowledge and consciousness in his book *Les États multiples de l'Être*: "knowledge, understood absolutely and in all its universality, is in no way synonymous with or equivalent to consciousness, whose domain is coextensive only with that of certain determined states of being, so that it is only in those states to the exclusion of all others, that knowledge is realized by means of what can properly be called 'becoming conscious' of anything. Consciousness, as we have understood the term until now, even in its most general sense and without restricting it to its specifically human form, is only a contingent and special mode of knowledge under certain conditions, a property inherent to a being envisaged in certain states of manifestation; all the more reason, then, to say that it is not applicable in any degree to unconditioned states, that is, to all that goes beyond Being, since it is not even applicable to the whole of Being. Knowledge, on the contrary, considered in itself and independently of the conditions attaching to any particular state, can admit of no restriction, and to be adequate to total truth must be

---

[1] On the contrary, Coomaraswamy translated *Chit* with "Intelligence" (*vide infra*).

coextensive not only with Being but also with universal Possibility itself."[1]

As we will see shortly, René Guénon did not avoid the traditional notion of *Chit*, but he specified:

> *Comme le mot "raison," le mot "conscience" peut être parfois universalisé, par une transposition purement analogique, et nous l'avons fait nous même ailleurs pour rendre la signification du terme sanscrit Chit; mais une telle transposition n'est possible que lorsqu'on se limite à l'Être, comme c'était le cas alors pour la considération du ternaire* Sachchidânanda.

What does this "analogy" mean for "consciousness"? First, that *Chit* and all the "superconscious" levels can be described "analogically" only, without really realizing (being aware of) them (as an invidual), as in the case of the deep sleep when the human individual does not remember anything about that "consciousness"[2]; second, this analogy

---

[1] "The Nirguna (Para-) Brahma is undetermined in any sense whatever, transcending both being (*sat*) and non-being (*asat*), though conceivable as non-being (*asat*) when contrasted with the *saguna* Brahma, Self-determined Self: of this absolutely undetermined Brahma we can only say "is" (*asti, Katha Up* VI.12 and 13), and then only by analogy. The *saguna* (*apara*) Brahma, Âtmâ, Self-determined (*svayambhû*) whose essence and nature equally are Being (*sat*), Intelligence (*cit*) and Bliss (*ananda*), Autonomous, Immortal absolutely, is spoken of as Îshvara, the Lord, Mahâpurusha, Great Person, or in the religious extensions by a personal name, as Vishnu, Shiva, and so forth. The *nirguna* and *saguna* Brahma (using the singular advisedly) are not two but identical, as cause and effect are One" (Ananda K. Coomaraswamy, *Yakshas*, Oxford University Press, 1993, *The Cult of Life: What Are the Waters?*, pp. 186-206).

[2] *La même retraite du sens interne se remarque aussi dans le sommeil profond et dans l'évanouissement extatique (avec cessation complète de toute manifestation extérieure de la conscience). Ajoutons que cette cessation n'implique cependant pas toujours, d'une façon nécessaire, la suspension totale de la sensibilité corporelle, sorte de conscience organique, si l'on peut dire, quoique la conscience individuelle proprement dite n'ait alors aucune part dans les manifestations de celle-ci, avec laquelle elle ne communique plus comme cela a lieu normalement dans les états ordinaires de l'être vivant; et la raison en est facile à comprendre, puisque, à vrai dire, il n'y a plus de conscience individuelle dans les cas dont il s'agit, la conscience véritable de l'être étant transférée dans un autre état, qui est en réalité un état supra-individuel. Cette conscience organique à laquelle nous venons de faire allusion n'est pas une conscience au vrai sens de ce mot, mais elle en participe en quelque façon, devant son origine à la conscience individuelle dont elle est comme un reflet; séparée de celle-ci, elle n'est plus qu'une illusion de conscience* (*L'Homme*, pp. 145-146).

should be metaphysically regarded as "reversed," which means that if the individual consciousness seems fundamental for the human being and *Chit* is nowhere in sight, *Chit* is in fact everything and omnipresent while the individual consciousness is nothing.[1]

Analogically, *Chit* is to the "Universal Man,"[2] what individual consciousness is to a human being,[3] and we could say that the individual consciousness refers to the cosmologic viewpoint, while *Chit* corresponds to the metaphysical point.[4]

Even the individual consciousness is not at hand for the modern man (not to mention then the superconsciousness), because realizing the individual consciousness, which the Tantra illustrates by taking possession of the six *chakras*, means to reconquer the primordial state, realizing the totality of the human state (the integral individual being), and not merely functioning with a consciousness completely enslaved to the corporeal domain.[5] As a manner of speaking, we could utter this

---

[1] ... *toute véritable analogie doit être appliquée en sens inverse: c'est ce que figure le symbole bien connu du "sceau de Salomon"... de même que l'image d'un objet dans un miroir est inversée par rapport à l'objet, ce qui est le premier ou le plus grand dans l'ordre principiel est, du moins en apparence, le dernier ou le plus petit dans l'ordre de la manifestation* (René Guénon, *Le Symbolisme de la croix*, Guy Trédaniel, 1989, p. 21). *Il y a donc analogie, mais non pas similitude, entre l'homme individuel, être relatif et incomplet, qui est pris ici comme type d'un certain mode d'existence, ou même de toute existence conditionnée, et l'être total, inconditionné et transcendant par rapport à tous les modes particuliers et déterminés d'existence, et même par rapport à l'Existence pure et simple, être total que nous désignons symboliquement comme l'"Homme Universel"* (ibid., p. 22).

[2] This *Chit* is "the true consciousness of the being" (*la conscience veritable de l'être*) Guénon was writing about (*vide supra*).

[3] *La réalisation effective des états multiples de l'être se réfère à la conception de ce que différentes doctrines traditionnelles, et notamment l'ésotérisme islamique, désigne comme l'"Homme Universel," conception qui, comme nous l'avons dit ailleurs, établit l'analogie constitutive de la manifestation universelle et de sa modalité individuelle humaine, ou, pour employer le langage de l'hermétisme occidental, du "macrocosme" et du "microcosme"* (ibid., p. 20).

[4] ... *surtout s'il s'agit de l'état humain, même pris dans le développement intégral de toutes ses modalités, ou d'un autre état individuel, n'est encore proprement que "cosmologique," et ce que nous devons envisager essentiellement ici, c'est une transposition métaphysique de la notion de l'homme individuel, transposition qui doit être effectuée dans le domaine extra-individuel et supra-individuel* (ibid., p. 21).

[5] For the common man, consciousness is awakened only in his corporeal modality: *Nous avons fait, dans ce que nous venons de dire, une distinction entre l'individualité intégrale et sa*

apparent paradox: to reach the Consciousness (*Chit*) it is necessary to annihilate the consciousness (*ahankâra*),[1] which shows the incommensurable difference between the individual domain and the universal one, or between *Corpus-Anima* and *Spiritus*, and suggests that the "states of consciousness" in the supra-individual realm should be called "spiritual states" instead, while the "states of consciousness" should refer to the *Corpus-Anima* realm.[2] This paradox stresses that a realization (*prendre conscience*)[3] of the spiritual or supra-individual states is

---

modalité corporelle, la première comprenant en outre toutes les modalités subtiles; et, à ce propos, nous pouvons ajouter une remarque qui, bien qu'accessoire, aidera sans doute à comprendre ce que nous avons principalement en vue. Pour l'homme ordinaire, dont la conscience n'est en quelque sorte "éveillée" que dans la seule modalité corporelle, ce qui est perçu plus ou moins obscurément des modalités subtiles apparaît comme inclus dans le corps, parce que cette perception ne correspond effectivement qu'à leurs rapports avec celui-ci, plutôt qu'à ce qu'elles sont en elles-mêmes (Guénon, *Initiation et Réalisation spirituelle*, p. 232). Arturo Reghini saw the initiatory path to immortality as a journey of the initiate's consciousness through successive phases: *Pour qui a quelque expérience de ce genre, il n'y a aucun doute à avoir sur l'existence, dans la Divine Comédie et dans l'Enéide, d'une allégorie métaphysico-ésotérique, qui voile et expose en même temps les phases successives par lesquelles passe la conscience de l'initié pour atteindre l'immortalité* (René Guénon, *L'ésotérisme de Dante*, Gallimard, 1981, p. 28).

[1] Even though this "annihilation" is, in reality, "union" and "integration." *Pratyahara* (the withdrawal of the senses) and *dharana* (concentration), as stipulated by Patanjali and found in other spiritual paths, illustrate this "annihilation."

[2] Guénon underlined that, for the supra-individual states, it cannot be question of "consciousness" in the proper sense of the word (...*états supra-individuels. Pour ces derniers, il ne peut plus être question de "conscience" au sens propre de ce mot*). "The operation of these powers in us ['the powers of the soul'] is what we call our consciousness (*caitanyam, samjnânam, vijnânam*), i.e., conscious life in terms of subject and object. This consciousness, with which all ethical responsibility is bound up, arises at our birth and ceases when 'we' die" (Coomaraswamy, *Metaphysics*, p. 337). Yet even in the individual domain we could say that the spiritual path means a gradual increase in knowledge: *Utkarshati ha vai jnânasantatim*, "he heightens, that is to say, increases the current of knowledge" (*Mândukya Upanishad Kârikâ* I.10, referring to *Taijasa*), culminating with the "state of the *Brâhmana*," of pure Knowledge; "Knowledge (*jnâna*) and the threefold knowable (*jneya*) being known, one after another, the knower possessed of the highest intellect spontaneously attains to the state of knowledge (*Turîya*) everywhere and in all things in this very life" (*Mândukya Upanishad Kârikâ* IV.89).

[3] As Ramana Maharshi said: "Then we attain knowledge or realisation of the Self."

inconceivable for man as individual being,¹ but quite accessible if we comprehend that the human state is just one of many, and we must refer to the "total being"² (the triad *Corpus-Anima-Spiritus*) in order to understand how *Sachchidânanda* could be realized.³

In the *Mândukya Upanishad Kârikâ*, it is said: "The knowledge that has Brahma for its content is birthless and everlasting. The birthless (Self) is known by the birthless (knowledge).⁴ Arthur Avalon wrote about the *Mândukya Upanishad*: "This Upanishad gives an analysis of the states of Consciousness on all planes, and should be studied in connection with Gaudapâda's *Kârikâ* on the same subject with Shankarâchârya's Commentary on the latter."⁵ Indeed, this *Upanishad* is fundamental for our subject and we should point out that René

---

¹ "The immortal cannot become mortal, nor can the mortal ever become immortal. For, it is never possible for a thing to change its nature" (*Mândukya Upanishad Kârikâ* III.21).

² *Ainsi, l'individu, en tant qu'individu, ne peut aucunement sortir des conditions qui le font être tel; mais l'être qui est un individu humain est aussi autre chose en même temps, et c'est à ce titre qu'il peut rendre effective la communication qui existe virtuellement entre son état humain et ses autres états* (Guénon, *Fragments Doctrinaux*, p. 226).

³ The individual consciousness has no power in the supra-individual world. Guénon wrote in a letter: ... *je ne veux parler que de ce qui est individuel; il ne peut donc pas être question alors de l'élément intellectuel proprement dit, qui est supra-individuel; vous objectez à cela que "l'individu est virtuellement tout-connaissant"; mais on ne peut pas dire cela, car, si c'est vrai de l'être humain, ce n'est pas en tant qu'individu, mais bien, au contraire, en tant qu'il se rattache aux états supra-individuels et qu'il a la possibilité d'entrer en possession de ces états, lesquels ne constituent avec l'état individuel qu'un seul et même être total. Maintenant, l'élément intellectuel est précisément ce qui relie entre eux tous ces états de l'être total, mais c'est pour cela qu'il n'appartient au domaine d'aucun de ces états pris en particulier; il rencontre seulement ce domaine en un point, qui en constitue d'ailleurs le centre véritable. C'est seulement cette rencontre ou cette incidence, avec la réfraction qui en est la conséquence, qui peut, lorsqu'il s'agit de l'état individuel humain, devenir consciente; et c'est là, d'ailleurs, une condition nécessaire pour que cet état puisse servir de base à une réalisation atteignant les états supra-individuels. Pour ces derniers, il ne peut plus être question de "conscience" au sens propre de ce mot* (*Fragments Doctrinaux*, p. 49).

⁴ III.33; and here it is Shankarâchârya's commentary: "The Knowers of Brahma say: the absolute knowledge (*jnâna*)... is non-different from Brahma, the absolute Reality (*Satya*). This is supported by such Scriptural passages as, 'Like heat from fire, knowledge (*jnâna*) is never absent from the knower (*Âtmâ*),' 'Brahma is Knowledge and Bliss,' 'Brahma is Truth (Reality), Knowledge, and Infinity'... the unborn knowledge (*ajena*) is the very nature of the Self."

⁵ *The Serpent Power*, p. 78, *La puissance du serpent*, p. 81.

Guénon based his major work about the Hindu tradition, *L'Homme et son devenir selon le Védânta*, on the *Mândukya Upanishad*. However, for the present work, the study of this *Upanishad*, together with Gaudapâda's *Kârikâ* and Shankarâchârya's *Bhâshya*, aims to reveal how the essential terms were translated for the contemporary world. In many cases, the notions used were "consciousness" and a "mass of consciousness" (*prajnâna-ghana*),[1] but also *vijnâna* was translated, like in Buddhism, as "consciousness,"[2] even though its prime meaning is "right knowledge, discrimination, discernment," even "wisdom."[3] Therefore, the only way to accept the word "consciousness" is to be conscious of its essence – the infinite Knowledge, which means that through "intellectual" knowledge the "being" reaches the consciousness of what is to be known (*prendre conscience*),[4] where the highest state is

---

[1] Avalon, *The Serpent Power*, p. 80, *La puissance du serpent*, p. 83; *The Mândûkyopanishad with Gaudapâda's Kârikâ and Shanka's Commentary*, translated and annotated by Swâmî Nikhilânda, Sri Ramakrishna Ashram, Mysore, 1955 (*prajnânaghana*, "a mass of all consciousness unified," p. 22, "with the cessation of the activity known as memory, the perceiver (in the waking and dream states) is unified with Prâjna in the Âkâsha of the heart and becomes a mass of consciousness," p. 29); *Eight Upanishads*, volume II, with the Commentary of Shankarâchârya, translated by Swâmî Gambhîrânanda, Advaita Ashrama, Calcutta, 1973 ("a mass of mere consciousness," *prajnânaghanah*, p. 188); Paul Martin-Dubost, *Çankara et le Védânta*, Seuil, 1973 (*prajnânam brahma*, "Le Brahma est Conscience"). Sometimes, as a compromise, *prajnâna* is translated as "supra-consciousness" (S. N. Dasgupta, *Hindu Mysticism*, Frederick Ungar Publishing Co., 1959, p. 38).

[2] *Mândukya Upanishad* IV.46 and 50 (*The Mândûkyopanishad*, pp. 262, 266; *Eight Upanishads*, pp. 362, 366).

[3] *Vijnâna*, Guénon wrote, is the "distinctive knowledge" and therefore is applied specifically to the individual or formal domain (*Prajnâna ou la Connaissance intégrale s'oppose ici à vijnâna ou la connaissance distinctive, qui, s'appliquant spécialement au domaine individuel ou formel, caractérise les deux états precedents*, *L'Homme*, p. 115).

[4] For this reason translations sometimes identify Knowledge with Consciousness: "Jnâna means the essence of Knowledge, i.e., the consciousness which is the very nature of Âtmâ or the Self" (*The Mândûkyopanishad*, p. 193; *Eight Upanishads*, p. 311); or it is said that Knowledge is identical to Consciousness and to *Âtmâ* (*The Mândûkyopanishad*, p. 309). Because of this confusion, "consciousness" was sometimes completely substituted with "knowledge": *Chit*, "Knowledge absolute"; "*Âtmâ*, the Existence-Knowledge-Bliss Absolute"; "thy own Self, which is Knowledge Absolute" (*Vivekachûdâmani of Shri Shankaracharya*, pp. 23, 110). Yet Shankarâchârya also said: "The Self must be known by pure consciousness (*cetasâ*)";

Sachchidânanda, when the knower, the knowing and what is to be known are united in One pure Consciousness,[1] and beyond which there is only the infinite Knowledge or the Unconsciousness.[2] Accordingly, René Guénon translated *prajnâna-ghana* as "a mass of integral Knowledge,"[3] while the Consciousness (*Chit*) is the mouth of *Prâjna* (the "Knower"),[4] and in this sense we should understand the expression *prendre conscience* as assimilating (like the mouth absorbing food) what is to be known and realizing the *Sachchidânanda*, this

---

Par ce passage (la sushumnâ *et la couronne de la tête où elle aboutit), en vertu de la Connaissance acquise et de la conscience de la Voie méditée (conscience qui est essentiellement d'ordre extra-temporel, puisqu'elle est, même en tant qu'on l'envisage dans l'état humain, un reflet des états supérieurs)* (Guénon commenting on the Hindu tradition, *L'Homme*, p. 162).

[1] This "pure Consciousness" could be conceived as "pure spiritual Light" (*prabhâtam svayam*, "fully illuminated by Itself," *Mândukya Upanishad* IV.81, "this knowledge, *Jnâna*, is all-light," *Mândukya Upanishad* IV.100). "The supreme Reality [is] characterized by the identity of the knower, knowledge and the object of knowledge" (*Mândukya Upanishad* IV.1).

[2] In the Fourth, *Turîya*, "is accomplished simultaneously the cessation of the distinction between the knower, the known and the knowledge. Thus it will be said later on, 'Duality cannot exist when *Gnosis* [metaphysical knowledge], the highest Truth (non-duality) is realised'" (Shankarâchârya's commentary, *The Mândûkyopanishad*, p. 50, *Eight Upanishads*, p. 208). *Turîya* is pure Knowledge; "Brahma is Truth, Knowledge and Infinity" (*Satyam jnanam anantam brahma*, *Taittirîya Upanishad* II.1.1; *Vivekachûdâmani* 514).

[3] ... *un ensemble synthétique (unique et sans détermination particulière) de Connaissance intégrale* (*L'Homme*, p. 115).

[4] ... *et dont la bouche (l'instrument de connaissance) est (uniquement) la Conscience totale* (Chit) *elle-même (sans intermédiaire ni particularisation d'aucune sorte), celui-là est appelé* Prâjna *(Celui qui connaît en dehors et au delà de toute condition spéciale)* (*ibid.*, pp. 115-116). Here it is Shankarâchârya's commentary: "It is called the *Cetomukha* [the consciousness mouth] because it is the doorway to the (cognition) of the two other states of consciousness known as dream and waking... It is called *Prâjna*, the knower *par excellence*... or it is called *Prâjna* because its peculiar feature is consciousness undifferentiated" (*The Mândûkyopanishad*, p. 23); in the *Eight Upanishads* (p. 189), *Prâjna* is not the knower but "conscious *par excellence*." Much better, Robert Ernest Hume in his *The Thirteen Principal Upanishads* (Oxford University Press, 1971) translated, in this fifth shruti of the *Mândukya Upanishad*, *prajnâna-ghana* as "a cognition-mass" and *Prâjna* as the "Cognitional" (p. 392).

corresponds to the "effective consciousness"[1] or to the consciousness of the Identity of the Being, which constitutes the "sense of eternity."[2] This "sense of eternity" cannot be described but has to be realized, and so, there is no doubt that the Consciousness itself cannot be described but it has to be realized, which means for the modern world that it has no alternative but to face a *Mysterium Conscientia*, as Arthur Avalon wrote: "the claim that Consciousness as such exists can only be verified by spiritual experience," and: "if it be asked how consciousness can obscure itself partially or at all, the only answer is *Acintyâ Shakti*, which Mâyâvâdins as all other Vedântists admit. Of this, as of all ultimates, we must say with the Western Scholastics, *omnia exeunt in mysterium*."[3]

---

[1] ...*ce n'est pas le lien avec le Principe qu'il s'agit en réalité de rétablir, puisqu'il existe toujours et ne peut pas cesser d'exister mais c'est, pour l'être manifesté, la conscience effective de ce lien qui doit être réalisée* (Guénon, *Initiation et Réalisation spirituelle*, p. 52).
[2] ...*c'est par la conscience de l'Identité de l'Être, permanente à travers toutes les modifications indéfiniment multiples de l'Existence unique, que se manifeste, au centre même de notre état humain aussi bien que de tous les autres états, cet élément transcendant et informel, donc non-incarné et non-individualisé, qui est appelé le "Rayon Céleste"; et c'est cette conscience, supérieure par là même à toute faculté de l'ordre formel, donc essentiellement supra-rationnelle, et impliquant l'assentiment de la loi d'harmonie qui relie et unit toutes choses dans l'Univers, c'est, disons-nous, cette conscience qui, pour notre être individuel, mais indépendamment de lui et des conditions auxquelles il est soumis, constitue véritablement la "sensation de l'éternité"* (*Le Symbolisme de la Croix*, Guy Trédaniel, 1989, p. 155).
[3] *Shakti and Shakta*, pp. 336-337.

CHAPTER IX

THE TRADITIONAL MENTALITY

Mysterium Conscientia has been degrading with increasing speed at the end of *Kali-Yuga*,[1] in accord with the spreading of the modern mentality, a mentality that could be called today a "mentality of servants,"[2] where consciousness was understood as something banal,

---

[1] Let us make a note that the modern "international movement" Hare Krishna (1966) is called the "International Society for Krishna Consciousness" and was motivated by the Bengali "seer" Chaitanya Mahaprabhu; *chaitanya* means "consciusness," but Mahaprabhu founded a "school" of *Bhakti-Yoga* (corresponding to *bhakti chaitanya*), and he accepted disciples regardless of caste or religion.

[2] What Sri Aurobindo said about India a century ago is valid now for the whole world: "There is no national life perfect or sound without the *caturvarnya* [the four castes]... The cause of India's decline was the practical disappearance of the Kshatriya and the dwindling of the Vaishya... The Vaishya held his own for a long time, indeed, until the British advent by which he has almost been extinguished. When the *caturvarnya* disappears, there comes *varnasankara*, utter confusion of the great types which keep a nation vigorous and sound. The Kshatriya dwindled, the Vaishya dwindled, the Brahmin and Shudra were left. The inevitable tendency was for the Brahmin type to disappear and the first sign of his disappearance was utter degeneracy... to gravitate towards Shudrahood. In the *Kaliyuga* the Shudra is powerful and attracts into himself the less vigorous Brahmin... For the *Satyayuga* to return, we must get back the *brahmatej* (the spiritual force) and make it general. For the *brahmatej* is the basis of all the rest... if either the Kshatriya or the Brahmin goes... the nation is doomed unless it can revive or replace the missing strength. And of the two the Brahmin is the most important... But if the Brahmin becomes the Shudra, then the lower instinct of the serf and the labourer becomes all in all... When spirituality is lost all is lost" (Rishabhchand, *Sri Aurobindo, His Life Unique*, Sri Aurobindo Ashram, 2007, pp. 305-307).

sentimental and vaguely moral, something demagogical.[1]

The English word "mentality" came into use, it seems, at the end of the 17th century, when the profane point of view was in full advance,[2] in concert with the fact that, in Occident, the complete and final rupture with the traditional way coincided with the treaties of Westphalia, which ended the Thirty Years War in 1648.[3] In a genuine traditional civilization, there was no need for such a term as "mentality," since there was no way of thinking other than the sacred way, and only when the profane viewpoint took advantage of the decline of the cycle did it become necessary to introduce such as a syntagm as "traditional mentality" in comparison to the "modern mentality" (or "profane mentality").

The word "mentality" is closely related to "man," where "man" should be understood as Sanskrit *mânava* "a mental being," image of Hindu *Manu*, the Lord of the World; *Manu* is not so much a mythological or historical character, but represents a principle, called the "cosmic intelligence" that reflects the spiritual and pure Light,[4] which means that a normal, "traditional" mind is the one subordinated and connected to the divine Intellect and to the Principle, while a

---

[1] See, for example (and there are too many examples), Jean Parvulesco's pathetic sayings: *Sous le feu d'un regard nourri par une conscience supérieure, la vie de René Guénon apparaît comme un parcours singulièrement incompréhensible; c'est que la vie de René Guénon s'identifie totalement avec la grade mission qui avait été la sienne: ramener la conscience européenne actuelle à ses origines antérieures; dans ce combat profondément caché, ce sont les consciences inconnues, chacune de son côté qui, ayant été embrasées par le feu clandestinement agissant de l'œuvre de René Guénon, ont fini, ensemble...* (David Gattegno & Thierry Jolif, *Que vous a apporté René Guénon?*, Dualpha, 2002, pp. 123-125).
[2] *Ce qui est tout à fait extraordinaire, c'est la rapidité avec laquelle la civilisation du moyen âge tomba dans le plus complet oubli ; les hommes du XVIIᵉ siècle n'en avaient plus la moindre notion, et les monuments qui en subsistaient ne représentaient plus rien à leurs yeux* (René Guénon, *La Crise du monde moderne*, Gallimard, 1975, p. 30).
[3] At that time, it is said, the last genuine Rose-Cross retired to Orient, wherever this "Orient" might be. See René Guénon, *Le Roi du Monde*, Gallimard, 1981, p. 71; Sédir, *Histoire et Doctrines des Rose-Croix*, Bibliothèque des Amitiés Spirituelles, 1932, p. 40.
[4] Guénon, *Le Roi*, p. 13. Fabre d'Olivet, *Histoire philosophique du genre humain*, Éditions Traditionnelles, Paris, 1991, I, p. 238.

"modern" and "profane" mind is the one that has broken this bond and, with an obtuse arrogance, sees itself as independent and suzerain.[1]

As we said before, the devils are not so much the physical appetites, but the psychical ones, and all the spiritual methods stress the importance of pacifying the mind. The mental waves, the elusive, turbulent thoughts, imagination[2] and the emotions are the greatest enemies of spiritual realization: these are the temptations, the sirens' songs, and the devils.[3] The mind is the fanatical sustainer of duality that allows the Devil to feel legitimated: "As in dream the mind acts through Mâyâ presenting the appearance of duality, so also in the waking state the mind acts, through Mâyâ [the art of illusion], presenting the appearance of duality" [and of an individual consciousness], and only in the "deep sleep" state the mind ceases to act and "becomes identical with fearless Brahma."[4] An untamed mind, unsubordinated to the divine Intellect, independent and arrogant, maintains the illusion of reality; that is why the Christian tradition states: "Blessed are the poor in spirit: for theirs is the kingdom of heaven."[5]

---

[1] We see the similarity with the Luciferian revolt. From the Church Fathers' perspective, the "fall" of man represented the revolt of reason against *nous* [the Intellect and not the mind as sometimes this one is confused with], and the separation of *nous* from God makes man a devil or a beast [here we have to understand *nous* as becoming hidden and the mind separated, apparently, from God] (Hierotheos, *The Illness and Cure of the Soul in the Orthodox Tradition*, Birth of the Theotokos Monastery, 2004, pp. 62, 70).

[2] *Nous rappellerons encore que, dès lors qu'il s'agit de questions d'ordre initiatique, on ne saurait trop se défier de l'imagination* (René Guénon, *Initiation et réalisation spirituelle*, Éditions Traditionnelles, 1980, p. 57).

[3] Ananda K. Coomaraswamy wisely proved that *anima* (the soul, mentality and sentiment, the "tempter") represents Hell and the devils. This soul has to be "lost" in order to be saved; this soul has to be "killed" and "tamed" in the Holy War (*jihâd*). As Rûmî said, "this soul is hell" and "the soul and Shaitân are both one being." The killing of this soul is his redemption, when the fallen angels, Lucifer, Phosphorus or Scintilla, become again what they were before, the light of the supernal Sun.

[4] *Mândûkya Up.* III.29-35.

[5] *Matthew* 5:3. Here, "poor in spirit" means precisely to have a "weak mind," that is, a tamed mind, and not being "high-spirited" (with all its profane significances).

The mind is a powerful "tool," and we may assume that, even if contaminated by the modern environment, it has the capability to grasp the qualities of the "traditional mentality"; however, a modern mind is seriously damaged and distorted, which makes the task of understanding different states of mind, and especially sacred states of mind, almost impossible or at least particularly faulty[1]; in a similar way, the faith of a modern religious person[2] is different, and often extremely different, from the faith of the traditional medieval Christians or of the primeval Christians, for this modern faith is disturbingly limited and lame, and therefore incapable of provoking miracles. Consequently, even for people with the *sattvic* vocation passing from a merely theoretical and rational understanding to a realization of the "traditional mentality" is in many cases impossible; and the theoretical understanding itself is commonly deficient and inadequate.

In a normal and coherent world, not only the word "mentality," but the syntagm "traditional mentality" would be superfluous, because, on the one hand, a civilization is the product and the expression of a certain mentality, and on the other hand, tradition and civilization are almost interchangeable terms,[3] which makes "traditional civilization" also a tautological expression. However, we are forced to use this adjective "traditional" to qualify a society, a doctrine, a mentality, gestures and thoughts that developed from what was transmitted uninterruptedly from the origin of this cycle, allowing the perpetuation of a "non-human" element, without which we cannot talk about "tradition," the lack of any divine blessing (*barakah*) characterizing the

---

[1] "What an illiterate Indian or American Indian peasant knows and understands would be entirely beyond the comprehension of the compulsorily educated product of the American public schools" (Ananda K. Coomaraswamy, *Traditional Art and Symbolism*, Princeton Univ. Press, 1986, p. 287).

[2] We could say "man" instead of "person" since we consider "man" a generic name for the human being, male or female, "man" being etymologically related to "mind" and "moon." We have to stress right away that the "politically correct" concept belongs to the modern mentality and, like this mentality, is volatile and manipulated by adverse forces.

[3] René Guénon, *Introduction générale à l'étude des doctrines hindoues*, Véga, 1932, pp. 74-75.

present modern society and mentality.¹ Furthermore, we could say that at the same time with the *barakah* there is an intellectual light or ray penetrating and sustaining the traditional civilization and the "traditional mentality," this light providing the tradition or the doctrine with an intellectual essence,² where "intellectual" has to be understood not as something "rational" but as a "supra-rational" principle.³

As *barakah* or the spiritual influence descends by countless degrees so does the intellectual ray⁴; moreover, for the same state of the being there are various intensities of the divine "vibrations" in concert with the quality of the "receptor."⁵ In the medieval Christian society, where traditional organizations like Free-Masonry and the Order of the Temple flourished, the Occidental mentality was carved by the Judaic and Greco-Roman chisels,⁶ where the shaped material was mainly composed of Anglo-German peoples⁷; accordingly, this mentality was less prepared for the highest intellectual activity (the metaphysical

---

¹ The "non-human" element is the spiritual influence carried by rites, their completion involving "the action of an influence belonging to a superior order, which can be properly called 'non-human,' both in the case of the initiatory rites and of the religious ones" (René Guénon, *Aperçus sur l'initiation*, Éditions Traditionnelles, 1992, p. 54).
² See our work *Free-Masonry: A Traditional Organization*, p. 39.
³ The modern mentality is very unstable and, consequently, the language and the meaning of the words change drastically (Guénon, *Introduction générale*, 1932, p. 49), which imposes caution in comprehending some important terms (like "intellect," "tradition," "metaphysics," "consciousness," "cult," etc.).
⁴ In the Hindu tradition, this spiritual influence is sometimes called "food," a food that can be eaten in all the worlds, in all the beings, and in all the selves (*Chândogya Upanishad* 5.18.1).
⁵ The parable of the sower is a good illustration: "Behold, a sower went forth to sow; And when he sowed, some seeds fell by the way side, and the fowls came and devoured them up: Some fell upon stony places, where they had not much earth: and forthwith they sprung up, because they had no deepness of earth: And when the sun was up, they were scorched; and because they had no root, they withered away..." (*Matthew* 13:3-6).
⁶ René Guénon, *Introduction générale à l'étude des doctrines hindoues*, Guy Trédaniel, 1987, p. 11.
⁷ Goths, Franks, Saxons, Vandals, Angles, Lombards, Suebi, Burgundians, etc. On the other hand, the Near West (*Occidens Proximus*) had the Slavic peoples as carving material.

level)¹ and for pure contemplation, even though there were eminent exceptions.²

The modern mentality, driven unwittingly by a peculiar "inspiration," has a strong tendency for generalization and idealization, for labels and categories, while absolute formulas like "*everybody* (or *nobody*) knows that ...," "you *always* say ...," or "men *never* do ..." are very common today; also, for a particular event an entire community is blamed, instead just an individual: "the Christians," not a specific Christian, "the Muslims," not a specific Muslim, "the Jews," not a specific Jew,³ or general judgments are uttered, such as "the Catholic priests are impious," not a specific priest, and "I am not going to church because the Orthodox priests are boorish," not a specific priest, and so on. Of course, in an ideal society, all the priests should be saints and all the teachers (διδάσκαλοι) sages and masters, but we must not confuse the individual with the function, especially at the end of *Kali-Yuga* when the disarray is so intense. Therefore, the human factor has to be taken into account, as we already underlined in a previous volume,⁴ especially when we envision the traditional societies of the last two millennia, which explains why we prefer to name *Oriens* and *Occidens* as limits of René Guénon's comparison between the Occident

---

[1] There is a fundamental difference between activity and action.
[2] ... *dans l'Europe du moyen âge, ... la métaphysique n'y a jamais été dégagée aussi nettement qu'elle devrait l'être de la théologie, c'est-à-dire, en somme, de son application spéciale à la pensée religieuse, et que, d'autre part, ce qui s'y trouve de proprement métaphysique n'est pas complet, demeurant soumis à certaines limitations qui semblent inhérentes à toute l'intellectualité occidentale; sans doute faut-il voir dans ces deux imperfections une conséquence du double héritage de la mentalité judaïque et de la mentalité grecque* (Guénon, *Introduction générale*, 1932, p. 76).
[3] Evidently, this has nothing to do with the situations involving doctrinal perspectives, when Muslims are all infidels (from a Christian viewpoint), or Christians are all infidels (from a Islamic standpoint), or when all Christians have been considered "execution victims" from the beginning (from the Roman imperial perspective, see Henri Daniel-Rops, *The Church of Apostles and Martyrs*, Image Books, 1962, vol. I, p. 205); not to say that any traditional society, by definition, had to regard itself as the one and only keeper of the truth, and, consequently, all the others were heresies.
[4] We should specify that the human factor is not always just human.

and the Orient, since he purposely described a symbolic picture.¹ Referring back to the medieval Christian society, which was not at all a perfect traditional civilization, it is safe to say that the human factor played a substantial role in its relative rapid decline; moreover, even though we can define medieval Christianity as a traditional civilization, and a sacred one as a whole, we have to accept some imperfections, not of its mentality, but of its humanity. The French king Philippe le Bel is a good example, since he was known as a very pious man, but he destroyed the Order of the Temple²; also, the authors of various medieval chronicles transmitted prejudiced information,³ but a "traditional mentality" did not mean a lack of human opinions, narrow-mindedness and partiality, which indicates why the "historical method" is not the best way to study a traditional society.⁴

The "traditional mentality" was kept alive and unbroken not by the multitude, by the people at large, by quantity, which, despite its *prakritian* inertia, was very sensitive to the human factor's vacillation, but by the intellectual elite, by the quality, by the spiritual authority (exoteric and esoteric)⁵ – the human factor could provoke accidents and local disturbances, but could not change or desecrate the

---

¹ In his *Le règne de la quantité et les signes des temps* (Gallimard, 1970, pp. 15-16), Guénon explained what he understands by Orient (i.e. *Oriens*), in accord with a symbolic geography, as the abode of a spiritual and intellectual mentality.
² Let us not forget that the early *Cosa Nostra* members were also very pious.
³ It is hard today, almost impossible to understand the Templars' state of mind, yet even their contemporaries who wrote about them could not grasp it because of the interference of the human factor. It is known that the Incas had an "official history," which was memorized and marked with the *quipus*, a "history" in which all the previous events and the past of the conquered people were absent, a "history" that was manipulated to be favourable to the Inca caste, but which, in fact, was proof that in a traditional society, the "mythical history" was the only real one, while the "human history" was something minor and volatile.
⁴ However, this mentality had nothing to do with the modern "rationalism" and "sentimentalism," as so erroneously Wirth thought: *la mentalité du moyen âge n'eut certes ni la précision, ni la netteté de la nôtre* and *ce qu'ils n'ont pas compris rationnellement, ils ont pu le sentir* (Oswald Wirth, *Les Mystères de l'Art Royal*, Dervy, 1977, pp. 53-54).
⁵ Therefore, any restoration of the disabled mentality must be inspired from above and would be doomed to failure if orchestrated from here down-below.

fundamental state of mind and orientation towards God[1]; only when the elite became disabled or even disappeared, was the diabolic inspiration able to manipulate the human factor to defile the mentality.

A "traditional mentality" was instituted in the child's mind from the beginning, and even in more recent centuries the fairy tales that a mother told her child were reminiscent of better ages, when human life was not just some result of economic and materialistic conditions, of filthy greed for social or political "power," but part of a sacred perspective where all activities, gestures, words, functions, métiers, etc. were sacred, directly related to the divine archetypes, supported by spiritual influences and supervised by gods.[2] As long as this sacred perspective and the divine inspiration were active, all the human "accidents," driven by ignorance, arrogance, thirst for power (that prospered along the centuries as the most diabolic vice), lust, stupidity, and so on, could be mended; a traditional society, Christian, Islamic or Hindu, was not "paradise on earth," which explains why it can be expected that the gluttonous, the unjust, the dishonest or the avaricious could be found in such a society; even the "Golden Age" (*Satya-Yuga*, the "age of truth") was not perfect and "revolts" took place.[3] We mentioned that even the medieval chronicles were affected by partisanship or misunderstandings with regard to their own traditional society; so much the more will modern man, enchained by his mentality, take into consideration only these "accidents," since they are somehow familiar and in concert with his way of thinking, foolishly disregarding the essence of a traditional civilization.[4] Therefore, the only sustainable position is René Guénon's metaphysical rostrum from

---

[1] The vocation of the prophets Hosea, Jeremiah and Ezekiel, or of St. Paul, did not prevent them from living the life of their contemporaries (see Lucien Cerfaux, *The Christian in the Theology of St. Paul*, Herder and Herder, 1967, p. 104).
[2] See René Guénon, *Mélanges*, Gallimard, 1976, p. 72, where he said that in a traditional society, like the Islamic civilization or the medieval Christian civilization, even the most common acts had a religious character.
[3] See our *Free-Masonry*, p. 268.
[4] In fact, modern man is impotent and incapable of thinking otherwise, his mind being monstrously distorted and shrunken.

where it is possible to intellectually comprehend without error (and without erring) a "traditional mentality."

Throughout his work, René Guénon constantly condemned and exposed the modern mentality, but it is obvious that in this last half-century, after his death, the decline was replaced by an increasingly rapid and destructive fall, with an abandon and haste that only the end of times could induce, and therefore the signs of the times are submerging us like an avalanche of decay.

The modern mentality is completely antitraditional,[1] which means that it "escaped" its normal vassalage and has no more guidance from above and no more links with the spiritual center; it means that the mind devolved from the normal stage of reflecting the "supra-rational" intellect to the "Luciferian" stage (the "age of reason"), reaching now the "Satanic" stage of the "infra-rational," which corresponds to an infantilized way of thinking and the loss of the "art of memory."[2] This "infra-rational" is illustrated by the final demagogic engorgement of the various "isms" (materialism, uniformism,[3] sentimentalism, moralism, evolutionism,[4] globalism, naturalism, psychologism,[5] empiricism, utilitarianism, aestheticism, museographic exhibitionism, informationism, "virtual realism"), the escalation of the "political

---

[1] The real distinction between the modern and traditional mentalities is "one of sickness from health" (Coomaraswamy, *ibid.*, p. 293).
[2] Hence the huge success of computer games and of "memory sticks." The oral transmission, which was the main mode by which the tradition was conserved, implied an ample and active use of memory.
[3] "In the various kinds of proletarian government, on the other hand, we meet always with the intention to achieve a rigid and inflexible uniformity; all the forces of 'education,' for example, are directed to this end" (Coomaraswamy, *ibid.*, p. 291); about "uniformism" see Guénon, *Le règne*, pp. 71-78. This infrahuman "uniformism" is the opposite of the suprahuman "unanimism" of the traditional societies, where a "unanimous society" is based on order, hierarchy and vocation, and the members of this society unanimously participate to the unique sacred doctrine derived from the eternal principles.
[4] The main "isms" became well established in the 18th century, when the "grand dupery" was in full expansion (René Guénon, *Orient et Occident*, Guy Trédaniel, 1993, p. 24).
[5] See Guénon, *Aperçus sur l'initiation*, p. 146.

correctness" bluff, of vulgarisation (everything "for dummies," a general "popularism"[1]), of profane and individual beliefs,[2] the ultimate spread of the lack of privacy, of chattering, of gossiping, of "twittering", of broadcasting the most intimate and confidential details, in concert with the abhorrence of anything "secret"[3]; and everything is encased by "quantism."[4] Finally, we should not forget another "ism," the "traditionalism," which is used successfully today by the adverse forces.[5]

In view of all that, the modern mentality is an obstacle and an adversary which makes the study of traditional doctrines and societies an almost impossible task[6]; and we could relate the expression "narrow minded" to this mentality, considering its veritable and profound significance, which is in utter opposition to what the modern people are manipulated to acknowledge: it means a limited and restricted way of thinking,[7] directed downwards only, since the *sattvic* path became

---

[1] See Guénon, *Introduction générale*, 1987, pp. 263-264.
[2] René Guénon sufficiently explained what extremely antitraditional "individualism" is, which includes "originality," "authorship," private ideas and doctrines; and, as modern mentality would have it, when it was necessary to explain the origins of the traditional scriptures, arts, métiers, and rites, this sort of "individualism" became "collectivism." "In a normal society, one no more 'thinks for oneself' than one has a private arithmetic. In a proletarian culture, one does not think at all, but only entertains a variety of prejudices [the "political correctness"], for the most part of journalistic and propagandistic origin, though treasured as one's 'own opinions.' … most men live as though they possessed a private intelligence of their own (Heracleitus, *Fragment* 92)" (Coomaraswamy, *ibid.*, p. 294).
[3] *En fait, l'intention défavorable qu'on y attache communément procède uniquement de ce trait caractéristique de la mentalité moderne que nous avons défini ailleurs comme la "haine du secret" sous toutes ses formes* (Le Règne de la Quantité et les Signes des Temps, ch. XII)" (Guénon, *Aperçus sur l'initiation*, p. 79).
[4] We understand by this somehow barbaric neologism "quantism" everything related to analytic, digital, number, quantity, quantifying (Latin *quantificare*: *quantus*, "how much" + *facere*, "to make").
[5] See René Guénon, *Articles et Comptes rendus I*, Éditions Traditionnelles, 2002, p. 55 and *Le règne*, p. 277.
[6] Guénon, *Introduction générale*, 1987, p. 1.
[7] *Ibid.*, p. 18.

forbidden and is blocked by the solid crust that now envelopes the world.[1]

Nonetheless, this indisputable and increasing limitation was concealed by developing "unlimited" skills in the "art" of deceiving, of fantasising, of empty talking, of distorting the truth, of changing the meaning of historical events, and so on. Thus it was possible to depict the epoch of medieval traditional civilization as the "dark ages" and to promote the Renaissance and the Reformation as illuminating movements, when, in fact, the Renaissance was the executioner of many traditional elements and the mutilator of intellectual perception, which with amazingly speed[2] was replaced with the "age of reason."[3]

From a principial perspective though, this return to Greek antiquity, correlated with deceptive and mischievous efforts to sink the medieval times into oblivion, are all part of a heritage naturally established many Ages ago, when a caste-like partition occurred, in accord with the

---

[1] There is today a very well organized public system to shape the younger generations' minds towards an infra-human way of thinking; this subject needs a volume to illustrate how such a "Mephistophelian" system works, and its accord with modern "psychologism," yet, to illustrate the diabolical character of such an enterprise, we should stress that the inferior pole (the "substance") is unintelligible, and searching downwards the fundamental answers regarding our world, etc., is a vain task, since we should search upwards, where the intelligible "essence" is (see Guénon, *Le règne*, pp. 30, 33).

[2] Guénon considered this rapid change one of the significant enigmas of history (*ce qui est étonnant, c'est la rapidité avec laquelle est venue cette incompréhension, si frappante chez les écrivains du XVIIe siècle; cette coupure radicale entre la mentalité du moyen âge et celle des temps modernes n'est certes pas une des moindres énigmes de l'histoire*, Aperçus sur l'initiation, p. 190); the solution for this enigma is related to the "collective suggestion" that deformed the mentality, since, as Guénon said, it is not possible to think that suddenly some madness hit an entire continent (Guénon, *Orient et Occident*, pp. 26, 45, *Le règne*, p. 278, *La crise*, p. 114). René Guénon gave an accurate definition of the modern mentality in an article called *Tradition et Traditionalisme* (published in 1936, in Études Traditionnelles, and incorporated in *Le règne*, p. 277 and reprinted in *Articles et Comptes rendus I*, Éd. Trad., 2002, p. 55): *la mentalité moderne elle-même, dans tout ce qui la caractérise spécifiquement comme telle, n'est en somme que le produit d'une vaste suggestion collective, qui, s'exerçant continuellement au cours de plusieurs siècles, a déterminé la formation et le développement progressif de l'esprit antitraditionnel, en lequel se résume en définitive tout l'ensemble des traits distinctifs de cette mentalité.*

[3] Guénon, *Introduction générale*, 1987, p. 19.

mental constitution of various peoples, and we could say that such a mental inaptitude regarding the pure intellectuality[1] and the innate ability for practical and material accomplishments and progress (since we cannot deny this type of progress[2]) were not so much consciously acquired but imposed by the Master Puppeteer's laws.[3] This variety of mentalities is a consequence of the infinity of the Universal Possibility,[4] and also of the law of manifestation: the universal manifestation exists only if the undifferentiated equilibrium of the three *gunas* is broken, which means that the immutable harmony is broken and an indefinite number of disharmonies come to existence.

The Master Puppeteer's laws influence the mind in two major ways: first, at the same point in the cycle, there is a hierarchy of mental aptitudes, differentiated by an increasingly narrow-mindedness and limitation from top to bottom, even though the mentality as a whole could be traditional; second, with the descending course of the cycle, the human mentality inevitably declines, but, before losing any traditional characteristics, it continues to maintain its orthodoxy as long as the tradition is able to adapt to the new conditions of the cycle that shape the new mentality; this adaptation is done, usually, to the

---

[1] *Ibid.*, pp. 23, 26, 75.
[2] The obscuration of the intellectual light is somehow proportional with the decadence of the castes and the expansion of sentimentalism and of materialistic progress (see, for example, Guénon, *Orient et Occident*, p. 87). Today, we see an advanced "intellectual myopia" (Guénon, *Le règne*, p. 65) or "intellectual atrophy" (Guénon, *Initiation*, p. 43); and Guénon underlined that, with the evolving of the cycle, the entire cosmic manifestation, and the human mentality, which is included in this manifestation, will follow a descendent course (*ibid.*, p. 155).
[3] There are no simplistic explanations regarding the mentality. The modern mentality has as one of its main characteristics the need of simplification, but, in fact, the axiom "Nature always tends to act in the simplest way," used by Johann Bernoulli, called the "principle of Leibniz" by D'Alembert and quoted by Guénon (*la nature agit toujours par les voies les plus simples*, *Le règne*, p. 104), has nothing to do with worldly simplicity.
[4] *Aussi toute limitation de la Possibilité universelle est-elle, au sens propre et rigoureux du mot, une impossibilité; ... Il est facile de voir, en outre, que ceci exclut toutes les théories plus ou moins "réincarnationnistes" qui ont vu le jour dans l'Occident moderne, au même titre que le fameux "retour éternel" de Nietzsche et autres conceptions similaires* (René Guénon, *Le symbolisme de la croix*, Guy Trédaniel, 1989, p. 92).

detriment of traditional purity and of the "traditional consciousness," when man becomes less and less conscious of the sacred domain and its intellectuality, of his participation in it, and of the active correlation between the cosmic and human orders, reaching in the end, together with a modern mentality, a "moral conscience," and a profane point of view.[1]

The reality of this variety of mentalities implies that it is impossible for people with incompatible mentalities to communicate, and therefore someone with a modern mentality cannot comprehend a traditional civilization,[2] even if the various events and activities of that civilization seem to be the same as those found in the present *Occidens*; "history repeats itself" is a treacherous slogan, used to excuse the modern methods of studying the (dead or alive) traditional civilizations by extrapolating the researchers' way of thinking and profane viewpoint.

This extrapolation, as well as the depiction of the extraterrestrial worlds, is based on an increasingly vivacious imagination, which, as paradoxical as it seems, became a major ally of the mind (reason) in shaping the modern mentality. The word "imagination" is used here with its modern and common meaning,[3] which has nothing to do with what Coomaraswamy was saying about "the art of thinking in images" as the "linguistic of metaphysics."[4] We need to make a clear distinction between the traditional "image," which is a symbol of a higher reality, and the modern "visual effects," which are taking over any ideational activity today; in the modern world, as an upside-down world, the language of symbols (images) that defined the traditional way towards the supra-rational domain "descended to the verbal logic of

---

[1] Guénon, *Initiation*, pp. 85-88, 96-97. The modern mentality generates the absurd and false impression that a profane domain has an authentic existence.

[2] Guénon, *Introduction générale*, 1987, p. 32, *Le règne*, pp.174-175.

[3] This meaning started to gain ground after the "temporal barrier," represented by the 14th century, was crossed. See also Henri Corbin about *mundus imaginalis* ('alam al-mithal).

[4] Coomaraswamy, *ibid.*, p. 296. See also, but with caution, Mircea Eliade, *Images and Symbols*, Princeton Univ. Press, 1991, pp. 17-20.

'philosophy,'"[1] and then verbal communication was replaced with "visual language" leading towards the infra-rational domain.

We should not forget that, in a traditional society, spiritual teaching was aided by the "art of memory," which beneficially used "images" (Latin *imago*) as supports, while the imagination (understood as fantasy or utopian invention) was considered an enemy[2]; not to say that imagination made impossible any type of real intellectual contemplation, helping the natural inclination of the *Occidens* toward action and agitation.[3] Furthermore, imagination was successfully used to establish the modern anti-initiatory beliefs that defiled and reduced the genuine initiatory doctrines and organizations to all sorts of elements like "magic," "powers," "philosophies," and Free-Masonry is a well-known example of how the profane imagination works[4]; and it is bizarre to see how this anti-initiatory imagination, normally a "creator" of non-corporeal worlds and events, instigated very materialistic fantasies to denigrate the initiatory organizations, a famous example being the reverie regarding the Templars' treasure.

---

[1] Coomaraswamy, *ibid.*
[2] "When constructs of the imagination are not allowed to enter the memory and mind, a man is not hindered" (see *On Cleaving to God*); see also the Hesychastic way, where the fantasies are considered a consequence of the fall; the more hidden (obscured) becomes the *nous*, the more vivacious appears the imagination; the imagination is a rational "creator" of God [it is a "creator" of idols] (Hierotheos, *ibid.*, pp. 70-73, 123-125) (we should add that even the theological idea of "creation" instead of "manifestation" is an adaptation of a metaphysical concept to the Western mentality; see Guénon, *Introduction générale*, 1987, p. 113). The modern mentality replaced "conceiving" (Latin *concipere*) with "imagining" [or "concept" with "fantasy"].
[3] The *Occidens* is very fond of exterior action, hating any contemplation; however, contemplation had an important role in the Holy Grail tales and also in the Orthodox Church (see Guénon, *Initiation*, pp. 200-201), suggesting a kernel belonging to *Oriens*.
[4] As Guénon said, you need a traditional mentality to understand the initiatory concepts and to acquire initiatory knowledge (*Aperçus sur l'initiation*, pp. 204, 210).

CHAPTER X

OUR DAYS ARE NUMBERED

The Templars' treasure is, for the modern mentality, nothing else than a pitiable materialistic treasure, because today nothing is so important, so valuable, so yearned after, so attractive, so hypnotic, as money, which has declined and is depleted of the traditional spirit, therey becoming the most vicious exponent of an upside-down world, where the command "thou hast ordered all things in measure and number and weight" and the syntagm "the days are numbered" lost all significance other than the quantitative one, a sign of acute degeneration as René Guénon underlined:

> *Les modernes, en général, ne conçoivent pas d'autre science que celle des choses qui se mesurent, se comptent et se pèsent* [our highlighting], *c'est-à-dire encore, en somme, des choses matérielles, car c'est à celles-ci seulement que peut s'appliquer le point de vue quantitatif; et la prétention de réduire la qualité à la quantité est très caractéristique de la science moderne.*[1]

Later, Guénon elaborated:

> *cette enumeration* [measure, number and weight], *qui se réfère manifestement à des modes divers de la quantité, n'est, comme telle, applicable littéralement qu'au seul monde corporel mais, par une transposition appropriée, on peut y voir encore une expression de l'"ordre" universel.*[2] [Guénon earlier observed: *Les termes* Numerus, Mensura, Pondus, *peuvent être considérés*

---

[1] René Guénon, *La Crise du monde moderne*, Gallimard, 1975, p. 134.
[2] *Le règne de la quantité et les signes des temps*, Gallimard, 1970, p. 45.

comme désignant les divers modes fondamentaux de la quantité ; on peut donc leur faire correspondre respectivement les divisions principales des sciences mathématiques : arithmétique, géométrie, mécanique].

Indeed, the Biblical saying, "thou hast ordered all things in measure and number and weight,"[1] refers to the corporeal world, because the present terrestrial human beings live in this particular world, and any spiritual realization starts from this corporeal state,[2] but it did not mean that, in a traditional society, the quantitative point of view predominated, or that the traditional man did not grasp a deeper significance of this formula, which, let us not forget, is not a profane but a Biblical, sacred statement.[3]

The operative Masonry is a perfect illustration: the operative Masons' métier or art was overwhelmingly based on number, measure and weight, yet these "quantitative" elements were symbols of higher realities, because they were projections in our world of "the Number without number, Measure without measure and Weight without weight," and the operative Masons, without disregarding the reality of

---

[1] *Wisdom of Solomon* 11:20. See our *Free-Masonry*, p. 124. St. Augustine said: "It is a great thing and a privilege of few people to surpass everything that can be measured to contemplate the Measure without measure; to surpass everything that can be numbered to contemplate the Number without number; to surpass everything that can be weighed to contemplate the Weight without weight" (*De Genesi ad litteram*, IV, III, 7-8). Johannes Scotus Eriugena deeply meditated upon this formula, which he interpreted in a metaphysical way (*Periphyseon*, II, 590 C). Among other things, he stated that God is not quantity, being without dimensions and parts (numbers) (Érigène, *De la division de la Nature, Periphyseon*, Livre I et Livre II, PUF, 1995, pp. 99, 377). René Guénon wrote to Ananda K. Coomaraswamy: *Ce que vous me citez d'Eckhart*, "Size without size," *me rappelle une expression arabe dont je ne pourrais d'ailleurs pas vous dire l'origine exacte, car on l'emploie assez couramment:* fî zamâni ghayri zamân, wa fî makâni ghayri makân = *"dans un temps sans temps, et dans un espace sans espace"* (January 22, 1939).

[2] For this reason Christ took a corporeal form.

[3] Guénon considered the prayer as a collective subtle force, and he introduced the quantitative aspect, because he said that the more members the collectivity has, the more powerful the force is, and specified that *il est d'ailleurs évident que cette considération "quantitative" indique essentiellement qu'il s'agit bien du domaine individuel, au delà duquel elle ne saurait plus aucunement intervenir* (*Aperçus sur l'initiation*, Éditions Traditionnelles, 1992, pp. 166-167).

these "quantitive" aspects, were well aware of the "qualitative" essence involved from above, not to say that Geometry, which was identified with Masonry, was obviously much more than a quantitative discipline.[1]

The traditional mind had no doubt or hesitation in admitting the limitations of the corporeal world, its "inferiority" and its inadequate and reduced capabilities, characteristics which were not considered with distress, but as given realities witnessing the undeniable truth that, climbing the universal ladder towards Measure without measure, we will find levels less and less limited (but still measured).[2] It was an obvious truth that, in the corporeal world, our thinking, our mind and our life are limited, finite elements, and their greatest usefulness was to be used as a starting point for the spiritual voyage towards the unlimited domain,[3] and it was never too early to begin this journey, since "our days were numbered."

> Lord, make me to know mine end, and the measure of my days [Remind me that my days are numbered], what it is: that I may know how frail I am[4]; So teach us to number our days, that we may apply our hearts unto wisdom[5]; Seeing his days are determined, the number of his months are with thee, thou hast appointed his bounds that he cannot pass.[6]

---

[1] Guénon said: *une telle géométrie, bien loin de ne se référer qu'à la pure quantité, est au contraire essentiellement "qualitative"; et nous en dirons tout autant de la véritable science des nombres, car les nombres principiels, bien que devant être appelés ainsi par analogie, sont pour ainsi dire, par rapport à notre monde, au pôle opposé de celui où se situent les nombres de l'arithmétique vulgaire* (Guénon, *Le règne*, p. 14).

[2] The *Corpus Hermeticum* says that *man ascends to heaven and he measures it* (R. P. Festugière, *La révélation d'Hermès Trismégiste*, I, L'Astrologie et les Sciences Occultes, Les Belles Lettres, 1983, p. 316); see also Johannes Scotus Eriugena.

[3] "Now it is natural to man to attain to intellectual truths through sensible objects, because all [*sic erat scriptum*] our knowledge originates from sense" (Saint Thomas Aquinas, *The Summa Theologica*, Encyclopædia Britannica, 1952, I, p. 9).

[4] *Psalms* 39:4.

[5] *Psalms* 90:12.

[6] *Job* 14:5.

We notice here one meaning of numbering or measuring: it means determination and limitation, that is, if the world is produced by the act of measuring, at the same time this measuring indicates a finite world with an end.[1] "Numbering the days," the days are produced, but also they are confined to finite borders and doomed to be devoured, since "the days are numbered" suggests, evidently, the end of time. There is here an apparent contradiction, which can be conciliated only if we understand that any symbol accepts two opposite viewpoints: from the *principial* perspective, the manifestation, the worlds, the Cosmos and so on are produced through a process of determination, of limitation, of numbering or measuring; from the world's standpoint, it is a process of indefinite multiplication. "So God created man in his own image, in the image of God created he him; male and female created he them. And God blessed them, and God said unto them, Be fruitful, and multiply, and replenish the earth."[2] "Yet the number of the children of Israel shall be as the sand of the sea, which cannot be measured nor numbered"[3]; "As the host of heaven cannot be numbered, neither the sand of the sea measured: so will I multiply the seed of David my servant."[4]

In fact, these two viewpoints come together at the end, since this indefinite multiplication means an increasing descent into quantity and this quantity is numbered.

It would be a mistake to reject or deny the reality of the corporeal domain, even if this reality is relative, and similarly, it would be a mistake to give exceptional or even exclusive importance to this domain, disregarding the universal hierarchy, which means that we have to accept the (limited) value of quantity in the "gross

---

[1] Indeed, to bring order from chaos means to measure the possibilities of manifestation, i.e. to determine the worlds, which, with everything they contain, will be realized or "actualized," the process of measurement appearing, *principially*, identical to that of manifestation.
[2] *Genesis* 1:27-8.
[3] *Hosea* 1:10.
[4] *Jeremiah* 33:22.

manifestation" (*l'état grossier*, as Guénon called it),[1] and moreover, we have to admit that even the discrete quantity has its *raison d'être*. In our "gross state," (our "sensitive world," the "world of senses") we need the discrete quantity, because otherwise how could we talk to each other, or function as corporeal beings?[2]

> Yah, Jehovah of hosts, the living Elohim, King of the Universe, Omnipotent, All-King and Merciful, Supreme and Extolled, Who is Eternal, Sublime and Most-Holy, formed and created the Universe in thirty-two mysterious paths of wisdom by three Sepharim, namely: Sfor, Sippur and Sapher[3] which are in Him one and the same. They consist of ten Sephiroth out of nothing and of twenty-two fundamental letters.[4]

---

[1] *L'"état grossier" en effet, n'est pas autre chose que l'existence corporelle elle-même, à laquelle l'individualité humaine, comme on le verra, n'appartient que par une de ses modalités, et non dans son développement integral* (René Guénon, *L'Homme et son devenir selon le Védânta*, Éditions Traditionnelles, 1991, p. 36).

[2] The human speech is made of separate words, that is, of discrete elements, otherwise there would be no communication; similarly, the written words are distinct parts, and so are the numbers. Johannes Scotus Eriugena said: "there is no creature, whether sensible (visible) or intelligible (invisible), which is not confined in something within the limits of its own nature by measure and number and weight" (*Periphyseon*, II, 590 B; Érigène, *De la division de la Nature, Periphyseon*, Livre I et Livre II, PUF, 1995, p. 377). Similarly, John Dee, in his *Preface to Euclid*, showed how the same principles of number, measure, and weight, which are found in Macrocosm, are to be found in man, as Microcosm (Frances A. Yates, *Theatre of the World*, The Univ. of Chicago Press, 1969, p. 22; see also the "fruitfull Preface made by M. I. Dee"); and Dee underlined that all the mathematical arts subserve Architecture as their queen. In addition, it is well known how the numbers successfully replaced any writing in the case of profound traditional civilizations like those that flourished in South America.

[3] The commentators say that these angelic names mean: Numbers, Letters and Words; the terms *sepher-saphar-sippur* (book – number – telling) are the "three books" by which God created the universe (*Mishna* 1:1). Indeed, *sepher* means missive, document, writing, book; *saphar* to count, to number (also, *saphar* a secretary, a scribe); *sippur* to tell (but goes beyond simple oral story telling, because it includes the ability to tell a story through writing).

[4] *The Sepher Yetzirah*, 1:1-2 (tr. by Isidor Kalisch); in W. W. Wescott's translation: "In two and thirty most occult and wonderful paths of wisdom did Jah the Lord of Hosts engrave his name: God of the armies of Israel, ever-living God, merciful and gracious, sublime, dwelling on high, who inhabiteth eternity. He created this universe by the three Sepharim, Number, Writing, and Speech."

Or

> *Par les trente-deux voies merveilleuses de la sagesse, Yah, Yehovah Tsebaoth, Dieu d'Israël, Dieu vivant, Roi du monde, Dieu de miséricorde et de grâce, élevé et exalté, qui demeure dans l'Eternité, sublime et saint est son Nom, a gravé (créé) sous trois formes* (Sepharim = livres): Sepher, Sephar *et* Sippur.[1]

Paul Vulliaud specified:

> *Il est vrai qu'il existe diverses interprétations de ces trois termes:* Ecriture, Nombre, Parole; – Livre, Scribe, Parole; – Nombre, Nombrant, Nombré; – Intelligence, Intelligent, *ce qui est* Compris; – Science, Sachant, *le* Connu.[2]

In conformity with the laws of symbols, the numbers, the letters and the words are powerful *signa*, "signs," which – as ingredients of the corporeal world – were fruitfully used to represent higher realities, and therefore the ternary *Nombre, Nombrant, Nombré* could have been considered. It is well known how the numbers were used, not only in the Judaic Kabbalah and in Pythagoreanism, but in all the main traditional doctrines to symbolize the divine principles. In the Christian tradition, the Holy Trinity, rejected by Islam as a violation of the idea of Unity, has a fundamental role and is, in fact, an illustration of how the numbers were transferred from the quantitative domain to the

---

[1] Paul Vulliaud, *La Kabbale Juive*, Émile Nourry, 1923, tome premier, p. 209.
[2] Vulliaud, *ibid.*, pp. 213-214. In his youth, when he wrote under the pen name of Palingénius, Guénon favoured this translation, "Number, Numbering, Numbered": *Ce ternaire [Sat, Chit* and *Ânanda] doit encore être rapproché de celui qui est constitué par le Nombre, le Nombrant et le Nombré, et dont il est question au début du Sépher Ietsirah* (*La constitution de l'être humain et son évolution posthume selon le Védânta, La Gnose,* oct. 1911); however, later, when he incorporated this article in *L'Homme et son devenir selon le Védânta,* Guénon, considering the "quantitative" implication, suppressed the suggestion, and he preferred to say: *En arabe, on a, comme équivalent de ces trois termes, l'Intelligence* (El-Aqlu), *l'Intelligent* (El-Âqil) *et l'Intelligible* (El-Maqûl): *la première est la Conscience universelle* (Chit), *le second est son sujet* (Sat), *et le troisième est son objet* (Ânanda), *les trois n'étant qu'un dans l'Être "qui Se connaît Soi-même par Soi-même"* (p. 119).

pure qualitative one.[1] René Guénon introduced also another type of ternary:

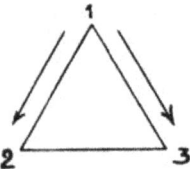

Le ternaire est constitué par un principe premier (au moins en un sens relatif) dont dérivent deux termes opposés, ou plutôt complémentaires… un tel ternaire pourra être représenté par un triangle dont le sommet est placé en haut.[2]

In the Judaic Kabbalah, it is said that God told Abraham: I am *One*, and I produced (created) the Sepher Yetzirah, and studied it. But you cannot comprehend it alone; you need a companion to study it together. Immediately, Abraham went to his master Schem and stayed three days with him. From that time, nobody could comprehend it alone; *two* sages are needed, and they cannot comprehend it in less than *three* years.[3]

Evidently, "our days are numbered"; yet, it seems that everything is numbered and not only downwards from One to multiplicity, but also

---

[1] *Parmi les différents ternaires qu'envisage la tradition hindoue, celui qu'on pourrait peut-être rapprocher le plus valablement de la Trinité chrétienne à certains égards, bien que le point de vue soit naturellement encore très différent, est celui de* Sat-Chit-Ânanda (voir *L'Homme et son devenir selon le Védânta*, ch. XIV) (René Guénon, *La Grande Triade*, Gallimard, 1980, p. 18).

[2] Guénon, *ibid.*, p. 23. He added: *et il en est ainsi, avant tout, en ce qui concerne la première de toutes les dualités, celle de l'Essence et de la Substance universelle, issues d'une polarisation de l'Être ou de l'Unité principielle, et entre lesquelles se produit toute manifestation. Ce sont les deux termes de cette première dualité qui sont désignés comme* Purusha et Prakriti *dans la tradition hindoue, et comme le Ciel* (Tien) *et la Terre* (Ti) *dans la tradition extrême-orientale; mais ni l'une ni l'autre, non plus d'ailleurs qu'aucune tradition orthodoxe, ne perd de vue, en les considérant, le principe supérieur dont ils sont derives (ibid.,* pp. 25-26).

[3] Vulliaud, *ibid.*, p. 204. In Masonry, the number *three* has a special importance. As Eriugena was saying, only the number 6 constitues a perfect number among the cardinal numbers, and 6 = 1 + 2 +3 (See for details Érigène, *De la division de la Nature, Periphyseon*, Livre III, PUF, 1995, p. 127 – Book 3, 655 D, 656).

towards One, as the operative Masons so well understood, which makes Mathematics a precious traditional science, totally different from what it is considered today, in the profane education, where less and less people are capable of grasping its mysteries.

Johannes Scotus Eriugena, like Boethius and Nicolaus Cusanus, like the operative Masons, and like René Guénon much later, perfectly understood the metaphysical merit of Mathematics[1] when managing sacred and divine subjects, and he presented it in his third book of the *Periphyseon*,[2] defining the Art of Arithmetic as "the science of numbers not of those which we count, but of those by which we count."[3] For Eriugena, the Biblical saying, "thou hast ordered all things in measure and number and weight," illustrates how the numbers, which are eternal in the monadic unity,[4] are created in multiplicity; the numbers subsist virtually and potentially in the monad, but they are actual and effective in creation, an actualization due to the Intellect.[5]

We should also recall what Nicolaus Cusanus stated:

---

[1] Robert Fludd was also a partisan of the mathematical arts, but in his case we see a tendency towards mechanical applications, and, at the same time, a profane action of unveiling the esoterical lore.
[2] Érigène, *ibid.*, pp. 119-121, 123-128.
[3] He added: "the wise say that it is not the numbers of animals, fruits, crops, and other bodies or things that belong to the science of arithmetic, but they assign to arithmetic only the intellectual, invisible, incorporeal (numbers) which are constituted in the science alone but reside in no subject... For not only does the Art of Arithmetic subsist as the immutable basis and primordial cause and principle of the other three branches of mathematics, namely, geometry, music, astronomy, but also the infinite multitude of all things visible and invisible assumes its substance according to the rules of numbers which arithmetic contemplates, as the supreme philosopher Pythagoras [a "father" of Masonry], the first inventor of this art, testifies when he gives good reason for asserting that the intellectual numbers are the substances of all things visible (sensible) and invisible (intelligible). Nor does the Holy Scripture deny this, for it says that all things have been made in measure and number and weight."
[4] The monad is the beginning, the middle and the end of all numbers, in concert with the rules of the Art of Arithmetic; the monad is eternal in the divine Wisdom. The Pythagorean monad is well known.
[5] We insisted to present Eriugena's judgment, because the monad he described is very similar with what René Guénon calls the Universal Possibility.

Therefore, in mathematics the wise wisely sought illustrations of things that were to be searched out by the intellect. And none of the ancients who are esteemed as great approached difficult matters by any other likeness than mathematics. Thus, Boethius, the most learned of the Romans, affirmed that anyone who altogether lacked skill in mathematics could not attain a knowledge of divine matters. Did Pythagoras, the first philosopher both in name and in fact, not consider all investigation of truth to be by means of numbers? Platonists and also our leading [thinkers] followed him to such an extent that our Augustine, and after him Boethius, affirmed that, assuredly, in the mind of the Creator number was the principal exemplar of the things to be created.[1]

René Guénon said in his first published book:

La même remarque peut d'ailleurs être faite également en ce qui concerne les mathématiques: celles-ci, bien que d'une portée restreinte, puisqu'elles sont exclusivement bornées au seul domaine de la quantité, appliquent à leur objet spécial des principes relatifs qui peuvent être regardés comme constituant une détermination immédiate par rapport à certains principes universels. Ainsi, la logique et les mathématiques sont, dans tout le domaine scientifique, ce qui offre le plus de rapports réels avec la métaphysique.[2]

---

[1] Nicholas of Cusa, *On Learned Ignorance*, I, 11. Cusanus underlined: *Nihil certi habemus in nostra scientia, nisi nostram mathematicam*. On the other hand, a profane philosopher like Hegel said: "To take numbers and geometrical figures – as the circle, the triangle etc., have often been taken – simply as symbols (the circle, for example, as a symbol of eternity, the triangle of the trinity) is so far harmless enough. But, on the other hand, it is foolish to fancy that in this way more is expressed than can be grasped and expressed as thought."

[2] *Introduction générale à l'étude des doctrines hindoues*, Guy Trédaniel, 1987, p. 118. After the war, René Guénon published a series of four books: *Le Règne de la quantité et les signes des temps*, in 1945 (a book considered by the "traditionalists" his "best-seller"; the "traditionalists" are the ones "who have only a tendency or a kind of aspiration toward tradition, without really possessing any authentic knowledge about it; we can measure through this the distance which separates the 'traditionalist' spirit from the true traditional spirit. ... In conclusion, the 'traditionalist' is only a simple 'researcher,' and for this reason he is always in danger of waywardness," Guénon, *Le règne*, p. 280); then, in 1946: *La Grande Triade*, *Aperçus sur l'initiation* and an unusual work, *Les Principes du calcul infinitésimal*. This last book was based on his 1915 thesis called *Examen des idées de Leibnitz sur la signification du calcul infinitésimal*, when he obtained a diploma *ès letters*, section Philosophy, option Mathematics. In fact, *Les*

There is no doubt that, for the western traditional civilization, that is, for Christianity, the geometrical and numerical symbolism was the essential fundament for the transmission of the esoteric lore, and also of the exoteric one, where Pythagoras, Plato and the operative Masons were the most known exponents of this symbolism (not to mention the Renaissance Cabala).[1]

Les Principes du calcul infinitésimal is much more than a revival of an old dissertation; it substantiates a symbolic understanding of metaphysical subjects. As we mentioned, we need the discrete quantities, illustrated by numbers, letters, and words, but at the same time, we are confronted, in our sensible (visible) world, with the continuous quantities, like those related to space and time, and, because of the impossibility to apply discrete quantities (numbers) in measuring continuous ones (space), the infinitesimal calculus was introduced, with its variables continuously increasing or decreasing. Our mind, anchored in the corporeal world, where all is numbered, measured and weighed, could view the universal Existence as composed of an indefinite series of discrete degrees, and the integral being as composed of an indefinite series of discrete states, during a spiritual realization the neophyte climbing a ladder, step by step. In fact, this representation is too "quantitative," and we have to consider that all the degrees or

---

Principes du calcul infinitésimal is much more than a revival of the old dissertation; it is a conclusion of the mathematical symbolism Guénon used in all his work.

[1] Therefore, Frithjof Schuon's criticism is not only misplaced and treacherous, but also erroneous: "Guénon was like a personification, not of a direct spirituality, but of an independent intellectual certainty, of a personal metaphysical evidence in a mathematical way, and this explains his teachings' approach, which is abstract and dependent on mathematics, as some of his character traits explain – indirectly and because of lack of compensatory elements. No doubt, he had a right to be biased, but this degraded with the broadening of his mission or of what he thought was his mission; he was no psychologist or aesthetician – in the best sense of these terms – which means that he underestimated both aesthetic values and moral ones, especially in relation to their spiritual functions. He had an innate disdain for everything human and 'individual,' and there are some points where this affected his metaphysics, as, for example, when he felt compelled to deny that the 'human condition' has a 'privileged position,' or that 'mind' – with reason as its essence – is a human privilege."

states are continuously connected, that there is continuity between all these degrees or states, and therefore we should consider a helicoidal movement, that is, a helix with an indefinite number of turns, each separated by an infinitesimal distance[1]; moreover, to emphasize the qualitative aspect, we should talk about a "multitude" of degrees or states.[2] However, as Guénon was saying, there is a moment of discontinuity in the development of the being or of the world, and this moment is *Fiat Lux*, the sudden transfer from chaos to order, which in the case of a being means the fulfilment of the spiritual realization, the Liberation[3]; we could extend Guénon's affirmation and say that, beside this *maximum maximorum* Transformation, each assimilation of a higher level of consciousness means a jump, suggesting the crossing of a discontinuity.[4]

There is no other way, for our human comprehension, than to recognize these two modalities of quantity: discrete and continuous. Accepting the terminology used by Matgioi when he commented on the hidden metaphysics of *Yi:Jing*, René Guénon considered that Infinity is the Active Perfection, *Qian*, and the Universal Possibility is the Passive Perfection, *Kun*, although in reality Infinity and the Universal Possibility perfectly overlap, and it is just more convenient for our human mind to consider such a dichotomy; therefore, *Qian* was represented by a continuous straight line (the "seamless garment"), and *Kun* by a broken straight line, which, by an analogical transposition, means that Infinity is without parts, a perfect continuum, while the Universal Possibility is the Infinity considered discontinuous, that is, seen as the integral of all the possibilities (as discrete elements, melted but not merged); also, the discontinuous quantity suggests much better

---

[1] For this geometrical representation, see in detail René Guénon, *Le symbolisme de la croix*. The infinitesimal variation from a turn to another of the helix correlates the discrete aspect with the continuous one.
[2] About the "multitude," see René Guénon, *Les Principes du calcul infinitésimal*, Gallimard, 1977, for example, chapter III (*La multitude innombrable*).
[3] René Guénon, *Le symbolisme de la croix*, Guy Trédaniel, pp. 141-142.
[4] See, for example, the teaching of the Kabalist Abulafia regarding the "science of jumping" (*dillug*).

the idea of finite and distinction, specifically for the universal manifestation, while the continuous quantity could better symbolize perfection and, therefore, the Principle.

Evidently, in the universal manifestation, there is no *Qian* or *Kun*, and not even *Tian* and *Di*, but only their measures, which, through reciprocated action and reaction, produce this manifestation, where we find the celestial (*Qian*, *Tian*) and terrestrial (*Kun*, *Di*) influences (the only ones that can be measured), and, in the universal Existence, there could not be *Qian* influence without *Kun* influence, or, vice versa, *Kun* influence without *Qian* influence, which means that in our world, as Eriugena insisted, there could not be *quantity* without *quality*, or *quality* without *quantity*.[1] We could say the same thing about the continuous and discrete quantities, and the best illustration of their coexistence is the "Chain of Worlds," the Hindu *aksha-mâlâ* or *rudrâksha-valaya*, and the Christian rosary: the beads or grains are the discrete aspect and the string the continuous one, the latter empowering the former to qualify as "multitude."[2] Each bead, symbolizing a world or a state of the being, represents just an infinitesimal element of the universal manifestation, all the elements being kept together by the Golden Chain, which provides the effective continuity of the states or worlds, and we must understand that, because of the limitation existing in the sensible world, where everything is finite (even if we could conceive it as indefinite), the unlimited and indefinite multitude, and the total continuity, are illustrated by the circular shape of the string of beads (or the "garland of roses"), which, though finite, suggests the indefinity by

---

[1] Érigène, *De la division de la Nature, Periphyseon*, Livre I et Livre II, PUF, 1995, pp. 148-150, 155, 159. For Eriugena, the *quantity* is a kind of secondary support of the *quality*, and each combination of the *quantity* and *quality* produces a *quantum* and a *quale*, and these two combined determine a corporeal element. In this specific text, Eriugena suggested the five conditions of existence.

[2] For the symbolism of the "Chain of Worlds" see René Guénon, *Symboles fondamentaux de la Science sacrée*, Gallimard, 1980, chapter LXI, *La Chaîne des mondes*.

permitting a continuous journey, each turn being essentially different from the previous one.[1]

The "Chain of Worlds" or *rudrâksha-mâlâ* is also the metaphysical instrument to number our "days," and even more, to number Brahmâ's "days." "Those who know a day of Brahmâ to end after one thousand ages, and the night to terminate after one thousand ages, are the persons who know day and night"[2]; a day of Brahmâ is considered to be a thousand *Mahâ-Yugas*, which translated in human years appears to value 1000 x 4,320,000 = 4,320,000,000 years. Guénon said: *l'indéfinité est souvent exprimée symboliquement par un nombre tel que dix mille, ainsi que nous l'avons expliqué ailleurs (cf.* Les Principes du Calcul infinitésimal, *ch. IX)*[3]; similarly, this huge number 4,320,000,000 is nothing else but a token of the indefinite multitude, which is a symbol of the infinity of the Principle, and should be perceived by our mind as a continuous quantity, because, like in the case of the *Prayer of the Heart*, this "numbering" of Brahmâ's "days" should become a continuous flow, a continuous Day, an integration that will permit the Great Jump.[4]

René Guénon, in the same chapter, *La Chaîne des mondes*, said: *Dans certains cas, ces sphères* [the beads or grains of the rosary] *sont remplacées par*

---

[1] The *Prayer of the Heart (Jesus Prayer)* is called the "Unceasing Prayer," because there should be no breaks but full continuity between words and between the present and the next "prayer"; it is said that if there is a discontinuity, the devil will penetrate through it in the mind, these discontinuities being the "fissures of the Great Wall" [Today, the great wall of China became a support of satanic influences, which are very active]. Regarding the devil's attack, Guénon was saying that *la peur constante (et, il faut bien le dire, trop souvent justifiée dans une certaine mesure), qu'ont la plupart des mystiques d'être trompés par le diable, prouve très nettement qu'ils ne dépassent pas le domaine psychique, car, comme nous l'avons déjà expliqué ailleurs, le diable ne peut avoir prise directement que sur celui-ci (et indirectement par là sur le domaine corporel), et tout ce qui appartient réellement à l'ordre spirituel lui est, par sa nature même, absolument fermé (ibid.,* p. 367).
[2] *Bhagavad-Gîtâ* 8:17.
[3] *Ibid.*, p. 371.
[4] Nevertheless, man is not allowed to number the days, either human or divine; and the translation of Brahmâ's days in terrestrial years, which is directly related to the doctrine of the cosmic cycles, does not reveal the secret of "numbering the days," because each cycle has not only a quantitative but also a qualitative and an invisible component.

des rondelles perforées en leur centre, et qui correspondent aux disques, considérés comme horizontaux par rapport à l'axe, dont nous avons parlé tout à l'heure.[1] Sometimes the discs, perforated in the center, that replaced the grains or beads were (golden) coins, or shells representing money, which – as "scientists" explained – allowed a better counting and storage for money, and it was a beautiful ornament. We do not disagree, but these functions were secondary:

> *On peut du reste penser légitimement qu'un tel collier a dû lui-même, à l'origine, n'être pas autre chose qu'un symbole de la "chaîne des mondes," puisque, comme nous l'avons dit bien souvent, le fait de n'attribuer à un objet qu'un caractère simplement "décoratif" ou "ornemental" n'est jamais que le résultat d'une certaine dégénérescence entraînant une incompréhension du point de vue traditionnel.*[2]

The use of money for a "necklace" (in fact, for a rosary) suggests that originally, for the traditional mentality, money had a spiritual and essential meaning, with the perforated coin symbolizing a cycle, a world or a state, and, moreover, a "sun."

In the Far-Eastern tradition, such a disc is the *banliang*[3]:

---

[1] *Ibid.*, p. 368.
[2] *Ibid.*, p. 368.
[3] *On remarquera que cette figure reproduit la forme des monnaies chinoises, forme qui est d'ailleurs originairement celle de certaines tablettes rituelles: entre le contour circulaire et le vide médian carré, la partie pleine, où s'inscrivent les caractères, correspond évidemment au Cosmos, où se situent les "dix mille êtres," et le fait qu'elle est comprise entre deux vides exprime symboliquement que ce qui n'est pas entre le Ciel et la Terre est par là même en dehors de la manifestation* (Guénon, La Grande Triade, p. 37).

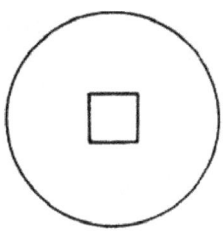

An ancient Babylonian bas-relief[1] presents the "sun god" Shamash holding a measuring rod and an assumed cord reel, while sitting in front of a large solar disc placed on an altar; this assumed cord reel was also considered to be a ring, in concert with the Biblical text: "And he [Judah] said, What pledge shall I give thee? And she [Tamar] said, Thy signet [ring], and thy bracelets, and thy staff that is in thine hand."[2]

Shamash was not only the sun-god, but also the god of justice,[3] with the rod and the ring regarded as token of justice and power (or righteousness). René Guénon discussed the same tablet: *Le soleil a été souvent représenté, en des temps et des lieux très divers, et jusqu'au moyen âge*

Similar to other parts of the world, before the *banliang*, the cowrie shell (*Cypraea moneta*), called *bei*, was used as money, and it is known that sometimes the cowrie shells were perforated and assembled on a string as "necklace" (*peng*). The name "cowrie" seems to be a deformation of the Sanskrit *kapardika*.

[1] The "Tablet of Shamash," found in the city of Sippar, is now at the British Museum.

[2] *Genesis* 38:18.

[3] Hammurabi received his code of laws from Shamash, and the king was represented himself in an attitude of adoration before Shamash as the embodiment of the idea of justice.

occidental, avec des rayons de deux sortes, alternativement rectilignes et nodules [see the above illustration and also chapter IV of the present work, where we showed the Christ-Sun with these two types of rays]; *un exemple remarquable de cette figuration se trouve sur une tablette assyrienne du* British Museum, *datant du Ier siècle avant l'ère chrétienne,*¹ *où le soleil apparaît comme une sorte d'étoile à huit rayons.* And this footnote follows:

> *Ce nombre 8 peut avoir ici un certain rapport avec le symbolisme chrétien du* Sol Justitiae *(cf. le symbolisme de la 8e lame du Tarot); le Dieu solaire devant lequel est placée cette figuration tient d'ailleurs dans une de ses mains "un disque et une barre qui sont des représentations conventionnelles de la ligne à mesurer et de la verge de justice"; au sujet du premier de ces deux emblèmes, nous rappellerons le rapport qui existe entre le symbolisme de la "mesure" et celui des "rayons solaires" (voir* Le Règne de la quantité et les signes des temps, *ch. III).*²

Either a cord reel or a ring (or a disc), this circular shape is associated with the rod and together define the attributes of the god of justice.³ In the *Archéomètre*,⁴ it is said:

> *Si l'on considère en particulier les attributions des deux premières castes, on voit que la caste sacerdotale a pour emblèmes le bâton augural, signe de l'esprit prophétique* (footnote: *le bâton augural, appelé* lituus *par les Romains, qui le tenaient des Etrusques, est devenu plus tard la crosse épiscopale; c'était l'attribut qui caractérisait l'interprète de la Volonté divine), et la coupe sacrificielle, signe des fonctions sacerdotales proprement dites* (footnote: *la coupe, qui contenait le* Sôma *dans le rite védique, est devenue le Saint-Graal dans la tradition*

---

¹ *Cette tablette est reproduite dans* The Babylonian Legends of the Creation and the Fight between Bel and the Dragon as told by Assurian Tablets from Nineveh (*publication du* British Museum) [Guénon's footnote].
² *Ibid.*, p. 362.
³ In the Christian tradition, the disc and the rod are united in the bishop's crosier (a shepherd's crook).
⁴ The name *Archeometre* is of Greek origins and means "the measure of the Principle"; Saint-Yves d'Alveydre wrote a work called *L'Archéomètre*, which was published posthumously in 1911, and in *La Gnose*, Guénon's Gnostic journal, a long article, *L'Archéomètre*, was published based on d'Alveydre, and having a collective authorship, in which Guénon (as Palingénius) participated, especially by adding important footnotes.

*chrétienne et rosicrucienne... Rappelons que le bâton est un symbole masculin, et que la coupe est un symbole féminin*¹), *tandis que les emblèmes de la caste royale sont l'épée, symbole du pouvoir militaire, et la balance, symbole du pouvoir judiciaire* (footnote: *L'union de l'épée et de la balance symbolise la Force² au service du Droit, comme on le voit dans la huitième lame du Tarot*).³

Regarding all this, René Guénon wrote:

*cette fonction, en effet, est celle qui appartient en propre à toute la caste des Kshatriyas, et le roi n'est que le premier parmi ceux-ci. La fonction dont il s'agit est double en quelque sorte: administrative et judiciaire d'une part, militaire de l'autre, car elle doit assurer le maintien de l'ordre à la fois au dedans, comme fonction régulatrice et équilibrante, et au dehors, comme fonction protectrice de l'organisation sociale; ces deux éléments constitutifs du pouvoir royal sont, dans diverses traditions, symbolisés respectivement par la balance et l'épée.*⁴

If we consider the attributes of Shamash, the sun-god and god of justice, and also the staff and the chalice of the spiritual authority, we see how the traditional spirit insisted on balancing the influences of the two Poles, *Purusha* and *Prakriti, Qian* and *Kun*; Guénon said too: *il* [le vajra] *doit donc être placé verticalement, ce qui s'accorde d'ailleurs avec son caractère de symbole masculin, ainsi qu'avec le fait qu'il est essentiellement un attribut sacerdotal*⁵; in footnote:

Son complémentaire féminin est, dans la tradition hindoue, la conque (shankha), *et, dans la tradition thibétaine, la clochette rituelle* (dilbu), *sur laquelle se voit souvent une figure féminine qui est celle de la* Prâjnâ-pâramitâ *ou "Sagesse transcendante" dont elle est le symbole, tandis que le* vajra *est celui*

---

¹ In the same footnote another footnote is mentioned from a previous part of the same article *L'Archéomètre. Dans le Tarot, le principe passif, figuré par la* coupe, *correspond à l'Air, mais le principe actif, figuré par le* bâton, *correspond à la Terre; l'*épée, *qui représente l'union de ces deux principes, correspond au Feu, et le* denier, *qui symbolise le produit de cette union, correspond à l'*Eau (*La Gnose*, no. 9, Juillet-Août 1910).
² Guénon said: *Le nom de la caste des Kshatriyas est dérivé de* kshatra *qui signifie "force"* (René Guénon, *Autorité spirituelle et pouvoir temporel*, Véga, 1976, p. 27).
³ *L'Archéomètre, La Gnose*, no. 1, Janvier 1911.
⁴ Guénon, *ibid.*, p. 28.
⁵ Guénon, *La Grande Triade*, p. 63.

de la "Méthode" ou de la "Voie"... Les Lamas tiennent le vajra *de la main droite et la clochette de la main gauche; ces deux objets rituels ne doivent jamais être séparés.*[1]

In the royal caste, the two attributes were the sword and the weighing scale, but in the Tarot cards, where the *baton* and the *cup* are present, the *sword* was paired up with the *coin* (*denier*[2]) that is, with the "(solar) disc," and not with the scale, which could be envisaged as a decline, but which, in fact, was based on three main reasons: first, the members of the third Hindu caste were also *dwija* ("twice born") and participants to the traditional spirit, as we also see in the Christian Middle Ages, where a tight collaboration between Templars and Masons flourished; second, with the evolvement of the cycle, the third caste became more and more prominent, just like the initiation centred on métiers, and as well as money[3]; third, the coin implicitly bore a symbolism related to justice and to the weighing scale (in a world breathing the pestilent air of the "Iron Age"[4] – when Astraea, the

---

[1] *Ibid.* It is well known that the staff and the scallop shell were the badge of the pilgrim.
[2] The *denier* was a Frankish coin created by Charlemagne in the Early Middle Ages; see the figure:

In the Roman currency system, the *denarius* (plural *denarii*) was a small silver coin first minted in 211 BC.
[3] *Il importe de remarquer que, dans une société régulière, la richesse n'est jamais regardée comme une supériorité; au contraire, elle appartient surtout aux Vaishyas, c'est-à-dire à la troisième caste, qui ne peut posséder qu'une puissance purement matérielle* (*L'Archéomètre, La Gnose*, no. 1, Janvier 1911).
[4] This air is similar to the south wind: "This air around us remains clear when the north wind is blowing in Creation because of the certain subtle nature of that wind which brings a clear sky, but when the south wind is blowing the whole air is as it were made thick and overcast by the mist-producing nature of this wind, which from a certain relatedness bears out of its own parts clouds over the whole inhabited world. Thus also, when the soul is set into activity by the inspiration of the True and

daughter of Themis, abandoned the earth – justice and balance were almost mythological and invisible realities).

The name of the ancient *talent*,[1] for example, came from Greek, where τάλαντον, *talanton* means "scale, balance" (Latin *talentum*); the weighing scale, even though used to measure money (weight and money were very strongly related), it was an instrument of justice, because in a traditional society the *true measure* was fundamental, including the case of currency.[2]

The *banliang* coin took its name from two character inscriptions (see the above figure) *ban* and *liang*, which means "half a *liang*," where *liang* was a Chinese unit of weight[3]; however, the character *liang* represented the image of a balance scale in equilibrium.[4]

For the modern mentality, it is almost impossible to comprehend how money could represent equilibrium and justice, when everybody knows that "life is not fair," an expression used exclusively from a quantitative and corporeal point of view. The days of Brahmâ are precisely numbered, each cycle containing a fixed number of terrestrial years, but when man's days are numbered there is no "fairness," since one could live more or less days than the other. This idea of (human) "injustice"[5] transpires in Christ's parable of the labourers in the

---

Holy Spirit it finds itself to be wholly outside the demonic mist, but when it is greatly inspired by the spirit of deception it is wholly covered over by the clouds of sin" (Diadochos of Photiki, *The Hundred Chapters*, chapter 75).

[1] The *talent* appears in the *New Testament*.

[2] The word "numismatic" comes from Latin *numisma* "coin, currency," from Greek *nomisma* "current coin, money" (in the sense of money "sanctioned by custom [as tradition] or usage"), from *nomos* "custom, law" (we see the connection money-justice, law); in Greek, νόμισμα meant: the current coin; an established weight or measure; legal measure; custom or law.

[3] The character *ban* means "to divide in two equal parts" (like the two pans of a balance scale) (Léon Wieger, *Caractères Chinois*, Kuangchi Cultural Group, 1932, p. 58).

[4] Wieger, *ibid.*, p. 99.

[5] "The corruptible courts are not able to judge in accord to the incorruptible court of God" (Diadochos of Photiki, *The Hundred Chapters*, chapter 64).

vineyard,[1] where Jesus uses money to transmit his teaching,[2] depicting the householder's "injust" deed of paying all the workers (regardless of how many hours they worked) the same amount of *denarii*.[3]

In the modern world, the Justice is missing and there is a strong feeling of injustice (life is not fair), but, paradoxically, this perception of injustice is from a very human, profane, sentimental and quantitative viewpoint, against any hierarchy or qualitative arguments.[4] René Guénon explained:

> *Nous ne pouvons pas, en effet, prendre un seul instant au sérieux les arguments d'ordre moral et sentimental, basés sur la constatation d'une prétendue injustice dans l'inégalité des conditions humaines. Cette constatation provient uniquement de ce qu'on envisage toujours des faits particuliers, en les isolant de l'ensemble dont ils font partie, alors que, si on les replace dans cet ensemble, il ne saurait y avoir évidemment aucune injustice, ou, pour employer un terme à la fois plus*

---

[1] *Matthew* 20:1-16. We may note that the parable describes the "Kingdom of Heaven": "For the kingdom of heaven is like unto a man that is a householder, which went out early in the morning to hire labourers into his vineyard..."

[2] The use of money in the parable illustrates, of course, the mentality of Jesus' audience in particular and of the world in general.

[3] The parable of the prodigal son (*Luke* 15:11-32) illustrates the same "injustice"; this parable is preceded by the parable of the lost coin, where a woman had ten *drachmas* and lost one and then found it, and we see again Jesus using money to exemplify his teachings; the prodigal son is, in fact, the "lost *drachma*." We should observe that in another parable the notion of hierarchy is present: "And unto one he gave five talents, to another two, and to another one; to every man according to his several ability" (*Matthew* 25:15), which for the profane mind would seem a contradiction of the previous parable and also of the parable of the talents, as exposed in *Luke* 19:13 ("he called his ten servants, and delivered them ten pounds," that is, equal share, a pound for each one), where hierarchy is related to the outcome.

[4] Let us refresh our mind with Guénon's sayings: *La même notion peut être appliquée, non pas seulement à un être unique, mais à une collectivité organisée, à une espèce, à tout l'ensemble des êtres d'un cycle cosmique ou d'un état d'existence, ou même à l'ordre total de l'Univers; c'est alors, à un degré où à un autre, la conformité à la nature essentielle des êtres, réalisée dans la constitution hiérarchiquement ordonnée de leur ensemble; c'est aussi, par conséquent, l'*équilibre fondamental, *l'*harmonie intégrale *résultant de cette* hiérarchisation, *à quoi se réduit d'ailleurs la notion même de justice quand on la dépouille de son caractère spécifiquement moral...* [our highlighting] (*Introduction générale*, 1987, pp. 186-188).

exact et plus étendu, aucun déséquilibre,[1] *puisque ces faits sont, comme tout le reste, des éléments de l'harmonie totale. Nous nous sommes d'ailleurs suffisamment expliqué sur cette question, et nous avons montré que le mal n'a aucune réalité, que ce qu'on appelle ainsi n'est qu'une relativité considérée analytiquement et que, au-delà de ce point de vue spécial de la mentalité humaine, l'imperfection est nécessairement illusoire, car elle ne peut exister que comme élément du Parfait, lequel ne saurait évidemment contenir rien d'imparfait. Il est facile de comprendre que la diversité des conditions humaines ne provient pas d'autre chose que des différences de nature qui existent entre les individus eux-mêmes, qu'elle est inhérente à la nature individuelle des êtres humains terrestres, et qu'elle n'est pas plus injuste ni moins nécessaire (étant du même ordre, quoique à un autre degré) que la variété des espèces animales et végétales, contre laquelle personne n'a encore jamais songé à protester au nom de la justice, ce qui serait d'ailleurs parfaitement ridicule.*[2]

---

[1] *Dans le domaine social, ce qu'on appelle la justice ne peut consister, suivant une formule extrême-orientale, qu'à compenser des injustices par d'autres injustices (conception qui ne souffre pas l'introduction d'idées mystico-morales telles que celles de mérite et de démérite, de récompense et de punition, etc., non plus que de la notion occidentale du progrès moral et social); la somme de toutes ces injustices, qui s'harmonisent en s'équilibrant, est, dans son ensemble, la plus grande justice au point de vue humain individuel* [Guénon's footnote; we should meditate on what "measure for measure" really means].

[2] Palingénius, *Les Néo-spiritualistes*, in *La Gnose*, septembre 1911. There is another parable of Christ, the parable of the talents, where money is used to illustrate the idea of "kingdom of heaven" ("For the kingdom of heaven is as a man travelling into a far country…"), of hierarchy, of last judgment (and second coming), and of the inherent possibilities each individual has at his birth, possibilities that could flourish or not (see *Matthew* 25:14-30 and *Luke* 19:12-27). Here, the human "injustice" is even more weighty, since the last servant, whom the lord casts "into outer darkness," accuses his master of "unfairness": "Lord, I knew thee that thou art an hard man, reaping where thou hast not sown, and gathering where thou hast not strawed" (this parable, even though abundantly discussed by various theologians, including the great St. John Chrysostom, deserves a metaphysical approach; for example, in the last quote, we find what later Meister Eckhart said about the purified soul: "The soul is purified in the body in order to reassemble what was scattered," while in Masonry, the task of the Masters consists in "spreading the light and gathering what is scattered"; the individual is doing the scattering and the Divinity is doing the gathering). There are also some comments on this parable, where the modern mentality is showing its lack of intelligence and "love of money" (St. Paul said: "The love of money is the root of all evil," *1 Timothy* 6:10).

CHAPTER XI

MONEY BEFORE MONEY

There is no doubt that today "Money is the Devil's Eye," as a Romanian proverb says.[1] René Guénon wrote an entire chapter about how the concept of "money" has decayed, from a traditional to a profane and modern level.[2] Today, after half a century,[3] the

---

[1] See E. B. Mawr, *Analogue Proverbs in Ten Languages*, Stock, 1885, p. 97; such a formulation is the equivalent of St. Paul's saying: "the love of money is the root of all evil" (*1 Timothy* 6:10); there are others like: "Worshipping the Golden Calf," or "He that loveth gold, shall not be justified" (*The Book of Sirach* 31:5); already at the beginning of the 17th century, Henri Neuhaus from Danzig (Gdansk) said in his *Advertissement pieux & utile Des Frères de la Rosée-Croix* (published in 1618, and then in 1623): *l'argent est le Roi du monde* (p. 28). Gatien de Courtilz de Sandras, in his *Mémoires de M^R. D'Argagnan*, said: *Il savait que, dans le siècle où nous sommes, l'argent était fort utile et qu'il n'y avait pas de plus grande consolation que celle-là* (Éditions Jean de Bonnot, 1966, I, p. 74).

[2] René Guénon, *Le règne de la quantité et les signes des temps*, Gallimard, 1970, chapter XVI (*La dégénérescence de la monnaie*). "It is worth noting that Guénon, in his study of the world's decadence (*Le Règne de la Quantité et Les Signes des Temps*), devotes a chapter to 'The Degeneration of Coinage' and shows how, once, every coin had a double use; it was both a quantitative unit of value and the vehicle of a certain spiritual significance (expressed by the symbols engraved upon it), so that trade between different peoples was never merely an exchange of goods (we know too well how fertile a source of discord such trade is), but also a means of communicating certain spiritual values" (Gai Eaton, *The Richest Vein*, Faber and Faber, 1949, p. 204).

[3] We insist upon this period of time ("half a century"), since it is obvious that after 1951 (when Guénon died) the materialistic progress and the fall of the cycle precipitated exponentially. If we think of all the electronic instruments and how they have almost brainwashed the young generations, we have to admit that this "half a century" has been the most aggressive and rapid phase of the cycle aiming at its

degeneration described by Guénon has reached its nadir, as illustrated by the present "economic" crisis (which started to become public and so visible in 2008) and the recurrent "bailouts," a crisis that refutes the absurd theory of "continued progress." In addition to the numerous political, psychological and social implications, which are not our concern, since our viewpoint is purely traditional, the crisis has reinforced an already well-known fact: money tops everything else, and the modern world loudly admitted that there is nothing so important as money, that the modern mentality cannot imagine a life without monetary slavery[1] and money as the main aspiration, which makes the "bailouts" vital for maintaining the profane and infrahuman lifestyle.[2]

It is futile to insist how today, more than ever, everything and everybody are valued based on quantity of money produced or acquired; Christmas is not about Christ, but about shopping (and starting as early as possible); a movie is not about message, but about box office records; a book is about the quantity of copies sold; and so on. Not to say that today the idea of "money donation" is spread worldwide, corrupting even the traditional domain, like the donation scheme that functions in Ayodhyâ, the mythical capital of Râma, in some of the Christian churches, and in other places.

There are innumerable examples illustrating how money today has become a central fixation of the modern mentality and how, together, mentality and money, they drastically fell towards pure quantity, even though, apparently, the humankind is less materialistic, since the electronic devices have created a virtual world, but this is an expected phase of the cycle, the solidification being replaced by dissolution,

---

destruction; the materialistic progress facilitated two things: first, an apparent reaction that allowed the pseudo-spirituality to develop and to prepare the transition to the last phase of this cycle: the dissolution; second, the reign of "virtuality" (the "e-life" and the "e-world") that seems "soft" in comparison to the solidification (the "hard") of the world.

[1] We merely need to mention the well established policy of "debts" and "credits," a complete "unnatural" policy.

[2] The only real progress made by the modern civilization is the constant rise in prices and debts.

where the anti-*Anima* and the infrahuman characteristics dominate.[1] Nonetheless, this propinquity between mentality and money suggests that money did not always have a profane and quantitative meaning, and even though it is impossible for the modern people to regard money differently, there was a time when the mentality was traditional and money had a spiritual value.

The most commonly accepted definition describes money as a "circulating medium of exchange," but this concept of "exchange" needs and deserves an explanation from the viewpoint of the traditional spirit. Dionysius the Areopagite transmitted a fundamental parable that we already quoted in our works:

> Imagine a great shining [supra-luminous] chain hanging downward from the heights of heaven to the world below. We grab hold of it with one hand and then another, and we seem to be pulling it down toward us. Actually it is already there in the heights and down below and instead of pulling it to us we are being lifted upward to that brilliance above, to the dazzling light of those beams.[2]

Dionysius' "image" is exceptionally powerful and accepts innumerable meanings that for a traditional mentality do not have to be detailed, because the "image" is comprehended as a whole, as "complication," at once, and not as a rational process developed in time, and, therefore, the question whether the traditional man understood the significance of the symbols and rites he used is a

---

[1] See our *Free-Masonry*, p. 246. We should not forget that the modern attitude regarding money, like the modern mentality, has nothing "spontaneous" in its manifestation, but is a "satanic" fabrication.

[2] And the divine Dionysius continues like this: "Or picture ourselves aboard a boat. There are hawsers joining it to some rock. We take hold of them and pull on them, and it is as if we were dragging the rock to us when in fact we are hauling ourselves and our boat toward that rock. And, from another point of view, when someone on the boat pushes away from the rock which is on the shore he will have no effect on the rock, which stands immovable, but will make a space between it and himself, and the more he pushes the greater the space will be" (*The Divine Names*, III, 1. See Pseudo-Dionysius, *The Complete Works*, Paulist Press, 1987, p. 68).

"wrong posed" question; the traditional man understood ("realized") not with his mind but with his intellectual intuition.

The super-luminous chain (a "golden" chain) is the *Axis Mundi*, and the symbolism of the chain, string, or thread probably belongs to the Primordial Tradition; we mentioned it in our works, in connection to the Master Puppeteer, to *aurea catena Homeri*, to Hindu *sûtrâtma* ("the thread-self" on which the worlds or the beings are threaded, the string passing through the central aperture of the heart – "the eye of the needle"), but also we have to be aware of the World as explication, with knots defining a mesh of strings and labyrinthian threads.[1]

As Ananda K. Coomaraswamy said, "Natural or artificial objects are not for the primitive [that is, for the traditional spirit], as they can be for us, arbitrary symbols of some other and higher reality, but actual manifestations of this reality"[2]; therefore, "that a safety pin or button is meaningless, and merely a convenience for us, is simply the evidence of our profane ignorance."[3] The pin or the button, Coomaraswamy explained, is a symbol of the Sun that "connects all things to himself and fastens them; he is the primordial embroiderer and tailor, by whom the tissue of the universe, to which our garments are analogous, is woven on a living thread"; and "the proof that the meaning of the safety pin had been understood [by the traditional man] can be pointed to in the fact that the heads or eyes of prehistoric fibulae are regularly decorated with a repertoire of distinctly solar symbols."[4] We have in our collection a hair pin, two thousand years old, 5.5 inches long, from an ancient Dacian city called Ratiaria, conquered by the Romans, who made it the capital of the province Dacia Ripensis; the pin has a wolf head,[5] with the eyes made of carneols, and holding a ring in his teeth: the ring clearly is the "Sun-Door."

---

[1] See, for example, Ananda K. Coomaraswamy, *The Iconography of Dürer's "Knots" and Leonardo's "Concatenation"*, The Art Quarterly, 1944, pp. 109-128.
[2] See Ananda K. Coomaraswamy, *Traditional Art and Symbolism*, Princeton Univ. Press, 1986, p. 295.
[3] *Ibid.*, p. 298.
[4] *Ibid.*, p. 299.
[5] The ancient Dacians' standard was a flying dragon with a wolf head.

"Just as the spider emits the thread (of the web) out of itself and again withdraws it into itself, just as the plants emerge from the earth, just as the hair grows from a man alive, likewise the universe emerges from the Imperishable."[1] There is nothing chaotic about the production and nurturing of the World; on the contrary, it is *ordo ab chao*, a process perfectly regulated and law-abiding, which means that the "image" of the spider and its web or of the "golden chain" is not just a symbol but pure reality, the reality of an invisible net of "channels" through which the divine grace or the spiritual influence flows, connecting the indefinite number of worlds and the indefinite number of modalities of a world, and so the "nurture" descends through the "golden chain" and feeds the universal manifestation and its innumerable layers[2]; which also means that the Dragon (identical to the solar tailor and to the wolf with the ring in his teeth) was sacrificed and indefinitely multiplied.

An aspect of such a sacrifice is the Christian Eucharist, where the bread and the wine are the spiritual ingredients, both symbol and reality, from the beginning of the world: "Then Melchizedek king of Salem brought out bread and wine. He was priest of God Most

---

[1] *Mundaka Up.* I.1.7.
[2] We may mention here the Hermetic tradition, where it is said that the "doctrine of divinity" is like a torrential flood coming down, and "from the celestial bodies there are spread throughout the world continual effluvia" (*Hermetica*, Shambhala, 1993, ed. and tr. by Walter Scott, p. 291, Frances A. Yates, *Giordano Bruno and the Hermetic Tradition*, The Univ. of Chicago Press, 1991, p. 35). Since Hermeticism was cosmologic and not metaphysical, Yates could talk about "continual effluvia of influences pouring down onto the earth from the stars" (*ibid.*, p. 45).

High."[1] Furthermore, the wine is the symbol of the "nurture" descending into the world, and Saint Bernard de Clairvaux said, in one of his sermons, that this wine from the highest flowed into the streets of the celestial city, and aforetime existed in abundance in a wine-cellar, in a spiritual place [the spiritual center].[2] There is more: the vine itself is a symbol of the web, as St. Bernard said:

> the vineyard of the Lord – that one, I mean, which encompasses the world, of which we are a part – a vine great beyond measure, planted by the Lord, bought with his blood, fertilized by grace and made fruitful by his Spirit.[3]

This web, this mesh, this vine, with the root in non-manifestation, is the sacred "infrastructure" that makes possible not only the descent and flow of the spiritual influences but also the "exchange" of invisible "energies" and "vibrations," since any disharmony, any action requires a return to harmony, a pacification, a reaction, any sacrificed head (the beheading) requires a reunification with the body, and so, as St. Paul explained, "For this Melchisedec, king of Salem, priest of the most high God, who met Abraham returning from the slaughter of the kings, and blessed him; To whom also Abraham gave a tenth part of

---

[1] *Genesis* 14:18-19. We should keep in mind that the multiplicity of wheat grains is melted in "one" white flour and the multiplicity of grapes is melted in "one" red wine, which means that Christian Communion is only in part a sacrifice where Jesus is "cut into pieces," and it is mainly a sacrifice that unites, imparts, and brings together a community. A complete sacrifice contains multiplication and reunification, in a way comparable with what Matgioi called *les actions et réactions concordantes* (*La Voie Rationnelle*, Éditions Traditionnelles, 1984, pp. 127 ff.).

[2] Jean Hani, *Les Métiers de Dieu*, Éd. des Trois Mondes, 1975, p. 156. About the "wine-cellar," see the *Song of Solomon* (*Canticles*) 2:4 and St. Bernard's sermon (no. 49).

[3] Sermon 65 on the *Song of Solomon*. See also, "Thou hast brought a vine out of Egypt: thou hast cast out the heathen, and planted it. Thou preparedst room before it, and didst cause it to take deep root, and it filled the land. The hills were covered with the shadow of it, and the boughs thereof were like the goodly cedars. She sent out her boughs unto the sea, and her branches unto the river" (*Psalms* 80:8-11); and, "I am the vine, ye are the branches: He that abideth in me, and I in him, the same bringeth forth much fruit: for without me ye can do nothing" (*John* 15:5).

all."¹ This "exchange" between Melchizedek and Abraham is a perfect illustration of what "barter" signified originally; and we notice again how the language of symbols is inexhaustibly rich, because we find here, besides the interpretation given by St. Paul and René Guénon's identification of Melchizedek with the Lord of the World,² another essential aspect, regarding the "exchange," which is profound spiritual and initiatory, and therefore Abraham's tithe is only an "adjuvant" of a higher reality.

The transmission of spiritual influence starts with a sacrifice (bearing in mind that "supports" are indispensable), and, as Guénon said, because Melchizedek brings wine, which symbolizes the esoteric knowledge, his sacrifice is an initiatory one³; the fact that the wine replaces blood⁴ seems to allude to the Primordial Tradition (represented by Melchizedek) as recognizing the pre-eminence of agricultural symbols, given that agriculture (mainly as gardening) seemed to precede the pastoral occupation.⁵

Ananda K. Coomaraswamy said:

> The First Sacrificers ... found in the Sacrifice their Way from privation to plenty, darkness to light, and death to immortality ... the Sacrifice ensuring the perpetual circulation of the "Stream of Wealth," the food of the gods reaching them in the smoke of the burnt offering, and our food in return descending from heaven in

---

[1] *Hebrews* 7:1-2 (*Genesis* 14:19-20).
[2] *Le Roi du Monde*, Gallimard, 1981, pp. 47 ff.
[3] *Ibid.*, pp. 47-48.
[4] Even though Christ (because addressing the Jews) "took the cup, and gave thanks, and gave it to them, saying, Drink ye all of it; For this is my blood" (*Matthew* 26:27-28).
[5] However, René Guénon considers Melchizedek's sacrifice beyond the distinction of the two laws, one of the sedentary people and one of the nomad people: *tel est le cas du sacrifice de Melchisédech, consistant en l'offrande essentiellement végétale du pain et du vin; mais ceci se rapporte en réalité au rite du Soma védique et à la perpétuation directe de la "tradition primordiale" au delà de la forme spécialisée de la tradition hébraïque et "abrahamique" et même, beaucoup plus loin encore, au delà de la distinction de la loi des peuples sédentaires et de celle des peuples nomads* (*Le règne*, p. 203).

the rain and thus through plants [agriculture] and cattle [pastoralism] to ourselves[1];

this is more an "exchange" than a circulation,[2] like in Melchizedek's case, when this one brings down from the highest bread and wine (the archetypal sacrifice) and his blessing (the spiritual influence), while Abraham, in exchange, gives a tenth part of all.

The supreme "exchange" is between God and the beings (along the "golden chain"), or even between the spiritual center and the beings (using the mesh or the vine), an exchange supervised by the spiritual authority, and only secondary between beings[3]; and this "exchange" will appear as a sacrifice, which "renders sacred" (Latin *sacrificium*) the world, and the beings, and the bonds.[4]

Lactantius connected "religion" with the Latin *religare*, meaning "to bind fast," and he was thinking about a "bond between humans and

---

[1] *Metaphysics*, Princeton, 1977, p. 107.
[2] A term used for the well-known hydrologic cycle (the water circulation).
[3] Jesus, as a newborn, is invested with the everlasting and unbroken Tradition by the three Magi, the wise men coming from the "east" (*Matthew* 2). The Magi form a hierarchy, implied by their gifts: gold for kingship (temporal authority), incense for priesthood (spiritual authority) and myrrh for the supreme function ("Lord of the World"). Those gifts (treasures) represent also the consecration of Christ as king, priest and prophet, as "Lord of the World" (Guénon, *Le Roi*, p. 36). The Magi's offers represent the spiritual influences from the supreme center; in compensation, Christ will offer his body as a sacrifice.
[4] "A number of them stand in order, each holding in his hand three darts; others take the man who is to be sent to Zalmoxis, and swinging him by his hands and feet, toss him into the air so that he falls upon the points of the weapons. If he is pierced and dies, they think that the god is propitious to them; but if not, they lay the fault on the messenger, who (they say) is a wicked man: and so they choose another to send away. The messages are given while the man is still alive. This same people, when it lightens and thunders, aim their arrows at the sky, uttering threats against the god; and they do not believe that there is any god but their own" (Herodotus *The Histories* IV.94). The arrows represent an "action" that needs a "reaction" from heaven, to complete the "exchange"; and the darts used for the sacrifice are related to the arrows, performing an offering along the "golden chain" in exchange for Zalmoxis' "reaction" (the spiritual influences).

God"[1]; however, René Guénon wondered: *La religion, d'après la dérivation de ce mot, c'est "ce qui relie"; mais faut-il entendre par là ce qui relie l'homme à un principe supérieur, ou simplement ce qui relie les hommes entre eux?*[2]; and, in his answer, he considered that, in the Greco-Roman antiquity, where the word comes from, the bond referred to both aspects. Albeit the etymology of the word "religion" is unsure, we may say that, indeed, the main function of religion is to facilitate the "bond" and, consequently, the "exchange" between God and the beings and between the beings participating in that religious community (a particular mesh)[3]; yet this "exchange" is even more powerful, operational and beyond measure in the case of an initiatory path.

This concept of a sacred "exchange" could not escape René Guénon, who wrote:

> Any exchange between beings subjected to time and space conditions is in fact a movement, or rather an ensemble of two reverse and reciprocal movements, which harmonize and compensate each other; here, the balance is therefore directly realized by the very fact of this compensation. The alternated movement of the exchanges can moreover relate to the three spiritual (or purely intellectual), psychical and corporeal domains in correspondence with the "three worlds": exchange of the principles, the symbols and the offerings, such is, in the real traditional history of terrestrial humanity, the triple foundation upon which is based the mystery of pacts, alliances and blessings, that is to say, in the end, the very distribution of the "spiritual influences" in action within our world.[4]

---

[1] "We are tied to God and bound to Him [*religati*] by the bond of piety" (*Divine Institutes* IV.28); St. Augustine agreed: "Religion binds us [*religat*] to the one Almighty God" (*Retractions* I.13).
[2] *Introduction générale à l'étude des doctrines hindoues*, Guy Trédaniel, 1987, p. 73.
[3] We should not forget the importance of the sacrifice; in Christianity, the Eucharist is a sacrifice from above, while the believer's offerings, his or her prayers, fasting, etc. represent the sacrifice from down-below.
[4] *Tout échange entre les êtres soumis aux conditions temporelle et spatiale est en somme un mouvement, ou plutôt un ensemble de deux mouvements inverses et réciproques, qui s'harmonisent et se compensent l'un l'autre; ici, l'équilibre se réalise donc directement par le fait même de cette compensation. Le mouvement alternatif des échanges peut d'ailleurs porter sur les trois domaines*

This text is fundamental for understanding what the definition of money as "circulating medium of exchange" really represents, as part of a universal sacred "exchange," and also how the law found in the Far-Eastern tradition and called by Matgioi *les actions et réactions concordantes* could be applied here. Guénon's text is, we repeat, fundamental, but it could pass almost unnoticed, as it was placed in a book about the decayed modern world and the signs of time (a subject that makes, for many, this specific book the most noteworthy of Guénon's works); yet we see, this text explains the very existence of the universal manifestation, the way the spiritual influences work and sustain this existence, the bond between it and the Principle, and we should note that Guénon introduced the word "mystery" in his text to warn the reader, like Dante did: *Aguzza qui, lettor, ben gli occhi al vero*[1]!

We reviewed what a "mystery" is for a traditional mentality; right now, we insist that René Guénon referred in his text to the "mystery of pacts, alliances and blessings, which, in fact, represent the very distribution of the 'spiritual influences' acting in our world." Only after the destruction of the Order of the Temple, which corresponds to a "temporal barrier" marking the end of the Christian traditional society, this "mystery" lost its sacred efficacy and meaning, and gradually became just the profane "payment." Therefore, the word "payment" (derived from Latin *pacare*) in English, but also in French, Spanish, and of course Italian, which in the Middle Ages still kept the Latin sense of

---

spirituel (ou intellectuel pur), psychique et corporel, en correspondance avec les "trois mondes": échange des principes, des symboles et des offrandes, telle est, dans la véritable histoire traditionnelle de l'humanité terrestre, la triple base sur laquelle repose le mystère des pactes, des alliances et des bénédictions, c'est-à-dire, au fond, la répartition même des "influences spirituelles" en action dans notre monde (*Le règne*, pp. 203-204).

[1] "Reader, if you seek truth, sharpen your eyes,/ for here the veil of allegory thins/ and may be pierced by any man who tries," Dante's *Purgatorio* VIII.19-21 (Mentor Classic, 1961, tr. John Ciardi). With regard to the law of *les actions et réactions concordantes*, we mention Ficino's idea of a continuous attraction, a "closed loop," "beginning from God, emanating to the World, and returning at last to God" (Marsilio Ficino, *Commentary on Plato's Symposium on Love*, Spring, 1994, p. 46).

"to appease, pacify, satisfy,"[1] became after the 14th century what it is today, a profane word describing a pecuniary exchange.[2]

We must persist: "to pacify" has to be understood first and foremost as a spiritual act related to Christ's "peace"[3] and to *Pax Profunda* of the Rose-Cross,[4] and therefore Guénon could refer to this as a "mystery"; an economic and financial "satisfaction" is just one of

---

[1] The Latin word *pacare*, "to please, pacify, satisfy," derives from *pax* "peace."
[2] In the modern (that is, profane) society, there is a general tendency to explain all the remaining sacred rituals, traditions, rules, etc. based on the ignorance and arrogance of the modern mentality; for example, fasting is considered a custom concerned with a healthy diet, and the spiritual meaning is just an artificial and somehow superimposed element, when, in fact, fasting, because is part of a spiritual process, has various applications at various levels, including the "healthy diet"; similarly, the construction of an edifice in a traditional society was conducted starting from the divine principles, complying with the metaphysical doctrine, with the principles of rhythm, proportions, and harmony, striving to realize the perfect equilibrium of the edifice (*coincidentia oppositorum*), to build "according to *true measure*," and as secondary consequences the building satisfied all the laws and rules of Physics and Mechanics (as understood in a modern sense); on the contrary, the modern and profane builder ignores the divine vision and uses an analytical and experimental approach, with all kinds of profane calculations (strength of materials, etc.), which make the edifice a vain, ugly and insecure result. Correspondingly, the pecuniary exchange only secondary, and as a natural consequence, had a social and economic function. However, we acknowledge some modern authors who, despite their mentality, admitted (even though in a confused manner), like Glyn Davies, that "money originated very largely from non-economic causes: from tribute as well as from trade, from blood-money and bride-money as well as from barter, from ceremonial and religious rites as well as from commerce, from ostentatious ornamentation as well as from acting as the common drudge between economic men" (*A History of Money*, University of Wales Press, 2002, p. XVIII); and Davies said also: "We face considerable difficulty in trying to span the chronological gap which separates us from a true understanding of the attitudes of ancient man towards religious, social and economic life, and similarly with regard to the cultural gap which separates us from existing or recent primitive societies. In both ancient and modern primitive societies human values and attitudes were such that religion permeated almost the whole of everyday life and could not as easily be separated from political, social and economic life in the way that comes readily to us with our tendency for facile categorization" (*ibid.*, p. 24).
[3] "My peace I give unto you: not as the world giveth" (*John* 14:27).
[4] Guénon, *Le Roi*, p. 24.

many collateral minor effects, as it is in the case of the so-called "bride-money."[1]

All these, and the following considerations, are indispensable if we want to escape the modern mentality and comprehend how in a traditional society, money was a part of the "mystery of pacts, alliances and blessings, which, in fact, represent the very distribution of the 'spiritual influences' acting in our world."[2]

The word "exchange," derived from Vulgar Latin (*ex-cambiare*), yet of unknown origin, describes an "act of reciprocal giving and receiving," which explains why Guénon chose to use it, having in mind the Far-Eastern law of *les actions et réactions concordantes*[3] and the "law of compensation."[4] René Guénon referred explicitly to the "law of compensation" only once, in a footnote; here is the text: "to return to biblical symbolism, the animal sacrifice is fatal to Abel, and the vegetal offering from Cain was not accepted; the one who is blessed dies, whereas the one who lives is cursed,"[5] and here is the footnote:

> Just as Abel slaughtered animals, he was himself slaughtered by Cain; there is here something as a manifestation of a "law of

---

[1] The "bride-money" is usually explained as payment to compensate the father who loses the daughter's services; in fact, the "bride-money," together with the "theft of the bride," is related to the spiritual symbolism of the bride (as *Madonna Intelligenza*) and to the initiatory quest. A spiritual "exchange" takes place; even today there is the custom in some countries to recover the stolen bride by paying "bride-money."

[2] We should remind our readers that, by definition, "traditional" is all that involves a "super-human" weight; money was for a long time a traditional element, and, consequently, its origin and use could not be explained by exclusively human factors.

[3] René Guénon observed: *La somme de toutes les actions et réactions est l'absolu Non-Agir.*

[4] There are plenty of examples to point up the "law of compensation": the revolt of the *Kshatriyas* was compensated by the revolt of the lower castes; the fact that the Masons functioned under the Templars' protection was compensated by the fact that, later, the Templars hid among the Masons; a sacred beheading is compensated by another beheading, and a head demands another head (see Ganesha); an abduction is compensated by a reparatory abduction (see *Râmâyana*); the Hindu tradition, fairy tales, the Greek mythology and the other sacred texts could provide many other illustrations.

[5] *Pour en revenir au symbolisme biblique, le sacrifice animal est fatal à Abel, et l'offrande végétale de Caïn n'est pas agréée; celui qui est béni meurt, celui qui vit est maudit.*

compensation" according to which partial imbalances, which are the fundamental basis of any manifestation, are integrated in the total balance.[1]

The story of Cain and Abel is legendary, prompting many commentaries that tried to exhaust its meaning, but for our topic Guénon's interpretation is fundamental, since, aside from his exposé on the "law of compensation" related to the sacred exchange, he emphasized the symbolism of the two brothers, Cain (representing the sedentary people, with their agricultural occupations) and Abel (representing the nomad people, with their pastoral activities).[2]

---

[1] *Comme Abel a versé le sang des animaux, son sang est versé par Caïn; il y a là comme l'expression d'une "loi de compensation" en vertu de laquelle les déséquilibres partiels, en quoi consiste au fond toute manifestation, s'intègrent dans l'équilibre total* (*Le règne*, p. 203). Guénon mentioned the notion of "compensation" before, just once, in *Autorité spirituelle et pouvoir temporel*, Véga, 1976, pp. 112-113, when he said: "According to the Far-Eastern doctrine, justice is the sum of all injustices, and, in the total order, any disorder is compensated by another disorder; this is why the revolution that overthrows the royalty is at the same time the logical consequence and the punishment, that is to say the compensation, of the previous revolt of this same royalty against spiritual authority (*suivant la doctrine extrême-orientale, la justice est faite de la somme de toutes les injustices, et, dans l'ordre total, tout désordre se compense par un autre désordre; c'est pourquoi la révolution qui renverse la royauté est à la fois la conséquence logique et le châtiment, c'est-à-dire la compensation, de la révolte antérieure de cette même royauté contre l'autorité spirituelle*).

[2] Guénon said that the works of the sedentary people are works developed in time, while those of the nomad people are works covering the unlimited space (*Le règne*, p. 199). Let us add an illustration: we used in the main text to which this note belongs the word "topic"; it derives, together with the word "theme," from a root meaning "place" (Gr. *thema, topos*), yet the "tale" itself develops in time. Regarding the story of Cain and Abel it is helpful to quote it from the *Septuagint*: "And Abel was a keeper of sheep, but Cain was a tiller of the ground. And it was so after some time that Cain brought of the fruits of the earth a sacrifice to the Lord. And Abel also brought of the first born of his sheep and of his fatlings, and God looked upon Abel and his gifts, but Cain and his sacrifices he regarded not, and Cain was exceedingly sorrowful and his countenance fell. And the Lord God said to Cain, Why art thou become very sorrowful and why is thy countenance fallen? Hast thou not sinned if thou hast brought it rightly, but not rightly divided it? be still, to thee shall be his submission, and thou shalt rule over him" (4:2-7). We see how the *Septuagint* makes a difference between Cain's sacrifice and Abel's offerings (gifts) (Cain killing Abel produces, seemingly, the conversion of the offers into a sacrifice; however, Guénon,

The very fact that the primordial people (*ativarna*,[1] *Hamsa*) separated in sedentary and nomadic groups, marked a time when the equilibrium was shattered, and the harmony was lost, and the events in the biblical story of Cain and Abel[3] only accentuated this situation. Hence René Guénon's conclusion: *L'équilibre, de part et d'autre, est donc rompu; comment le rétablir, sinon par des échanges tels que chacun ait sa part des productions de l'autre?*[4] The "law of compensation" imposed the birth of the "exchange," preventing this separation to become pure opposition, and "changing" the contraries to complements, as part of the "mystery of pacts, alliances and blessings," with all the pacifying, appeasing and conciliatory acts as expressions of the archetypal reality of the center, where all the contraries are resolved and the complements unified[5] into an absolute peace, perfect equilibrium and complete harmony, not to say that any pact was a reflection of the supreme covenant between God and man.

---

when he talked about *le sacrifice animal de Abel* and *l'offrande végétale de Caïn*, considered the reversed situation, where the killing of Abel is a compensatory sacrifice); also we notice the allusion to *hesychia*.

[1] "Beyond the castes" (Guénon, *Le règne*, p. 89).
[2] "The unique primordial caste" (René Guénon, *Études sur l'hindouisme*, Éditions Traditionnelles, 1979, p. 78).
[3] *Genesis* 4:1-17. Here, the sacrifices of Cain and Abel are called "offering."
[4] *Le règne*, p. 203. This important text of René Guénon was already written in 1922.
[5] See René Guénon, *Le symbolisme de la croix*, chs. VI and VII.

CHAPTER XII

MEASURE FOR MEASURE

As we saw, René Guénon rhetorically asked: "The balance, both sides, is therefore broken; how can it be restored, if not by exchanges that allow each to have its share of the other's productions?"

In the previous chapter, the traditional concept of "exchange" was situated in its normal sacred environment, yet in Guénon's question there is another keyword, in conjunction with "exchange," which is "balance," a concept just as fundamental as the other one, both metaphysically delineating the universal manifestation, and where "balance" is the 'A and 'Ω of the sacred "exchange"; the "mystery of pacts, alliances and blessings" is all about restoring the "balance" by suitable "exchanges."

A primordial rupture of mankind's equilibrium was the separation in sedentary and nomadic groups; consequently, there is no surprise that the oldest forms of "money" were grains and cattle.[1] From a

---

[1] There are many monographs about the history of money, which can illustrate how the cattle or grains were used as money. Glyn Davies, for example, mentions the Babylonian temples as "banks" storing, not money, but grains (*A History of Money*, Univ. of Wales Press, 2002, pp. 50-51); and: "Nowhere has grain achieved such a high degree of monetary use as in ancient Egypt. Despite the existence of metallic money, it was grain which formed the most extensively used monetary medium, particularly for accounting purposes, even after the Greeks had introduced coinage" (*ibid.*, p. 52) ... "When Egypt fell under the rule of a Greek dynasty, the Ptolemies (323-30 BC), the old system of warehouse banking reached a new level of sophistication. The numerous scattered government granaries were transformed into a network of grain banks with what amounted to a central bank in Alexandria where the main accounts from all the state granary banks were recorded" ... "the basic unit

worldly viewpoint, which implies multiplicity and quantity, grains could be connected to weight, while cattle to number. We already mentioned St. Augustine's interpretation of the famous passage "thou hast ordered all things in measure and number and weight" that became the lemma of the medieval world's traditional view with respect to architecture, music, or poetry.[1] At the same time, wheat and barley grains[2] served as the oldest forms of units of mass, which where connected to the concept of money.[3] As Guénon said,

> Les modes principaux de la quantité sont désignés expressément dans cette formule biblique: "Tu as disposé toutes choses en poids, nombre et mesure" (Sagesse, XI, 21), à laquelle répond terme pour terme (sauf l'interversion des deux premiers) le Mane, Thekel, Phares *(compté, pesé, divisé) de la vision de Balthasar* (Daniel, V, 25 à 28)[4];

there were some disputed opinions[5] that tried to explain the biblical "handwriting on the wall" as various measures of currency (and

---

of weight in the Greek speaking world was the 'drachma' or 'handful of grain'" (*ibid.*, p. 75) (*drachma* was the Greek currency before the Euro).

[1] Otto von Simson, *The Gothic Cathedral*, Harper Torchbooks, 1956, p. 25. Agrippa said: "The number of three is an incompounded number, a holy number, a number of perfection, a most powerful number... God orders the world by number, weight, and measure, and the number of three is deputed to the ideal forms thereof" (Henry Cornelius Agrippa, *Three Books of Occult Philosophy*, Llewellyn Publications, Edited and Annotated by Donald Tyson, 1998, p. 249).

[2] Obviously, there were also other types of grains used at one time or another in the present cycle. The Aztecs, for example, used the cacao beans as money.

[3] The Semitic (Akkadian and Hebrew) *shekel* was used as a unit of weight (weight of barley) and as money (attested in Mesopotamia around 3000 BC, but evidently it was used long before this date). René Guénon observed: *Sakal est l'hébreu* שקל*, qui a signifié "poids" avant de désigner une cetraine monnaie ("sicle")*. We could add the Latin *libra pondo* or the *talent*. The decree of Henry III of England said: "By consent of the whole Realm the King's Measure was made, so that an English Penny, which is called the Sterling, round without clipping, shall weigh Thirty-two Grains of Wheat dry in the midst of the Ear; Twenty-pence make an Ounce; and Twelve Ounces make a Pound."

[4] René Guénon, *L'Homme et son Devenir selon le Védânta*, Éditions Traditionnelles, 1991, p. 157.

[5] See, for example, Clermont Ganneau's interpretation in *Journal Asiatique*, 8, Paris, Imprimerie Nationale, 1886, p. 36.

weight): *mina, mina, shekel, half-mina (peres)*.[1] However, there is no doubt that, in fact, there were four, not three words written on the wall, where "mina, mina" could be translated not only as "numbered, numbered" but also as "count, the accountant," which basically is another way to say "measure for measure."[2]

---

[1] *Mene, Mene, Tekel u-Pharsin* (אנמ, אנמ, לקת, וסרפו) ("numbered, weighed, divided"; *Daniel* 5:25). As an illustration we present here the mina of Antiochus IV Epiphanes. We mentioned in our *Free-Masonry: A Traditional Organization* the desecration of the Temple in Jerusalem by Antiochus, who, in 168 BC, erected a statue of Zeus in the Holy of Holies; therefore, there is no surprise that Antiochus was the first Seleucid king to use divine epithets on coins, like Θεὸς Ἐπιφανής, "manifested god":

[2] In our *Free-Masonry*, we gave sufficient biblical examples to show how "measure for measure" worked in the case of the Jewish people; as a reminder, we mention Isaiah who considered the Assyrians as God's instrument. In the case of the "handwriting of the wall," the inscription as interpreted by Daniel was a prediction about the Persians capturing Babylon. Regarding the accounting, we should point out how important the idea of "balance" was for it, even though any sacred meanings were lost; also, it is known that in Sumeria, Assyria and Babylon "accountancy" was well developed (which does not mean that it was not used before their time), and it is interesting to note that it was applied to record the crops and herds (agriculture and pastoralism) with the help of clay tokens (a type of token represented one sheep, a different token meant ten sheep, another token valued ten goats etc.). All these tokens were strung on a string, which was a reflection of *sûtrâtmâ*: "All this is woven upon me, like numbers of pearls upon a thread," *Bhagavad-Gîtâ*, VII, 7; and Guénon explained: *Il est dit dans la* Bhagavad-Gîtâ: *"Sur Moi toutes choses* (Sarvamidam, *"ce tout," c'est-à-dire la totalité de la manifestation, comprenant tous les mondes, et non pas seulement "tout ce qui est en ce monde" comme il est dit dans une traduction publiée récemment "d'après Shri Aurobindo") sont enfilées comme un rang de perles sur un fil." Il s'agit ici du symbolisme du* sûtrâtmâ…: *c'est* Âtmâ *qui, comme un fil* (sûtra)*, pénètre et relie entre eux tous les mondes… Nous parlons ici des mondes en nous plaçant au point de vue macrocosmique, mais il doit être bien entendu qu'on pourrait tout aussi bien envisager de même, au point de vue microcosmique, les états*

The act of measuring was a primeval sacred activity and its meaning was part of the traditional spirit from the beginning of the cycle. In the Jewish tradition and, then, in the Christian one, the act of measuring was strongly underlined. Ezekiel's vision gives a very thorough and almost tedious series of measurements,[1] and the "measuring reed" is mentioned, an equivalent of the "golden reed"[2] and of the "measuring line."[3]

On a coin of Markianopolis (Moesia), struck by Heliogabalus, we see a woman holding the scales in her right hand, a *measuring-rod* in her left hand and there is a wheel at her feet; the woman was identified as Nemesis Aequitas, but she could be very well Dike or Tyche.[4] The coin bears a powerful symbolism, all its three elements (scales, measuring-rod, wheel[5]) having their source in the Primordial Tradition, and being related to our discourse about money.

---

de manifestation d'un être, et que le symbolisme serait exactement le même (*Symboles fondamentaux de la Science sacrée*, Gallimard, 1980, p. 365).
[1] *Ezekiel* 40:5-15, 40:19-37, 40:47-49, 41:1-5, 41:8-15, 42:15-20, 43:13-17, 45:1-3. See also *Revelation* 21:16-18, where the art of measuring is described. "No medieval reader could have failed to notice with what emphasis every Biblical description of a sacred edifice, particularly those of Solomon's Temple, of the Heavenly Jerusalem, and of the vision of Ezekiel, dwells on the measurements of these buildings" (Simson, *The Gothic Cathedral*, p. 37).
[2] *Revelation* 21:15.
[3] *Zechariah* 2:1-2.
[4] Jane Harrison, *Themis*, Merlin Press, 1989, p. 528. Tyche the goddess of fortune, fate and luck, was an archetype of the *palladium*, sometimes represented crowned with the turrets of a city-wall (about the symbolism of the wall see our *Free-Masonry*, p. 62) and holding a cornucopia (therefore, in French, to the normal meaning of the word *fortune*, "fate," was added that of "richness," i.e., "a lot of money"). We cannot develop here the symbolism of Tyche, but it is important to mention the strong relation with Dike (on occasion Tyche was identified to her), with the Moirae, Themis' daughters (at times Tyche was identified to a Moira). In the Far-Eastern tradition, there were "The Three Sages of Good Fortune" (Fu Xing, the god of good luck and happiness, Lu Xing, the god of prosperity, and Shou Xing, the god of longevity); however, it is imperative to underline that the tokens of "good luck" are just profanation and degeneration of the metaphysical primeval meaning of these types of symbols.
[5] The symbol known as "the wheel of fortune" is the tenth Major Arcana of the Tarot cards. Guénon said: *il y est aussi question de la "roue de la Loi,"* [*Dharmachakra*] *expression que le bouddhisme a empruntée, comme bien d'autres, aux doctrines antérieures, et qui,*

In the Egyptian tradition, Set used the art of measurement to sacrifice his brother Osiris[1]; it is said that, in fact, Set measured Osiris' shadow,[2] and there is a similarity with the old Romanian tradition regarding a Masonic sacrifice: to successfully build an edifice, a human being had to be buried alive under the foundation-stone, but a measuring-reed was used instead, having the length of somebody's shadow.[3]

In Masonry, the measuring-reed is illustrated by the "Twenty-Four-Inch Gage," where "twenty-four" is usually considered as representing "24 hours" and the ruler (gauge, rule) defines the "time well spent"[4]; in fact, we have here a celestial instrument (6, including its multiples, is a celestial number), with reference to the doctrine of the cosmic cycles,

---

originairement tout au moins, se réfère surtout aux théories cycliques... Notons également que la "roue de la Fortune," dans le symbolisme de l'antiquité occidentale, a des rapports très étroits avec la "roue de la Loi," et aussi, quoique cela n'apparaisse peut-être pas aussi clairement à première vue, avec la roue zodiacale (Symboles fondamentaux, pp. 86-87).

[1] Guénon compared Set with Cain; he noticed that the Greek name Typhon given to Set is an anagram for Python (*Symboles fondamentaux*, p. 158; for the curious contrast between the Egyptian Set and Seth, Adam's son, as the two sides of the same coin, see our work *Simbolismul ciclurilor cosmice și sfârșitul lumii*, Aion, 2008, p. 128). "Typhon secretly measured the body of Osiris and got made to the corresponding size a beautiful chest which was exquisitely decorated ... Osiris went in and lay down. Then the conspirators ran and slammed the lid on, and after securing it with bolts from the outside and also with molten lead poured on, they took it out to the river and let it go to the sea by way of the Tanitic mouth" (Plutarch, *De Iside et Osiride*, Univ. of Wales Press, 1970, p. 139).

[2] See, for example, Padraic Colum, *Orpheus, Myths of the World.*

[3] The shadow is an image of the human being's subtle modality. About the shadow and its meanings, see, for instance, J. S. M. Ward and W. G. Stirling, *Hung Society Or the Society of Heaven and Earth*, Kessinger Publishing, I, pp. 140 ff.

[4] Albert G. Mackey, *An Encyclopedia of Freemasonry*, The Masonic History Company, 1925, II, p. 811; Bernard E. Jones, *Freemasons' Guide and Compendium*, Cumberland House, 2005, p. 430; Irène Mainguy, *La Symbolique maçonnique du troisième millénaire*, Dervy, 2006, p. 332. The "Twenty-Four-Inch Gage" is the first tool presented to the Masonic neophyte, and it is also the first weapon used to kill the Grand Master Hiram Abif. Similarly, we could say that the cross is Christ's "tool" (not a tool of death, since the Cross, it is said, was made of the wood taken from the Tree of Life; René Guénon observed: *La croix, placée entre le Soleil et la Lune occupe la place centrale de l'"Arbre de Vie", représentant l'"axe du monde"*).

which are regulated[1] by the *true measure*, and like in other cases the qualitative influence is visible.[2] It is easy to understand why the Masonic gauge was associated to Ptah's staff (or "measuring-rod"): Ptah was the Egyptian god of craftsmen, and in particular of stone-masons.[3]

The fact that a measuring-rod could symbolize the "shadow" of a man, that is, the subtle modality of a human being, is in accord with Protagoras of Abdera's sayings: "Of all things the measure is Man, of the things that are, that they are, and of the things that are not, that they are not," which became the well known adage, "Man is the

---

[1] The word "ruler" is strongly related to "regulation," Sanskrit *râja* and Latin *rex*. For this reason, the "Twenty-Four-Inch Gage" was considered a representation of justice, truth and balance.

[2] We may mention that Shakespeare regarded the "measuring rule" as one of the carpenter's main tools: "Speak, what trade art thou? Why, sir, a carpenter. Where is thy leather apron and thy rule?" (*The Tragedy of Julius Caesar*, I.1). Guénon showed the relation between carpenter and mason, and it is known that Vishwakarma, "the Great Architect" of the Hindu tradition was a carpenter, and so was Jesus' father (René Guénon, *Études sur la Franc-Maçonnerie et le Compagnonnage*, Éditions Traditionnelles, 1978, II, pp. 9 ff.).

[3] There is no doubt that Ptah's symbolism is quite remarkable. He was the sovereign god of Memphis, and it is worthy to note that Memphis represented a spiritual center (one of its names was *Mekhat Tawy* "the Balance of the Two Lands"), founded by the Lord of the World, manifested as Menes (*Le titre de "Roi du Monde," pris dans son acception la plus élevée, la plus complète et en même temps la plus rigoureuse, s'applique proprement à Manu, le Législateur primordial et universel, dont le nom se retrouve, sous des formes diverses, chez un grand nombre de peuples anciens; rappelons seulement, à cet égard, le Mina ou Ménès des Égyptiens, le Menw des Celtes et le Minos des Grecs*, René Guénon, *Le Roi du Monde*, Gallimard, 1981, p. 13); the same Menes built the famous temple of Ptah, *Hewet Ka-Ptah* ("He [Menes] founded in it that city which is now called Memphis... Then secondly he [Menes] established in the city the temple of Hephaistos [Ptah] a great work and most worthy to mention," Herodotus, *The Histories*, II, 99). It is said, in the Egyptian tradition, that Ptah produced the World, first in his heart, then opening his mouth and uttering the word ("the primordial sound" of the Hindu tradition and the Word of St. John) (it is also said that Horus is a manifestation of Ptah's heart and Thoth of his tongue). Ptah "gave birth to the gods, He made the towns, He established the nomes, He placed the gods in their shrines, He settled their offerings"; Ptah, as a Great Architect of the Universe, who made the World, was the sovereign god of stonecutters, sculptors, blacksmiths, architects, boat builders, and other artisans; his high priest at Memphis was then called *wer kherep hemw*, "Greatest of the Controllers of Craftsmen."

Measure of All Things." Yet this "man" to truly be the "measure" of everything must be equivalent to Ptah, the Great Architect who "crafted" everything, and moreover, he must be the Universal Man, who is the measure of manifestation ("the things that are") and of non-manifestation ("the things that are not"); in this sense Guénon transposed Protagoras' sayings to the metaphysical level,[1] but he cautioned that, strictly speaking, *on ne puisse parler d'une "mesure" du non-manifesté, si l'on entend par là la détermination par des conditions spéciales d'existence, comme celles qui définissent chaque état de manifestation.*

Indeed, Guénon and Coomaraswamy specified that Infinity is the "non-measurable"[2] and what is "measured" represents what is

---

[1] *C'est seulement dans cet état d'universalisation, et non dans l'état individuel, que l'on pourrait dire véritablement que "l'homme est la mesure de toutes choses, de celles qui sont en tant qu'elles sont, et de celles qui ne sont pas en tant qu'elles ne sont pas," c'est-à-dire, métaphysiquement, du manifesté et du non-manifesté, bien que, en toute rigueur, on ne puisse parler d'une "mesure" du non-manifesté, si l'on entend par là la détermination par des conditions spéciales d'existence, comme celles qui définissent chaque état de manifestation. D'autre part, il va sans dire que le sophiste grec Protagoras, à qui l'on attribue la formule que nous venons de reproduire en transposant le sens pour l'appliquer à l'"Homme Universel," a été certainement très loin de s'élever jusqu'à cette conception, de sorte que, l'appliquant à l'être humain individuel, il n'entendait exprimer par là que ce que les modernes appelleraient un "relativisme" radical, alors que, pour nous, il s'agit évidemment de tout autre chose, comme le comprendront sans peine ceux qui savent quels sont les rapports de l'"Homme Universel" avec le Verbe Divin (cf.* notamment St Paul 1er Épître aux Corinthiens, XV) (L'Homme, 1991, pp. 133-134; *C'est l'"Homme Universel," symbolisé par cette croix, mais non l'homme individuel (celui-ci, en tant que tel, ne pouvant rien atteindre qui soit en dehors de son propre état d'être), qui est véritablement la "mesure de toutes choses," pour employer l'expression de Protagoras que nous avons déjà rappelée ailleurs, mais, bien entendu, sans attribuer au sophiste grec lui-même la moindre compréhension de cette interprétation métaphysique,* Le symbolisme de la croix, Guy Trédaniel / Ed. Véga, 1989, p. 99). See also *La Grande Triade* (Gallimard, 1980, p. 191): *dans la Grande Triade extrême-orientale, l'Homme est parfois assimilé au rayon de la "roue cosmique," dont le centre et la circonférence correspondent alors respectivement au Ciel et à la Terre. Comme le rayon émané du centre "mesure" le Cosmos ou le domaine de la manifestation, on voit encore par là que l'"homme veritable" est proprement la "mesure de toutes choses" en ce monde.*

[2] "The true measure of loving God is to love Him without measure" (Saint Bernard, *On the Love of God*, Mission Press, 1943, ch. 1, p. 4). Only God is "Measure without measure, Number without number, and Weight without weight... since God is not measured, numbered or ordered by any other principle, neither by Himself, and God knows that He is not limited by any measure, number, or order... because He only really exists in all the existents as Infinity that surpass all the existents" (Érigène, *De la division de la Nature*, Livre I et Livre II, PUF, 1995, p. 377). Johannes Scotus Eriugena's work helps to understand Guénon's writings.

"ordered," that is, the cosmos,[1] which explains why money for the traditional societies was a means to sustain the "order" and the "equilibrium." René Guénon stated that "equilibrium, harmony, justice, are three forms or aspects of the same thing,"[2] and the early relation between weight and money is an expression of the *true measure*, which is an image of the divine justice, not to say that the balance scale (called *Tulâ* in Sanskrit[3]) was, together with the sword, the symbol of justice.[4]

Ultimately, because everything in the world has reality only if it maintains its bond with the principles, from a traditional mentality perspective the axiom "thou hast ordered all things in measure and number and weight" (and implicitly money) is a reflection of the divine equilibrium, harmony and justice, which in the Hindu tradition were comprised in a concept, almost impossible to define, called Dharma,[5]

---

[1] Guénon, *Le règne*, pp. 42-43.
[2] *Ibid.*, p. 204.
[3] Guénon, *Le Roi*, p. 83. *Siphra Di-Tzeniutha* begins with: "Nous avons appris: le Livre du Secret est celui de l'équilibre de la Balance. Nous avons appris: avant qu'il n'y ait eu 'Balance,' la face n'était point tournée vers la face… Cette Balance a été suspendue en un lieu qui n'est pas [Nya]" (Paul Vulliaud, *Traduction intégrale du Siphra Di-Tzeniutha*, Michel Allard, 1977) (*The Zohar*, II, 177b-179a). This "place that does not exist" is the "non-location" of the Center, as Guénon explained when he corrected Pascal's formulation: *C'est le centre qui n'est proprement nulle part, puisque, comme nous l'avons dit, il est essentiellement "non-localisé"; il ne peut être trouvé en aucun lieu de la manifestation, étant absolument transcendant par rapport à celle-ci, tout en étant intérieur à toutes choses* (*Le symbolisme de la croix*, p. 150), and: *non seulement dans l'espace, mais dans tout ce qui est manifesté, c'est l'extérieur (ou la circonférence) qui est partout, tandis que le centre n'est nulle part, car il est non-manifesté (C'est "le lieu qui n'est pas" (Nya), dans lequel réside l'équilibre de la Balance, comme il est dit au commencement du* Siphra D'zénioutha*)* (*Le symbolisme de la croix*, published in *La Gnose*, 1911, signed Tau Palingénius).
[4] The *true measure* was what the ritual of the Hung society called "perfect accord" or "perfect measure": "By its aid we prove the Empire of the Qings [darkness] untrue, While it shows the Empire of Ming [light] to be in perfect accord" (Ward, *Hung Society*, I, p. 49). Guénon asked: *n'est-ce pas la "Citadelle solaire" des Rose-Croix qui doit "descendre du ciel en terre," à la fin du cycle, sous la forme de la "Jérusalem céleste," réalisant la "quadrature du cercle" selon* la mesure parfaite [our highlighting] *du "roseau d'or"*? (*Formes traditionnelles et cycles cosmiques*, Gallimard, 1980, p. 137).
[5] The notion of *dharma* is fundamental for the normal functioning of the world, in fact, for the universal manifestation with everything this one comprises. René Guénon explained: *car toutes les applications du* dharma *se rapportent toujours au monde*

that in many ways corresponded, in ancient Greece, to Themis, and, in ancient Egypt, to Maat.[1]

---

manifesté... Âtmâ *est non-manifesté, donc immuable; et* dharma *en est une expression, si l'on veut, en ce sens qu'il reflète l'immutabilité principielle dans l'ordre de la manifestation* (Études sur l'Hindouisme, Editions Traditionnelles, 1979, p. 70); *Comme le montre le sens de la racine verbale* dhri *dont il est dérivé, ce mot, dans sa signification la plus générale, ne désigne rien d'autre qu'une "manière d'être"; c'est, si l'on veut, la nature essentielle d'un être, comprenant tout l'ensemble de ses qualités ou propriétés caractéristiques, et déterminant, par les tendances ou les dispositions qu'elle implique, la façon dont cet être se comporte, soit en totalité, soit par rapport à chaque circonstance particulière. La même notion peut être appliquée, non pas seulement à un être unique, mais à une collectivité organisée, à une espèce, à tout l'ensemble des êtres d'un cycle cosmique ou d'un état d'existence, ou même à l'ordre total de l'Univers; c'est alors, à un degré où à un autre, la conformité à la nature essentielle des êtres, réalisée dans la constitution hiérarchiquement ordonnée de leur ensemble; c'est aussi, par conséquent,* l'équilibre fondamental, l'harmonie intégrale [our highlighting] *résultant de cette hiérarchisation, à quoi se réduit d'ailleurs la notion même de justice quand on la dépouille de son caractère spécifiquement moral... Le sens de la "loi" étant ainsi précisé, et d'ailleurs dégagé de toutes les applications particulières et dérivées auxquelles il peut donner lieu, nous pouvons accepter ce mot de "loi" pour traduire* dharma, *d'une façon encore imparfaite sans doute, mais moins inexacte que les autres termes empruntés aux langues occidentales; seulement, encore une fois, ce n'est nullement de loi morale qu'il s'agit, et les notions mêmes de loi scientifique et de loi sociale ou juridique ne se réfèrent ici qu'à des cas spéciaux* (Introduction générale a l'étude des doctrines hindoues, Guy Trédaniel, 1987, pp. 186-188).

[1] "He [Zeus] married bright Themis [Divine Law and Order] who bare the Horae (Hours) [Cycles, Seasons], and Eunomia (Order), Dike (Justice), and blooming Eirene (Peace), who mind the works of mortal men, and the Moerae (Fates) to whom wise Zeus gave the greatest honour, Clotho, and Lachesis, and Atropos who give mortal men evil and good to have [as Guénon said: *mais celui-ci [le mythe des Parques] semble bien ne se rapporter qu'aux fils de la trame, et son caractère "fatal" peut en effet s'expliquer par l'absence de la notion de la chaîne, c'est-à-dire par le fait que l'être est envisagé seulement dans son état individuel, sans aucune intervention consciente (pour cet individu) de son principe personnel transcendant,* Le symbolisme de la croix, p. 89]" (Hesiod, The Homeric Hymns and Homerica, William Heinemann Ltd, 1936, p. 145, Theogony, 900-905). We notice that Themis has the three traditional components (daughters): Order, Justice, and Peace, and we may add that Themis was associated to the Oracle of Delphi and even considered its mistress before Apollo. Moses Finley, despite his many errors, such as considering the mythological Greek Age to be "Dark Ages" and having an anthropological approach, honestly said that "Themis is untranslatable. A gift of the gods and a mark of civilized existence, sometimes it means right custom, proper procedure, social order, and sometimes merely the will of the gods (as revealed by an omen, for example) … There was themis – custom, tradition, folk-ways, mores, whatever we may call it, the enormous power of 'it is (or is not) done' [Guénon's explanations for *dharma* are valid for *themis* also]" (The World of Odysseus, Viking Press, 1978, pp. 78, 82). A similar author, Jane Harrison, said: "[Themis] is the substratum [as Guénon said, *dharma* derived from the root *dhri*, which signifies to

There is a noteworthy aspect of Maat, associated with Justice, when she represents *the true (just, correct) measure of weight*, balancing (as a small statue) the soul of the dead, and we see how the *true measure* of money could be an application of Justice. Guénon said: *si une idée comme celle de "justice" convient parfois pour rendre le sens de* dharma, *ce n'est qu'en tant qu'elle est une expression humaine de l'équilibre ou de l'harmonie, c'est-à-dire d'un des aspects du maintien de la stabilité cosmique.*[1] Hence, we can understand the "confusion" that covered the real meaning of the Greek goddesses Themis, Astraea, Dike, Tyche and Nemesis, who appeared to be equivalent or even interchangeable[2]; and, at least in one aspect, there is correspondence between Astraea (*Virgo*) holding the scale (*Libra*) and Maat, the Mistress of the scales.[3]

---

support, to sustain] of each and every god, she is in a sense above as well as below each and every god" (*Themis*, p. 485). The Egyptian Maat represented at the same time truth, balance, law, justice, and order (she brought order from chaos); she symbolized the natural way of manifestation, in accord with the divine principles (*Dao, dharma*). Maat's feather was used in weighing the "soul" of the dead. Similarly to *dharma*, Maat sustained the universal manifestation in all its aspects, providing the fundamental equilibrium of the universe, and governing as applications the human society, the ritual life, the cycle of the seasons, the heavenly and earthly influences; she was the supreme principle of universal harmony that brought together all the local injustices, disharmonies and unbalances.

[1] *Études sur l'Hindouisme*, p. 72. *Car il y a identité entre les notions de justice, d'ordre, d'équilibre, d'harmonie, ou, plus précisément, ce ne sont là que des aspects divers d'une seule et même chose, envisagée de façons différentes et multiples suivant les domaines auxquels elle s'applique (Tous ces sens, et aussi celui de "loi" sont compris dans ce que la doctrine hindoue désigne par le mot* dharma) (*Autorité spirituelle et pouvoir temporel*, Véga, 1976, p. 112).

[2] "On coin types the figures of Dike, Nemesis, Tyche, Adrasteia, are only distinguishable by the places at which they were minted" (Harrison, *Themis*, p. 528).

[3] Nemesis is the counterpart of Dike. Astraea, the daughter of Themis, abandoned the earth during the "Iron Age," and became, during the last attempt to bring back the traditional spirit, the Justice impersonated by the Virgin Queen Elizabeth of England. When Astraea abandoned the decayed mankind, she ascended to heaven and became the constellation *Virgo*, while the scales of justice she carried became the nearby constellation *Libra*. (see Frances A. Yates, *Astraea*, Penguin Books, 1977, pp. 10, 30, 64, 71); the Justice abandoning our world is in an unambiguous concert with the decay of the notion of money. Dante said: "Further, the world is disposed for the best when Justice reigns therein; wherefore, desiring to glorify that age which seemed to be dawning in his own day, Virgil sang in his *Bucolics*, 'Now doth the Virgin return and the kingdoms of Saturn.' For they called Justice the Virgin, and

The Virgin Queen Astraea is depicted in the Tarot cards with the sword and the scales, and we may notice that she corresponds to the eighth card,[1] alluding to the qualitative meaning of numbers, where 8 is the symbol of justice, but we should understand here justice as stability and harmony, as illustrated in various traditions, including the Christian one, where the octagonal churches of the Templars are well known[2]; for Dante, 8 is the Virgin's number.[3]

The idea of *true measure*, implying justice and balance, was at the basis of weighing out money. The words "to spend," "expense," "pound," likewise the French "dépenser," derived from Latin *expendere*, "to weigh out money,"[4] but if we want to truly understand *expendere* in a traditional society we should accept in addition to the evident quantitative aspect a qualitative one, which makes money more than

---

called her also Astraea. The kingdoms of Saturn meant those happiest times which men named the Golden Age. Justice is pre-eminent only under a Monarch; therefore, that the world may be disposed for the best, a Monarchy, or Empire is needed (Dante, *De Monarchia*, I. 11).

[1] Gérard Van Rijnberk, *Le Tarot*, Guy Trédaniel, 1981, pp. 125, 236.

[2] See our *Free-Masonry*, p. 145. We said there that the eight primary *guas* or trigrams of the Far-Eastern tradition were placed in an octagonal form. Guénon also described an Assyrian image of the sun with eight rays, and he related the number eight to the Christian symbolism of *Sol Justitiae*; it is interesting that the solar god situated near this image had in one hand "a disc and a rod, which are the conventional representations of the measuring ruler and the rod of justice," and Guénon recalled the relation between "measure" and the "solar rays" (*Symboles fondamentaux*, p. 362), which should be in addition connected to the importance of the right measurements. One of the main significances of the number 8, Guénon underscored, is that of "justice" and "equilibrium," directly attached to the idea of Center (*Écrits pour Regnabit*, Archè, 1999, p. 93). Agrippa said: "The Pythagoreans call eight the number of justice, and fullness: first, because it is first of all divided into numbers equally even [harmony]... Hence the custom of Orpheus, swearing by eight deities, if at any time he would beseech divine justice" (*Three Books of Occult Philosophy*, p. 281; Agrippa added: "the number eight, by reason it contains the mystery of justice, is ascribed to Jupiter," *ibid.* p. 315).

[3] See this sonnet that is considered referring to Dante: *O tu, Tu del ciel donna; Tu sai, Or mi soccorri*, where we observe the acrostic OTTO (P. Vinassa De Regny, *Dante e il simbolismo pitagorico*, Fratelli Melita Editori, Genova, 1990, p. 85). Saint Bernard said about justice: "Hence the Prophet, speaking to God who is eternal happiness, says: 'Justice and judgment are the foundation of your throne'" (*Sermon 27*).

[4] It comes from Latin *expendo*, "to balance carefully, to judge, to pay out."

just the money known by the modern mentality, and the concept of measure much more than the exclusive quantitative measurements used by the modern world to judge and characterize everything (so terribly illustrated by all those "isms").

Therefore, "a handful of grain"[1] is the *true measure* as weight, but implicitly it transmits an initiatory teaching and a spiritual influence, because in the "Golden Age" the grain had a spiritual meaning by itself, before an explication was needed[2]; also, "a handful of grain" suggested more than just quantity, being somehow a continuous quantity that implied a qualitative component.

Before we continue, we should accentuate as strong as possible an element that seems obvious, but which too often is forgotten or misused: we cannot expect to find perfection and paradisiacal life in our corporeal terrestrial world, but also we cannot be so arrogant as to think that our human condition is sufficient by itself and could exist without the support of a higher principle; consequently, our terrestrial existence cannot be purely quantitative, and even though the present cycle is fast approaching its conclusion, it will contain a qualitative aspect till the end, but, at the same time, we are forced to use the quantitative characteristic (which is inherent to our existence[3]) to

---

[1] "There shall be a handful of grain (corn) in the earth upon the top of the mountains" (*Psalms* 72:16).

[2] With the evolvement of the cycle, the "complication" became more and more "explication," and we witness the development of the so-called "tautological symbolism." The hart with a precious stone on his forehead is such a tautology, because the hart by itself symbolizes the spiritual Sun, and the precious stone is just an explication of this meaning; so is the representation of Apollo with ram's horns; and so on.

[3] For man, as a corporeal human being, it is impossible to disregard the quantitative aspect. Guénon had the same problem when he described prayer as a way to use a collective force (i.e. the "church" force, where the church should be understood as Greek *eklesia*, "the assembly of people," hence French *église*), *une force constituée par les apports de tous ses membres passés et présents, et qui, par conséquent, est d'autant plus considérable que la collectivité est plus ancienne et se compose d'un plus grand nombre de members* (*La prière et l'incantation*, published in *La Gnose*, January 1911, and signed Tau Palingénius); later on, Guénon realized the quantitative aspect involved and added: *il est d'ailleurs évident que cette considération "quantitative" indique essentiellement qu'il s'agit bien du domaine*

translate and transmit principial realities, and only then will we fully understand the divine command: "thou hast ordered all things in measure and number and weight."

René Guénon considered the concept of "measure" from a universal viewpoint, as found in various traditions, and also from a terrestrial one, as an application of the former, and in which case what is measured is the space, a continuous quantity, using discontinuous quantities, that is, the numbers, since, Guénon stressed, "the number is definitely the basis of any measurement."[1]

The numbers could be viewed from a "qualitative" perspective, and it is well known that the Pythagorean numbers, as principles of all things,[2] are purely qualitative, or from a "quantitative" angle, in conformity with Saint Thomas Aquinas' saying, *numerus stat ex parte materiae*, which suggests that the numbers are the substantial basis of the world and they should be considered as purely quantitative.[3]

Moreover, as Guénon said, it is not the "quantity"[4] that is measured, but, on the contrary, it is by means of "quantity" that all things are measured, and so "the measure with respect to number, in an inverse analogical sense, is what the manifestation with respect to its essential principle is"[5]; therefore, René Guénon placed the "quantity," that is, the number among the five "conditions of existence" defining our corporeal world.[6]

---

individuel, au delà duquel elle ne saurait plus aucunement intervenir (René Guénon, *Aperçus sur l'initiation*, Éditions Traditionnelles, 1992, pp. 166-167).

[1] Guénon, *Le règne*, p. 41.
[2] Guénon, *ibid.*, pp. 12, 26.
[3] Guénon, *ibid.*, pp. 26, 34.
[4] Here "quantity" refers to "substance," while "quality" to "essence," as the two poles of our state of existence.
[5] Guénon, *ibid.*, p. 41.
[6] He said about "quantity": *La quantité n'est en définitive, aussi bien d'ailleurs que l'espace et le temps, qu'une des conditions spéciales de l'existence corporelle* (*Le règne*, pp. 32, 42). Guénon previously wrote: "The number constitutes the true basis for what the modern physicists call 'matter,' and for what the scholastic philosophers called more accurate 'quantified matter'; we could then, using a language closer to the Occidental mode of expression, substitute matter with number in the list of the conditions of corporeal existence"; and Guénon continued: "For the moment we do not insist upon this

In an explicit and immediate sense, measure relates to spatial characteristics,[1] and therefore geometry is strongly related to measure, being, as Guénon called it, the "science of measurement,"[2] yet we have to consider here a "sacred geometry,"[3] where God is the Grand Architect of the Universe,[4] while Geometry is identical to Masonry (as underlined in the old manuscripts), and the Masonic tools are not any tools, but images of the divine tools, used to measure the *true measure*

---

subject; we intend, if the circumstances will permit, to consecrate a special study to it" (*Le nombre forme la base véritable de ce que les physiciens modernes appellent "matière," et que les philosophes scolastiques appelaient plus précisément "matière quantifiée"; on pourrait donc, si l'on voulait s'exprimer en un langage plus occidental, substituer la matière au nombre dans la liste des conditions de l'existence corporelle. Pour le moment nous n'insisterons pas davantage sur celles-ci; nous avons l'intention, si les circonstances nous le permettent, de consacrer à cette question toute une étude spéciale*) (René Guénon, *L'Homme et son devenir selon le Védânta*, Ed. Bossard, 1925, p. 246). Two observations: first, this quotation is from the chapter XXV, called *La délivrance selon les Jainas*, a chapter that later Guénon excluded from his book (our extract is from the first edition); second, here, in this excluded chapter, is the only place where Guénon listed together the five conditions of existence, that is, time, space, number, form, and life. It is true that he wrote, under the name of Palingénius, an article called *Les conditions de l'existence corporelle*, published in 1912 in *La Gnose*, where he listed the five conditions as: space, time, matter, form, and life (René Guénon, *Mélanges*, Gallimard, 1976, p. 112; see also his *Les néo-spiritualistes*, published in *La Gnose*, August to November 1911 and February 1912, signed Tau Palingénius: *L'existence des êtres individuels dans le monde physique est en effet soumise à un ensemble de cinq conditions : espace, temps, matière, forme et vie, que l'on peut faire correspondre aux cinq sens corporels, ainsi d'ailleurs qu'aux cinq éléments; cette question, très importante, sera traitée par nous avec tous les développements qu'elle comporte, au cours d'autres études*), but he never resumed this study under his real name, even though he promised many times to do so (in addition to what he said in the above excerpt, he announced it again and again; see *L'Homme*, 1991, p. 80, *Études sur l'Hindouisme*, p. 55, *Le symbolisme de la croix*, pp. 41, 75, 79, 95, *Les états multiples de l'être*, Guy Trédaniel / Ed. Véga, 1989, pp. 28, 65).

[1] See Guénon, *Le règne*, p. 40.
[2] In ancient Greek, *geo* means "earth," and *metria* "measurement." See Guénon, *ibid.*, pp. 45-47.
[3] Guénon, *ibid.*, p. 13 and the above footnote with the quotation from *Le règne*, p. 14, about the sacred geometry as a pure qualitative art, like the true science of numbers.
[4] "Who hath measured the waters in the hollow of his hand, and meted out heaven with the span, and comprehended the dust of the earth in a measure, and weighed the mountains in scales, and the hills in a balance?" (*Isaiah* 40:12).

and the sacred proportions, thus bringing order from chaos, and establishing balance and harmony.

Indeed, to bring order from chaos means to measure the possibilities of manifestation, i.e. to determine the worlds, which, with everything they contain, will be realized or "actualized," the process of measurement appearing, *principially*, identical to that of manifestation.[1] To measure in the sense of "to determine" comes from the Latin *determine*, which derives from *termino*, meaning "to limit, to restrict", while *determinatio* means "border, limit," and of course the process of manifestation or of measurement means a limitation of Infinity.[2]

However, besides the explicit sense of measuring the space, and besides this metaphysical sense of the measure, there are other related meanings that highlight the ideas of justice and balance, since it is one thing to measure the possibilities of manifestation and organize and put the actualized possibilities in order, and another to regulate them after the actualization, to keep them in quest for balance and harmony, to sustain the tendency toward harmony and balance through compensation.[3] This is the invisible activity of the Center, where the

---

[1] Guénon, *ibid.*, pp. 39, 42. Moreover, this "measurement" is associated to the law of the "concordant actions and reactions," as Guénon explained when he mentioned the symbolism of the celestial and terrestrial numbers: the numbers 2 and 3 represent the Earth and Heaven in themselves, while 5 and 6 are the Earth and Heaven in their reciprocated action and reaction that produce the very universal manifestation; therefore, 5 and 6 are the "measures" of Earth and Heaven (since they are not measurable in themselves, and only their determinations, i.e. the celestial and terrestrial influences, are subject to measurements), which explains why the earthly forms, which are linear, are measured by multiples of 5, whereas the celestial forms, which are circular, are measured by multiples of 6 (*La Grande Triade*, pp. 77-80). Consequently, the three combinations used in Masonry to associate the square and the compass in the center of the Lodge illustrate, among other things, these measurements and the law of the concordant actions and reactions. We should also mention that, at the beginning, there was a duodecimal currency system.

[2] We add the Latin *meto*, "to measure, to decide." Any decision is a limitation, a determination.

[3] "As a whole, the equilibrium is composed of the sum of all the unbalanced parts, and each partial disorder concurs, willy-nilly, to a perfect order" (Guénon, *Études sur l'hindouisme*, p. 15). Johannes Scotus Eriugena explained that, even though the subdivisions, when they are observed separately, are in opposition to each other,

balance scale stands, marking the Invariable Middle (*Zhong Yong* of the Far-Eastern tradition), and in this context we should understand the Latin words *mediocris* and *moderatus*, which, with the reign of the modern mentality, lost their real significance, but which initially referred to the idea of "regulation"[1] and also meant "keep within due measure." The Latin *mediocris* comes from *medius*, "middle," related to Sanskrit *madhya* and German *mitte*, where *medius* means also "neutral, balanced, measured," while *moderatus* is related to *modus*, "measure," "rhythm."[2] In Romanian, for "moderate, measured, balanced" is used the word *cumpătat*, considered a derivation of Latin **compitare*, where *puto* means not only "to prune, to cleanse" but also "to think, to consider, to judge" and "to count, to reckon."[3]

The concept of measure, because of its relation with balance, middle, justice, and harmony, is strongly associated with the "law of compensation": "For with what judgment ye judge, ye shall be judged: and with what measure ye mete, it shall be measured to you again,"[4]

---

they participate in the universal harmony (Érigène, *De la division de la Nature, Periphyseon*, Livre III, PUF, 1995, p. 97).

[1] The word is related etymologically to *rex*, king, who obviously "regulated" the kingdom.

[2] It seems that from the same root *med*, "to measure, to limit, to advise" derived *medicus* ("physician") and "to meditate."

[3] Because of these meanings, it is possible that the Latin words *mens* ("mind, to judge, to meditate"), *mensis* ("month"), and *mensura* ("measure") derive from the same root (see Guénon, *Écrits*, p. 140). The idea of *moderatus* (balanced, measured) could be found in John Cassian the Roman's *Conferences*, where he writes about the "right measure" and also about the "wise discretion" ("discretion" understood in its etymological sense, as "right judgment," "discrimination" like the Hindu *viveka*, and "right, balanced measure").

[4] *Matthew* 7:2. We must not consider here a moral viewpoint of any sort, but just an application of the *principe de l'égalité de l'action et de la réaction. Un exemple du second cas est ce qu'on appelle le "principe de l'égalité de l'action et de la réaction," qui est si peu un "principe" qu'il se déduit immédiatement de la loi générale de l'équilibre des forces naturelles: chaque fois que cet équilibre est rompu d'une façon quelconque, il tend aussitôt à se rétablir, d'où une réaction dont l'intensité est équivalente à celle de l'action qui l'a provoquée; ce n'est donc là qu'un simple cas particulier des "actions et réactions concordantes," qui ne concernent point le seul monde corporel, mais bien l'ensemble de la manifestation sous tous ses modes et dans tous ses états* (Guénon, *Melanges*, p. 98; *Les Principes du Calcul infinitésimal*, ch. XVII).

which is echoed in Shakespeare's *Measure for Measure*[1]; yet it is important to observe that, as expected, Shakespeare's play has a secret meaning that, even though it led the profane mind to consider *Measure for Measure* to be one of Shakespeare's three "problem plays," could shed light on comprehending the initiatory symbolism of "vengeance" in the Masonic ritual. Let us not forget that the Evangelic words we just quoted have on top the command: "Judge not, that ye be not judged,"[2] which is not opposing the "law of compensation," but covertly suggests the final goal, that is, the Center, the Balance, and the Peace, where there are no oppositions and to where one arrives by renouncing the fruits of any action.[3] In Shakespeare's case, "measure for measure" is applied on a mundane level, but eventually we see a pacification corresponding to the paradisiacal and "hypermetrical" level,[4] with the Shakespearean weddings very similar in meaning to the one from the Hindu tradition.[5]

The significance of "measure for measure" is immeasurable though, since it could be applied to innumerable levels; for example, the command "Judge not, that ye be not judged" does not contradict the

---

[1] "The very mercy of the law cries out/ Most audible, even from his proper tongue,/ 'An Angelo for Claudio, death for death!'/ Haste still pays haste, and leisure answers leisure;/ Like doth quit like, and Measure still for Measure./ Then, Angelo, thy fault's thus manifested;/ Which, though thou wouldst deny, denies thee vantage./ We do condemn thee to the very block/ Where Claudio stoop'd to death, and with like haste./ Away with him!" (5. 1. 415-424).
[2] *Matthew* 7:1.
[3] "Renunciation and Yoga through action both lead to the highest bliss: but, of the two, Yoga through action is superior to renunciation of action. He should be known as a perpetual renouncer, who has no aversion and no desire. For, O you of mighty arms! he who is free from the pairs of opposites is easily released from (all) bonds" (*Bhagavad-Gîtâ*, V, 2-3).
[4] This is what makes this play a "problem play."
[5] "The holy marriage, the synthesis (*samadhi*) of the conjoint principles, immortal and mortal 'selves' implied in CU. VII. 25. 2 is even more poignantly described in BU. IV. 3. 21: 'That is his hypermetrical form'" (Ananda K. Coomaraswamy, *Spiritual Authority and Temporal Power in the Indian Theory of Government*, Munshiram Manoharlal, 1978, p. 83).

concept of the Last Judgment, where the "measure for measure"'s connection to "justice" finds its finest illustration.[1]

There is no coincidence that in various traditions this Last Judgment implies a balance scale weighing the souls and the deeds[2];

---

[1] Indeed, the real and righteous Judgment is of divine nature and identical to the Center, and thus, in the world, it is only a "tendency" to pacify all disharmonies. Therefore, Christ said: "Ye judge after the flesh [that is, the mundane judgment; "Judge not according to the appearance [flesh], but judge righteous judgment" (*John* 7:24)]; *I judge no man* [our Italics]. And yet if I judge, my judgment is true: for I am not alone, but I and the Father that sent me" (*John* 8:15-16). And consequently: "He that is without sin among you, let him first cast a stone at her" (*John* 8:7). "Then saith he unto them, Render therefore unto Caesar the things which are Caesar's [i.e. money in a traditional sense]; and unto God the things that are God's" (*Matthew* 22:21). See also "Whosoever therefore shall confess me before men, him will I confess also before my Father which is in heaven. But whosoever shall deny me before men, him will I also deny before my Father which is in heaven" (*Matthew* 10:32-3).

[2] "And he [the Elect One] shall judge all the works of the holy above in the heaven, And in the balance shall their deeds be weighed" (*The Book of Enoch*, tr. R. H. Charles, Kessinger Publishing, p. 120); and before this: "these shall bring the measures of the righteous, And the ropes [used by the angels to measure] of the righteous to the righteous" (*ibid.*, p. 119). In one of the Hung society's rituals, the candidate's soul is weighed too; also it is said: "This Pair of Scales represents Justice and enables us to weigh the Qing against the Ming, to detect the false from the true" (*Hung Society*, I, pp. 78-9, 167) [the author said: "The Triad scales are most ingenious, and fit into a kind of double wooden spoon"; a very similar type could be found in India, with a wooden case]. One of the fundamental elements of any initiation is to open the eye of the heart to discriminate between true and false (in the Christian tradition, this is the hidden meaning of Juda's kiss). We can see the weighing of the souls on the façade of the 12th Century cathedral St. Trophime of Arles (photo MAT; see also *Hung Society*, III, p. 20):

and that the soul has to pay coins to pass the barriers in the "other world." The weighing of the souls and of the deeds implies a payment, as "measure for measure," and there is indeed equivalence between payment and measurement[1]; also, since the posthumous journey of the soul is a replica of the initiatory voyage, the payment, for passing through various barriers, is the echo of an initiatory gesture: as White Arab pays a coin to Saint Sunday so the neophyte pays an obol to Demeter, both in the *Lesser* and the *Greater Mysteries* of Eleusis, and this payment primarily had a sacred and operative significance, related to the holy exchange and to the authentic role of the password.[2]

The scale is also present in the church of St. Cajetan, Goa (left) and in the Speyer Cathedral (right) (photos MAT):

[1] "Your iniquities, and the iniquities of your fathers together, saith the Lord, which have burned incense upon the mountains, and blasphemed me upon the hills: therefore *will I measure* their former work into their bosom" (or "Because they burned sacrifices on the mountains and defied me on the hills, *I will measure* into their laps the full *payment* for their former deeds") (*Isaiah* 65:7). "Woe to the wicked! Disaster is upon them! They *will be paid* back for what their hands have done" (*Isaiah* 3:11); "Give, and it will be given to you. A *good measure*, pressed down, shaken together and running over, will be poured into your lap. For with *the measure* you use, it *will be measured* to you" (*Luke* 6:38); "For the *wages* of sin is death" (*Romans* 6:23) [our *Italic*]. In a Romanian fairy tale (*The Story of White Arab*), the hero, just before he faces the initiatory trials, is visited by *Shekinah*, the "divine presence," represented by Saint Sunday (dressed as an old woman) and he gives her a coin, saying: "Take this, old woman; a small gift from me, but may God send you many good things" (*Folk Tales from Roumania*, Routledge and Kegan Paul, 1952, p. 5); the same Saint Sunday teaches the hero: "there is no action [deed, act] without payment" (*pentru că nu-i nici o faptă fără plată*) (*ibid.*, p. 28).
[2] George E. Mylonas, *Eleusis*, Princeton Univ. Press, 1974, p. 231. Also "the initiate had to pay a fee to the various functionaries for their services, and apparently the

entire expense for initiation amounted to fifteen drachmai. Thus we find that the Hierophant received from each initiate an obol per day (both for Lesser and Greater Mysteries), the Priestess of Demeter likewise received an obol per day, the Hierokeryx, as well as the Priest at the altar, the priestesses and the Phaethyntes hald an obol per day from each initiate. In the amount is included the price for a pig that served to purify the worshiper" (*ibid.*, pp. 237-238). We notice the sacrifice of the pig (Demeter's token); before he could be initiated, each mystai had to sacrifice a pig, after it was washed in sea water: it was a purification rite, where the mystai was identified with the sacrificed animal (*ibid.*, p. 149; Carl Kerényi, *Eleusis*, Princeton Univ. Press, 1991, pp. 55-56). The initiatory secret teaching, compressed in the image of the pig, was transmitted later through the money exchange: "when Eleusis was permitted (BC 350-327) to issue her autonomous coinage it is the pig that she chooses as the sign and symbol of her mysteries" (Jane Ellen Harrison, *Prolegomena to the Study of Greek Religion*, Princeton Univ. Press, 1991, p. 153). This rite (the sacrifice of the pig) was later related to Christmas in some countries. We should also mention the role of the coin and the importance of payment in the initiatory rituals of the operative Masonry.

CHAPTER XIII

MONEY MORE THAN MONEY

The *Eleusian Mysteries* are based on a sacred tale or myth, well known to the Western scholars, researchers, literators, and, of course, occultists, who analysed it as much as they could, from profane, historical, quasi-religious, and pseudo-esoteric angles; however, for the present work, we would like to underline one adjacent element of this sacred tale: its connection with Hermes.

Hermes is an interminable esoteric subject, given that Hermeticism played a major role in the consolidation of the medieval traditional spirit. With respect to the *Eleusian Mysteries*, let us recall that actually Hermes, and not Demeter, was the one who descended into Hades' kingdom, negotiated Persephone's homecoming, and brought her back to her mother.[1] There is another aspect that pair Hermes to

---

[1] This represents the *libretto* of an initiation ("descent" – "search" – "ascent"). See Homer's *Hymn to Demeter*: "He [Zeus] sent the Slayer of Argus [Ἀργειφόντης, *Argeiphontes*, one of Hermes' epithets] whose wand is of gold to Erebus, so that having won over Hades with soft words, he might lead forth chaste Persephone to the light from the misty gloom to join the gods" (Hesiod, *The Homeric Hymns and Homerica*, William Heinemann Ltd., 1936, p. 313); and Ovid (*Fasti* 4. 417 ff): "The winged Herald [Hermes] visits Tartarus as ordered [by Zeus to recover Persephone], returns quicker than hope, tells what he witnessed." Zeus, thereafter, appointed Hermes as the Guide of Dead Souls (hence, the name Hermes *Psychopompos*), who became not only the "driver of the herds" but also the "driver of the souls." We should add that Pythagoras, it is said, considered himself the son of Hermes, in connection with the doctrine of *metempsychosis* (and, "Hermes is the steward of souls, and for that reason is called Hermes the Escorter, Hermes the Keeper of the Gate [!], and Hermes of the Underworld"; see Diogenes Laertius, *Lives of Eminent*

Demeter: Hermes illustrates the nomad people, with their pastoral activities,[1] while Demeter indicates the sedentary people, with their agricultural occupations,[2] and we return to Guénon's sayings in this respect: *L'équilibre, de part et d'autre, est donc rompu; comment le rétablir, sinon par des échanges tels que chacun ait sa part des productions de l'autre?*[3]

Nonetheless, the sacred science of symbols teaches us that even though any symbol has a consort (either opponent or complement), the symbol contains in itself these two aspects, and Hermes is no exception to this rule, as his insignia, the caduceus (*kerykeion*) entwined by two serpents, attests, to say nothing of his representation with the staff and the purse, which suggests that Hermes is closely related to the idea of equilibrium and balance, achieved through "exchange."[4] The Minor Arcana cards, as we already mentioned, have as attributes the baton, the chalice (cup), the sword and the coin (denier), where the coin replaces the balance scale; we found in Suidas: "They say he [Hermes] was responsible for profit and an overseer of the businesses:

Philosophers, Harvard, 2000, II, pp. 323, 347). In Masonry, the Cooke Manuscript (the oldest one, next to Regius) says: "And this flood was called Noah's flood, for he, and his children, were saved there-in. And after this flood many years, as the chronicle telleth, these 2 pillars were found, and as the *Pilicronicon* saith, that a great clerk that [was] called Pythagoras found that one, and Hermes, the philosopher, found that other, and they taught forth the sciences that they found therein written."

[1] Hermes invented the tools of shepherds and herders, and also the shepherd's lyre (made from a tortoise-shell), the shepherd's pipes, and pastoral poetry and fable (music and poetry were part of the nomad characteristics; see Guénon, *Le règne de la quantité et les signes des temps*, Gallimard, 1970, p. 201). We make a note that, after Herodotus, Hermes was of Thracian origins: "They [the Thracians] worship no gods but Ares, Dionysos, and Artemis [the Thracian gods Ares, Sabazios and Bendis]. Their princes, however, unlike the rest of their countrymen, worship Hermes [probably the Thracian god Zalmoxis] above all gods and swear only by him, claiming him for their ancestor" (Herodotus, *Histories*, 5.7).

[2] Demeter taught Triptolemus the art of agriculture and, from him, the rest of Greece learned to plant and harvest crops.

[3] Guénon, *Le règne*, p. 203.

[4] In the Greek mythology, Hermes supervises the exchanges (but not only the ones regarding trade and commerce, as it is usually assumed); he is the god of merchants, weights and measures, and the inventor of the sacrifices.

consequently they set up the statue of him weighing a purse," a purse supposedly full of money. There is no doubt that Hermes with the staff (symbol of the Masculine Pole, *Purusha*) and the purse (symbol of the Feminine Pole, *Prakriti*) unites the two serpents, that is, the two influences, of Heaven and of Earth, the same way the spiritual authority unites them (the staff and the chalice).[1] In the Roman Empire, this image of Hermes (Mercury) with the staff and the purse appears on coins, as shown on an "antoninianus" of Gallienus[2]:

---

[1] We may add the black-and-white *moly*, a divine plant with black roots and a milky flower, which Hermes gave to Ulysses (*Odyssey* X.275-306).

[2] The "antoninianus" also tells us the story of the decadence of the Empire: it was made initially from silver to equal two *denarii*, but from the beginning the weight was lower than the *true measure*, and later it was debased to bronze (and later to copper – the "barbarous radiate"); also, the coin, introduced by Caracalla, usually featured the emperor as god ("Shew me the tribute money. And they brought unto him a penny. And he saith unto them, Whose is this image and superscription? They say unto him, Caesar's. Then saith he unto them, Render therefore unto Caesar the things which are Caesar's; and unto God the things that are God's," *Matthew* 22:19-21). Ironically, the "antoninianus" of the emperors Philip I the Arab and Claudius II Gothicus has on its reverse the "Aequitas" (Justice and Equity), represented as a woman with a balance scale, which was supposed to symbolize first the *true measure* and then justice:

Regardless of what we think today, this representation of Hermes minted on the "antoninianus" was far more spiritual than mercantile (despite the decadence of the Roman Empire), and therefore the purse was more than just a purse with money,[1] just like money wase more than just money in a traditional world.

Hermes, with his winged hat (*petasos*), cloak, winged boots, staff and pouch, is also a paradigmatic traveller, and, in a way, the medieval pilgrim, with his cloak, broad hat, staff, shell and pouch, is a replica of Hermes:

Hermes also had a shell as attribute, but a tortoise shell that became the first lyre[2]; the scallop shell as an attribute of the pilgrimage to Compostela, like the tortoise shell, must be traced to the Primordial Tradition's symbols, to which is connected Shiva's matted hair (like a

---

[1] We can trace the symbolic purse to some fairy tales.
[2] The tortoise shell, together with the dolphin (for dolphin's symbolism, see René Guénon, *Symboles fondamentaux de la Science sacrée*, Gallimard, 1980, pp. 170, 174, 359), can be seen on ancient Greek coins, such as on this one from Aegina (500 BC):

cowrie-shell, *kaparda*), Vishnu's conch (*shankha*), and Aphrodite's scallop shell.¹

Indeed, very likely the shell is one of the primordial symbols, which explains why cowries were found in prehistoric settlements and, above all, why they, like the *swastika*, were spread all over the world.² The shell (and the conch) essentially symbolizes the Principle, not so much as Itself, but as Universal Possibility, that is, as Origin of the universal manifestation,³ and, because this implies "birth,"⁴ the shell illustrates, from a microcosmic viewpoint, the idea of initiatory "rebirth."⁵ As we

---

¹ Obviously, the grooves in the shell, which converge to a single point, represent the various initiatory routes or the *principial* rays, and, as an application, the various ways of the pilgrims, eventually arriving at a single destination: the tomb of St. James in Santiago de Compostela.

² See, for example, Mircea Eliade, *Images and Symbols*, Princeton Univ. Press, 1991, chapter IV (first published in *Zalmoxis*, in 1938), *Observations on the Symbolism of Shells*. "Cro-Magnon man, for his part, has left us more than three hundred shells of *Littorina littorea*, which are perforated [our underlining]. Elsewhere, a female skeleton covered with shells has been found near the skeleton of a man wearing ornaments and a crown made of perforated shells [we should mention that a "legend" says that St. James of Compostela arrived from the sea covered in scallops]. This caused Mainage to wonder: 'Why was the skeleton of Laugerie Basse (Dordogne) wearing a necklace of Mediterranean shells, and the Cro-Magnon skeleton an ornament built up of ocean shells? Why have the excavations at Grimaldi (on the Côte d'Azur) yielded shells collected on the shores of the Atlantic? And how is it that, at Pont-à-Lesse in Belgium, they have found tertiary shells gathered in the vicinity of Rheims?'" (p. 137); evidently, what we have here is the sacred "exchange." Let us note that Eliade talks about the "magic powers" of the shell, but, of course, Evola's and Eliade's obsession with "magic" is just an expression of their limited comprehension capabilities.

³ It is well known that the Waters (to which the shell is directly related) represent the Universal Possibility.

⁴ "By a curious parallel, this sense of 'matrix' (the Sanskrit *yoni*) is also implied in the Greek word *delphus*, which is at the same time the name of the dolphin" (Guénon, *Symboles fondamentaux*, p. 174).

⁵ Hereof, Guénon mentioned: *dans la confusion qui, partie de l'Occident, gagne présentement l'Orient, nous pourrions voir le "commencement de la fin," le signe précurseur du moment où,*

previously said, the exoteric rites (concerning birth, death, wedding, etc.) are outer replicas of the initiatory rites, all zeroing in on "rebirth," which explains why the shells were involved with all these rites,[1] but also why the cowries were used since the "prehistorical" times, and everywhere, as "money."[2]

Even in modern times, in places invaded by the Western way of life, it is possible to find traces of the sacred symbolism "concealed in the shell": in Namibia, *himba* women sell ornaments[3] made of tree bark and shells[4]; in Saintes-Maries-de-la-Mer,[5] there is inside the church (where the relics of the Saintes Maries are) a special stone, called *oreiller des Saintes Maries* ("the Saintes Maries' pillow"), which has the form

---

suivant la tradition hindoue, la doctrine sacrée doit être enfermée tout entière dans une conque, pour en sortir intacte à l'aube du monde nouveau (*La Crise du monde moderne*, Gallimard, 1975, p. 156); *Pendant le cataclysme qui sépare ce* Manvantara *du précédent, le* Vêda *était renfermé à l'état d'enveloppement dans la conque* (shankha), *qui est un des principaux attributs de* Vishnu. *C'est que la conque est regardée comme contenant le son primordial et impérissable* (akshara), *c'est-à-dire le monosyllabe* Om, *qui est par excellence le nom du Verbe, en même temps qu'il est, par ses trois éléments (A U M), l'essence du triple* Vêda (*Écrits pour Regnabit*, Archè, 1999, p. 147); … *la conque* (shankha), *qui est évidemment en relation directe avec les Eaux, et qui est également représentée comme contenant les germes du cycle futur pendant les périodes de* pralaya *ou de "dissolution extérieure" du monde* (*Symboles fondamentaux*, p. 154). Let us add that the young cowrie shows a spire, another primordial symbol.

[1] See Eliade, *ibid.*, pp. 132, 134, 144.

[2] John Wilfrid Jackons, who studied conchology all his life, wrote in 1916 a paper called "The Money-Cowry (*Cypraea Moneta*, L.) as a sacred object among the American Indians." The word "porcelain" comes from Italian *porcellana*, the name for the cowrie-shell (Latin *porcellus* means "young pig").

[3] For the traditional spirit, any "ornament" was a symbol with spiritual significance, and only when this spirit disappeared it became just "decoration."

[4] Photo MAT:

[5] See our *The Wrath of Gods*, 2011, p. 278.

(and, evidently, the sacred significance) of the cowrie-shell (see below, fig. right[1]).

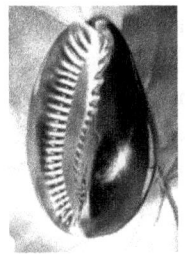 

The shells of cowries were used as sacred objects and money in India, China, America,[2] Europe and Africa[3]; the ancient Chinese character for money, *bèi*, represented a cowrie-shell:

[4]

---

[1] Photo MAT (on the left, the "front" of a cowrie). We should recall that the Saintes Maries came from the sea, a gesture repeated each year, even in our days.
[2] Whiteshell Provincial Park in Manitoba, Canada, is named after the cowrie-shell. In the Inca Empire the shells were, together with the textiles, sacred ingredients of the traditional life.
[3] As René Guénon observed: *L'identité primitive du symbolisme s'explique d'elle-même par l'universalité des idées exprimées*, and he gave as example the money to show that, even though universal, a symbol differed from one people to another by various details (*mais, quand il s'agit de symboles d'un caractère plus particulier et de certaines précisions de détails, il faut faire intervenir des relations ayant existé entre les peuples anciens d'une façon beaucoup plus générale qu'on ne le croit ordinairement – ex. similitude des monnaies chez un grand nombre de peuples, avec des différences spéciales caractéristiques de chaque peuple*).
[4] Léon Wieger, *Caractères chinois*, Kuangchi Cultural Group, pp. 328 (numéro 161), 909. See cowries below (photo MAT):

In time, the actual shell was replaced by copies made of wood, bone, stone and eventually metals, especially bronze, which became the common currency in China (the "bronze shell"). The use of metals implied two things: complying with the *true measure* and the explicit description of the initial symbol. If the cowrie-shell by itself transmitted a spiritual message, the metal shells and coins, with the descent of the cycle, had to carry the symbolism in a more explicit manner, engraved on the surface of the metal, which obviously meant that the "ornamentation" of the coins was not a result of individual initiatives and tastes, but obeyed sacred laws, originally preserved by the spiritual authority; furthermore, to stress the qualitative aspect, metal money was initially not coins to be counted (quantitatively), but weighed metals, maintaining the *true measure*,[1] which implied not discrete but, in a way, continuous quantity.[2] René Guénon flawlessly epitomized:

> In the traditional civilizations, the intervention of the spiritual authority with reference to money can be immediately linked to what we just talked about; money itself, indeed, is somehow the very representation of the exchange, and as a result one can understand, in a more accurate way, the actual role of the symbols the money carried and which circulated with it, thus giving the exchange a completely different meaning than the one representing just the "materiality" and which is all that is left in the secular conditions

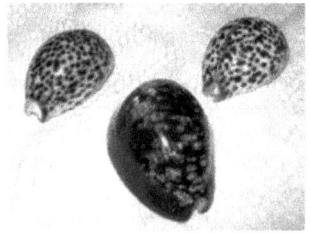

---

[1] This *true measure* included not only the true weight, but also the purity of the metal used. The periods of spiritual decadence were illustrated by debasing this purity.
[2] The ancient coin *stater*, for example, literally means "balancer" or "weigher."

that rule, in the modern world, the relationships between peoples as well as individuals.[1]

Just like the cowrie-shell, cattle and grains were primordial "money," allowing the compensatory "exchange" between the sedentary and nomad people, but also between traditional people in general: *L'équilibre, de part et d'autre, est donc rompu; comment le rétablir, sinon par des échanges tels que chacun ait sa part des productions de l'autre?* Both cattle and grains carried, like the cowrie-shell, a spiritual meaning by themselves, as "complication," seeing that Sri Aurobindo identified cattle with the flow of spiritual light,[2] while the grain played a major role in the ancient initiatory *Mysteries*.[3]

---

[1] *L'intervention de l'autorité spirituelle en ce qui concerne la monnaie, dans les civilisations traditionnelles, se rattache immédiatement à ce dont nous venons de parler ici; la monnaie elle-même, en effet, est en quelque sorte la représentation même de l'échange, et l'on peut comprendre par là, d'une façon plus précise, quel était le rôle effectif des symboles qu'elle portait et qui circulaient ainsi avec elle, donnant à l'échange une signification tout autre que ce qui n'en constitue que la simple "matérialité" et qui est tout ce qu'il en reste dans les conditions profanes qui régissent, dans le monde moderne, les relations des peuples comme celles des individus* (Guénon, *Le règne*, p. 204).

[2] This perspective helps us beteter decipher the myth about Hermes stealing Apollo's cattle.

[3] With regard to the symbolism of the grain, René Guénon wrote a key text: *Dans l'état présent de notre monde, la terre ne peut pas produire une plante d'elle-même et spontanément, et sans qu'on y ait déposé une graine qui doit nécessairement provenir d'une autre plante préexistante (Signalons, sans pouvoir y insister présentement, que ceci n'est pas sans rapport avec le symbolisme du grain de blé dans les mystères d'Éleusis, non plus que, dans la Maçonnerie, avec le mot de passe du grade de Compagnon* [the Hebrew word *shibbolet* literally means the part of a plant containing grains, such as an ear of corn or a stalk of grain; we may add the Masonic "sheaf of corn"]; *l'application initiatique est d'ailleurs évidemment en relation étroite avec l'idée de "postérité spirituelle." – Il n'est peut-être pas sans intérêt de noter aussi, à ce propos, que le mot "néophyte" signifie littéralement "nouvelle plante"); il a pourtant bien fallu qu'il en ait été ainsi en un certain temps, sans quoi rien n'aurait jamais pu commencer, mais cette possibilité n'est plus de celles qui sont susceptibles de se manifester actuellement. Dans les conditions où nous sommes en fait, on ne peut rien récolter sans avoir semé tout d'abord, et cela est tout aussi vrai spirituellement que matériellement; or le germe qui doit être déposé dans l'être pour rendre possible son développement spirituel ultérieur, c'est précisément l'influence qui, dans un état de virtualité et d'"enveloppement" exactement comparable à celui de la graine (Ce n'est pas que l'influence spirituelle, en elle-même, puisse jamais être dans un état de potentialité, mais le néophyte la reçoit en quelque sorte d'une manière proportionnée à son propre état), lui est communiquée par l'initiation (Nous pourrions même ajouter que, en raison de la correspondance qui existe entre l'ordre cosmique et l'ordre humain, il peut y avoir entre les deux termes de la comparaison que nous*

The evolvement of the cycle inexorable brought the decline of money, from cowrie-shell, cattle and grains[1] to metallic coins, where these illustrated the fall of the Ages, from golden to silver, bronze and finally iron coins.[2] In concurrence with the fall from the sacred reality to profane viewpoint, the symbolism waned and diluted from intrinsic (the cowrie-shell itself) to extrinsic images, which declined from fundamental symbols (like the *swastika*, or the cross, or even an animal figure) to anthropomorphic effigies well developed by the ancient Greeks[3] and then by the Romans (with their emperors represented as "gods")[4]; in the end, money lost everything sacred together with its function as "support" for spiritual influence.

---

venons d'indiquer, non pas une simple similitude, mais une relation beaucoup plus étroite et plus directe, et qui est de nature à la justifier encore plus complètement; et il est possible d'entrevoir par là que le texte biblique dans lequel l'homme déchu est représenté comme condamné à ne plus rien pouvoir obtenir de la terre sans se livrer à un pénible travail (Genèse, III, 17-19) *peut fort bien répondre à une vérité même dans son sens le plus littéral*) (*Initiation et realisation spirituelle*, Éditions Traditionnelles, 1980, pp. 53-54).

[1] There were other sacred "supports" to complete the "exchange," like the Quetzal feather.

[2] Today, however, with this "infrahuman" life-style, "e-money" and bitcoins are dominant. The collapse of the sacred viewpoint regarding money happened rapidly and mainly after the destruction of the Order of the Temple; René Guénon commented on it: *La question dont il s'agit est celle de la monnaie, et assurément, si l'on s'en tient au simple point de vue "économique" tel qu'on l'entend aujourd'hui, il semble bien que celle-ci soit quelque chose qui appartient aussi complètement que possible au "règne de la quantité"; c'est d'ailleurs à ce titre qu'elle joue, dans la société moderne, le rôle prépondérant que l'on ne connaît que trop et sur lequel il serait évidemment superflu d'insister; mais la vérité est que le point de vue "économique" lui-même, et la conception exclusivement quantitative de la monnaie qui lui est inhérente, ne sont que le produit d'une dégénérescence somme toute assez récente, et que la monnaie a eu à son origine et a conservé pendant longtemps un caractère tout différent et une valeur proprement qualitative, si étonnant que cela puisse paraître à la généralité de nos contemporains* (*Le règne*, pp. 147-148). We may note that, in China, "paper money" was used for the posthumous journey (J. S. M. Ward and W. G. Stirling, *Hung Society Or the Society of Heaven and Earth*, The Baskerville Press, 1925, III, p. 21).

[3] Nonetheless, the gods of Olympus were featured with their attributes.

[4] Subsequently, the Mediterranean Basin became a rich source of coins for the modern researchers. René Guénon amended their conclusions: *Le fait dont nous voulons parler est l'adoption, tout autour du bassin de la Méditerranée, d'un même type fondamental de monnaie, avec des variations accessoires servant de marques distinctives locales; et cette adoption, encore qu'on ne puisse guère en fixer la date exacte, remonte certainement à une époque fort ancienne, du moins si l'on ne tient compte que de la période qu'on envisage le plus*

Today, in the modern world, money illustrates the *inferus* or *infimus* "center,"[1] and for the traditional spirit, the modern money suggests the closing stage of the cycle.[2] Therefore, what we can do is only to recall the lost symbols, reenacting the traditional spirit.

Since we mentioned the Romans, we consider it is worthwhile to present a coin from the times when the Empire was not yet declared, an *as*[3] with Janus bifrons and his ship on its two sides[4]:

---

habituellement dans l'antiquité... Ce qui nous apparaît comme certain, c'est que le type monétaire commun dont il s'agit, qui comporte essentiellement une tête humaine d'un côté, un cheval ou un char de l'autre, n'est pas plus spécifiquement grec qu'italique ou carthaginois, ou même gaulois ou ibérique; son adoption a sûrement nécessité un accord plus ou moins explicite entre les divers peuples méditerranéens, encore que les modalités de cet accord nous échappent forcément. Il en est de ce type monétaire comme de certains symboles ou de certaines traditions, qui se retrouvent les mêmes dans des limites encore plus étendues (Introduction générale à l'étude des doctrines hindoues, Guy Trédaniel, 1987, pp. 30-31); *Cette étude* [Noel de la Houssaye, *Les Bronzes italiotes archaïques et leur symbolique*] *débute par des considérations sur les origines de la monnaie dans le bassin de la Méditerranée, question assez obscure, et pour laquelle, comme pour tant d'autres choses, il ne semble pas possible de remonter au-delà du VIe siècle avant l'ère chrétienne. En tout cas, l'auteur a bien compris que la* 'monnaie était pour les Anciens une chose sacrée,' [our highlighting] *contrairement à la conception toute profane que s'en font les modernes, et que c'est par là que s'explique le caractère des symboles qu'elle portait; on pourrait même aller plus loin, pensons-nous, et voir dans ces symboles la marque d'un contrôle exercé par une autorité spirituelle* (Formes traditionnelles et cycles cosmiques, Gallimard, 1980, pp. 163-165).

[1] See the example of London, where the central "City" is the business and financial heart of England. *Infimus*' antonym is *supremus* (supreme), but there is no equal opposition with regard to the idea of center; in the present case, *inferus* should be related to *infernus*.

[2] *Le cas de la monnaie, telle qu'elle est actuellement, peut encore servir ici d'exemple caractéristique: dépouillée de tout ce qui pouvait, dans des civilisations traditionnelles, en faire comme un véhicule d'"influences spirituelles," non seulement elle est réduite à n'être plus, en elle-même, qu'un simple signe "matériel" et quantitatif, mais encore elle ne peut plus jouer qu'un rôle véritablement néfaste et "satanique," qu'il n'est que trop facile de constater effectivement à notre époque; la monnaie elle-même, ou ce qui en tiendra lieu, aura de nouveau un caractère qualitatif de cette sorte puisqu'il est dit que "nul ne pourra acheter ou vendre que celui qui aura le caractère ou le nom de la Bête, ou le nombre de son nom"* (Apocalypse, XIII, 17), *ce qui implique un usage effectif, à cet égard, des symboles inversés de la "contre-tradition"* (Guénon, *Le règne*, pp. 209, 363).

[3] The Roman *as* or *libra* (from this *libra* comes the modern *pound*) was also the main unit of weight.

[4] About Janus' symbolism see Guénon, *Symboles fondamentaux*, p. 149; also see his review regarding the bronze coins we already mentioned in a previous note: *Ainsi, nous ne nous expliquons pas qu'on puisse dire que la proue d'un navire associée à la figure de Janus*

Guénon was saying, *la monnaie a eu à son origine et a conservé pendant longtemps un caractère tout différent et une valeur proprement qualitative*, and, indeed, the ancient symbols confronted and surpassed the vicissitudes of time, being there on coins, even though their *spirit* was less and less comprehended. However, anyone familiar with René Guénon and the traditional spirit can read these coins, either Bar Kochba's coinage, with the Temple on it (see fig. left), or the *Provincia Dacia* coin (see *infra* fig. right[1]), or the Trajanus Decius' *Dacia* coin, with the wolf head standard (see fig. middle).[2]

---

sur l'as romain "concerne Saturne, et lui seul," alors qu'il est pourtant assez connu que le navire ou la barque était un des attributs de Janus lui-même (*Formes traditionnelles*, p. 165).

[1] In our collection, we have a similar *sestertius*, called "Marcia Otacilia Severa" (she was the wife of the Roman emperor Philip the Arab), with Dacia in long robe and pointed Phrygian cap standing between an eagle and a lion; Dacia is holding the curved Dacian sword in the left hand and a vexillum marked DF (Dacia Felix) in the right hand (these attributes are seemingly in the wrong hands, due to an engraver's error; see fig. right, compared to fig. left, showing a *sestertius* of Philip II, son of Otacilia Severa):

[2] About the meaning of the curved sword and of the Dacian standard with a wolf head, see our *The Everlasting Sacred Kernel*, 2012, pp. 21, 53, 61; about the *Dacia Felix* see our *Agarttha, the Invisible Center*, p. 94 (Christian Rosenkreutz, it is said, went to Damcar, in *Arabia Felix*) and *Din negura de vremi*, p. 99; about the symbolism of the eagle and lion see *Free-Masonry: A Traditional Organization* and *The Everlasting Sacred Kernel*.

We mentioned *Provincia Dacia*, which directed us to end this chapter with the symbols of some medieval coins from the same Dacian area, bearing in mind how unfamiliar these are for the general reader:

This is not the place to discuss the symbols coins transmitted, but we should stress the close similarity with heraldry and the medieval guilds' marking, which belonged, like the "science of money," to the traditional sciences.[1]

---

[1] For example, the eagle holding a cross in its beak, standing on top of a helmet, which is on top of a shield, needs an entire chapter to elucidate the symbols and compare to the science of heraldry, and also to the vestiges found in fairy tales.

CONCLUSION

THE TEMPLARS' TREASURE

In a recent article called *Monetary Science, Fiscal Alchemy*,[1] "monetary science" is contrasted against "fiscal alchemy"; it is a good example how the traditional spirit was not only annihilated, but also its terminology profaned and used in an antitraditional way, because, as we said, the "science of money" was a traditional science like "alchemy," which referred to a spiritual process and not to the vulgar chemical reactions.

René Guénon, in a review, confirmed the existence of a "traditional monetary science," and underlined that its "secrets" have nothing to do with the materialistic and quantitative view about money, a view that has destroyed this traditional science, together with the traditional spirit.[2] The authentic "monetary science" is far from being

---

[1] Eric M. Leeper, Cambridge, MA, 2010.
[2] *Nous sommes fort loin de contester qu'il existe, ou qu'il ait existé, une "science monétaire" traditionnelle, et que cette science ait des secrets; mais ceux-ci, encore qu'ils n'aient rien à voir avec la "pierre philosophale," sont d'une tout autre nature que ce que nous voyons ici; bien plus, en répétant à satiété que la monnaie est chose purement "matérielle" et "quantitative," on va précisément dans le sens voulu par ceux que l'on croit viser, et qui sont en réalité les destructeurs de cette science traditionnelle aussi bien que de toute autre connaissance ayant le même caractère, puisque ce sont eux qui ont arraché de l'esprit moderne toute notion dépassant le domaine de la "matière" et de la "quantité." Ceux-là, quoiqu'ils ne soient point des "initiés" (car c'est de la "contreinitiation" qu'ils relèvent) ne sont nullement dupes eux-mêmes de ce "matérialisme" qu'ils ont imposé au monde moderne, pour des fins qui sont tout autres qu'"économiques"; et, quels que soient les instruments dont ils se servent suivant les circonstances, ils sont un peu plus difficiles à découvrir que ne le serait un "comité" ou un "groupe" quelconque d'Anglais ou de Juifs* (René

"materialistic" because it was under the control of the spiritual authority and not of the temporal power, which could still be proved by the inscriptions and symbols engraved on coins[1]; not to say that it was not fortuitously the type of metal used to mint money, since, even though their values were essentially symbolical (gold = Sun, silver = Moon), the metal had its own reality considering that through symbolism the elements of this world are connected to the superior realities.[2]

René Guénon insisted:

> the ancient coins are literally covered with traditional symbols, often chosen from among those that carry some particularly profound meaning; thus for instance it has been observed that among the Celts the symbols on the coins can only be explained if they are related to the doctrinal knowledge that belonged to the Druids alone, which implies a direct intervention of the Druids in the monetary domain. There is not the least doubt that the truth in this matter is the same for the other peoples of antiquity... This is fully in agreement with the fact of the inexistence of the profane point of

---

Guénon, *Études sur la Franc-Maçonnerie et le Compagnonnage*, tome I, Éditions Traditionnelles, 1980, p. 100).

[1] In his confused and errounous way, Oswald Spengler replaced the spiritual authority with "intellect" (or "mind") and the temporal power with "money" (*The Decline of the West*, Alfred A. Knopf, 1927, II, pp. 347, 358, 364); he also wrote: "Through money, democracy becomes its own destroyer, after money has destroyed intellect" (*ibid.*, II, p. 464).

[2] *Pour ce qui est de la véritable "science monétaire," nous dirons simplement ceci: si elle était d'ordre "matériel," il serait parfaitement incompréhensible que, tant qu'elle a eu une existence effective, les questions qui s'y rapportent n'aient point été laissées à la discrétion du pouvoir temporel (comment celui-ci aurait-il jamais pu être accusé d'"altérer les monnaies" s'il avait été souverain à cet égard?), mais, au contraire, soumises au contrôle d'une autorité spirituelle (nous y avons fait allusion dans* Autorité spirituelle et pouvoir temporel), *contrôle qui s'affirmait par des marques dont on retrouve un dernier vestige incompris dans les inscriptions qui, il n'y a pas bien longtemps encore, figuraient sur la tranche des monnaies; mais comment faire comprendre cela à quelqu'un qui pousse le "nationalisme" (encore une de ces suggestions destinées à la destruction systématique de tout esprit traditionnel) jusqu'à se livrer à un éloge dithyrambique de Philippe le Bel? Au surplus, c'est une erreur de dire que les métaux "monétaires" n'ont pas par eux-mêmes de valeur propre; et, si leur valeur est essentiellement symbolique (or et argent, Soleil et Lune), elle n'en est que plus réelle, car ce n'est que par le symbolisme que les choses de ce monde sont rattachées aux réalités supérieures* (*ibid.*).

view in strictly traditional civilizations: money itself, where it existed at all, could not be the profane thing it came to be later; and if it had been so, how could the intervention of a spiritual authority, which would then obviously have no concern with money, be explained, and how would it be possible to understand that many traditions speak of coinage as of something really charged with a "spiritual influence," the action of which could become effective by means of the symbols that constituted its normal "support"?[1]

In one of his lessons, Jesus Christ used the symbol engraved on a coin to separate the two levels, that of "spiritual authority" and of "temporal power":

> But he, knowing their hypocrisy, said unto them, Why tempt ye me? bring me a penny [Gr. *denarion*] that I may see it. And they brought it. And he saith unto them, Whose is this image and superscription? And they said unto him, Caesar's. And Jesus answering said unto them, Render to Caesar the things that are Caesar's, and to God the things that are God's."[2]

---

[1] *Les monnaies anciennes sont littéralement couvertes de symboles traditionnels, pris même souvent parmi ceux qui présentent un sens plus particulièrement profond; c'est ainsi qu'on a remarqué notamment que chez les Celtes, les symboles figurant sur les monnaies ne peuvent s'expliquer que si on les rapporte à des connaissances doctrinales qui étaient propres aux Druides, ce qui implique d'ailleurs une intervention directe de ceux-ci dans ce domaine; et, bien entendu, ce qui est vrai sous ce rapport pour les Celtes l'est également pour les autres peuples de l'antiquité… Cela s'accorde très exactement avec l'inexistence du point de vue profane dans les civilisations strictement traditionnelles: la monnaie, là où elle existait, ne pouvait elle-même pas être la chose profane qu'elle est devenue plus tard; et si elle l'avait été, comment s'expliquerait ici l'intervention d'une autorité spirituelle qui évidemment n'aurait rien eu à y voir, et comment aussi pourrait-on comprendre que diverses traditions parlent de la monnaie comme de quelque chose qui est véritablement chargé d'une "influence spirituelle," dont l'action pouvait effectivement s'exercer par le moyen des symboles qui en constituaient le "support" normal?* (René Guénon, *Le règne de la quantité et les signes des temps*, Gallimard, 1970, p. 148).
[2] *Mark* 12:15-17. It is known that Julius Caesar started to mint coins having his head on them, a sign of decadence, since the Roman coinage previously bore traditional symbols, like the two-headed Janus and the ship, or the she-wolf:

 (bronze, 240 BC)   (silver, 269 BC)   (Caesar, 44 BC denarius)

Clearly Jesus Christ did not pay any attention to the "materialistic" value of money, leaving this task to Judas, who was the "bag-keeper" of the apostles[1] and who illustrated how perilous it is to touch and handle money if you are not entitled to, the spiritual authority representing (in the case when the traditional spirit was efficiently present) the only valid custodian because of its sacred knowledge and mentality, while the lower "castes" were in danger of viewing money only in a "materialistic" sense; yet even the representatives of the spiritual authority, with a nature incompatible with their function, especially in *Kali-Yuga*, were attracted by money as a tool to gain "temporal power." In fact, without a conscious understanding of money as spiritual "supports," and as society degraded, it became more and more easier to be influenced by the "devilish" component of money; as mentioned in the *Gospels*, the tax collectors were considered the worst sinners, which no doubt must be related to the evil influence of money. Something similar happened to the blacksmith and to the executioner in the Middle Ages, who were considered connected to inferior forces, the former because his relation to metals and infernal fire,[2] the latter because of his attachment to death and blood.[3]

---

[1] "Then saith one of his disciples, Judas Iscariot, Simon's son, which should betray him, Why was not this ointment sold for three hundred pence, and given to the poor? This he said, not that he cared for the poor; but because he was a thief, and had the bag, and bare what was put therein" (*John* 12:4-6); "For some of them thought, because Judas had the bag, that Jesus had said unto him, Buy those things that we have need of against the feast; or, that he should give something to the poor" (*John* 13:29).

[2] "In many countries, a sort of partial exclusion from the community, or at least a 'pushing aside,' was practised and is still practised even now so far as metal-workers are concerned, and more particularly blacksmiths, whose craft is often associated with the practice of an inferior and dangerous kind of magic, which has eventually degenerated in most cases into mere sorcery" (*dans bien des pays, une sorte d'exclusion partielle de la communauté, ou tout au moins de "mise à l'écart," a existé et existe même encore contre les ouvriers travaillant les métaux, surtout les forgerons, dont le métier s'associe du reste souvent avec la pratique d'une magie inférieure et dangereuse, dégénérée finalement, dans la plupart des cas, en sorcellerie pure et simple*, Guénon, *Le règne*, p. 207).

[3] In the Middle Ages, the executioner (the hangman, *le bourreau*) had a low social status; while the guild artisans were "honourable" the executioner was not (he had to stand separately in church, to wear a distinctive mark on his clothes, a distinctive

The metals were also in relation with money, yet they had a "celestial" aspect, being in correspondence with the planets (to which the spiritual characteristic of money could apply),[1] and a "terrestrial" one (or, more precisely, a "subterranean" one), associated to the "subterranean fire"[2] and to the "hidden treasures"[3]:

> It may facilitate the understanding of what has just been said if it is pointed out that, according to traditional symbolism, the metals are in relation not only with the "subterranean fire" as already indicated, but also with the "hidden treasures"... all the "legends" (using the language of today) about these "treasures" clearly show that their "guardians," who are none other than the subtle influences attached to them, are psychic "entities" extremely dangerous for anyone to approach without the required "qualifications" and without taking the necessary precautions... the "guardians of the hidden treasure," who are at the same time the smiths working with the "subterranean fire," are represented in various "legends" sometimes as giants and sometimes as dwarfs.[4]

---

colour – red, to live outside the city, he could not become a priest, could not touch the food in the markets, and could not be buried in a consecrated soil); like the blacksmith, he was considered skilful in magic and healing practices.

[1] *Ce symbole de l'échelle semble être d'origine chaldéenne et avoir été apporté en Occident avec les mystères de Mithra: il y avait alors sept échelons dont chacun était formé d'un métal différent, suivant la correspondance des métaux avec les planètes* (René Guénon, *L'ésotérisme de Dante*, Gallimard, 1981, p. 24); *Les Kabires, d'autre part, tout en étant aussi des forgerons, avaient un double aspect terrestre et céleste, les mettant en rapport à la fois avec les métaux et avec les planètes correspondantes* (Guénon, *Le règne*, p. 208).

[2] This second aspect has degenerated in a "satanic" influence that enveloped money when the spiritual meaning disappeared: "For the love of money is the root of all evil: which while some coveted after, they have erred from the faith, and pierced themselves through with many sorrows" (*1 Timothy* 6:10). Nonetheless, the metals which money were made of had their own value, in addition to the symbolical implications (like the hierarchy: gold, silver, bronze, iron, corresponding to the four "ages"), a value measured, as we saw previously, as weight. One of the attributes of the spiritual authority was to guard this weight, to ensure it was not altered.

[3] René Guénon observed: *Dans les mystères des Kabires de Samothrace, il était question d'un trésor caché (cf. Kubêra ou Kuvêra, qui préside aux trésors souterraines).*

[4] *On comprendra peut-être mieux ce que nous venons de dire si l'on remarque que les métaux, suivant le symbolisme traditionnel, sont en relation non seulement avec le "feu souterrain" comme nous l'avons indiqué, mais encore avec les "trésors cachés"... toutes les "légendes" (pour parler le langage actuel) qui se rapportent à ces "trésors" montrent clairement que leurs "gardiens,"*

The "hidden treasure," even when guarded by psychic "entities," is, at the highest level, a symbol of the spiritual knowledge,[1] of the center of the world, an equivalent of the Holy Grail, and not at all a materialistic pile of money and precious stones[2]; but how could the modern people understand this truth, when they lack any "qualification" to unlock the door of the "forbidden room"?[3] This door started to close for the West at the end of the 13th century, when the Order of the Temple was in its second phase and when the "Lombard banking" began its antitraditional venture.

The term "Lombard" in relation to money is a convenient label alluding to the northern Italian region of Lombardy where the first successful medieval "pawn shops" (*Monte di Pietà*) originated,[4] and the

---

c'est-à-dire précisément les influences subtiles qui y sont attachées, sont des "entités" psychiques qu'il est fort dangereux d'approcher sans posséder les "qualifications" requises et sans prendre les précautions voulues… les "gardiens des trésors cachés," qui sont en même temps les forgerons travaillant dans le "feu souterrain" sont, dans les "légendes," représentés à la fois, et suivant les cas, comme des géants et comme des nains (Guénon, *Le règne*, pp. 210-211).

[1] René Guénon noted: *D'une façon générale, le symbolisme des trésors cachés se réfère toujours à la véritable connaissance et à la tradition initiatique (cf. les mystères des Kabires)*.

[2] "Lay not up for yourselves treasures upon earth, where moth and rust doth corrupt, and where thieves break through and steal: But lay up for yourselves treasures in heaven, where neither moth nor rust doth corrupt, and where thieves do not break through nor steal: For where your treasure is, there will your heart be also" (*Matthew* 6:19-21); "No man can serve two masters: for either he will hate the one, and love the other; or else he will hold to the one, and despise the other. Ye cannot serve God and mammon [the materialistic money]" (*Matthew* 6:24); "Again, the kingdom of heaven is like unto treasure hid in a field; the which when a man hath found, he hideth, and for joy thereof goeth and selleth all that he hath, and buyeth that field" (*Matthew* 13:44).

[3] *…des "entités" psychiques qu'il est fort dangereux d'approcher sans posséder les "qualifications" requises et sans prendre les précautions voulues; mais en fait, quelles précautions des modernes, qui sont complètement ignorants de ces choses, pourraient-ils bien prendre à cet égard? Ils sont trop évidemment dépourvus de toute "qualification," ainsi que de tout moyen d'action dans ce domaine, qui leur échappe en conséquence de l'attitude même qu'ils ont prise vis-à-vis de toutes choses; il est vrai qu'ils se vantent constamment de "dompter les forces de la nature," mais ils sont certes bien loin de se douter que, derrière ces forces mêmes, qu'ils envisagent en un sens exclusivement corporel, il y a quelque chose d'un autre ordre, dont elles ne sont réellement que le véhicule et comme l'apparence extérieure* (Guénon, *Le règne*, p. 210).

[4] The "Lombard" pawn shop system extended from city to city; it became, for example, well established in Cahors, hence the name *Cahorsins* given to Christian

"pawn shop" banking system was a way to avoid the religious prohibition to gain money without work (as all the modern banks and other institutions, including the governments, do today).[1] It was a strong attack against the traditional spirit, a very efficient way to help the birth of the modern world with its profane viewpoint, which succeeded in an amazing short period of time to make people forget the spiritual side of money and become more and more deeply engulfed by the "satanic" aspect.[2] Note that the Italian families that participated in the "Lombard banking" were enemies of the Holy Roman Empire (the last bastion of the traditional society in Europe, at least by name) and they exiled Dante from Florence. What started in northern Italy expanded south to Genoa, Lucca and Siena, but Venice and then Florence were the most important factors of this antitraditional movement that had its best days after the obliteration of the Order of the Temple.[3]

---

moneylenders, and in the second half of the 13th century, spread to Western Europe reaching London and Amsterdam.

[1] The *Bible* (that is, the Judaic and Christian traditions) prohibited the usury, but the Jews considered acceptable to lend money with interest to the gentiles (*goy*) and so, in the Middle Ages, the Jews flourished as usurers, since the Church prohibited any Christian to profit by moneylending (recall the well-known episode about Jesus' expulsion of the moneychangers from the temple); in 1163, Pope Alexander III and the Council of Tours condemned usury, and in 1179 the pope excommunicated all obvious usurers; in 1311, the Council of Vienne stressed again that usury is a sin.

[2] It is understandable why the "Lombard banking" started in Italy, where a strong antitraditional mentality developed with the expansion of the "third class" in the main city-states (the so-called "bourgeoisie") and where the Jews could function well as moneylenders; the famous Renaissance, born in Italy, is a normal consequence. In contrast, in countries where the hierarchy still worked, especially in England, the Jews were condemned: in 1290, King Edward I expelled the Jews from England, because their activity as usurers; much later, in 1492, the Jews were banned from Spain. However, we should not generalize the role of the Jews in the "banking" process, since the "Lombard banking" was promoted by Italian usurers who supervised the higher level (dealing with kings and nobility), while the Jews (and again "some Jews" not "all Jews") were left with the lower level (pawn shops and later the goldsmith trade and the diamond market; however they flourished as moneylenders in Bukowina).

[3] The Medici of Florence became the most powerful banking family after the 14th century. They attracted the Jews to come to Italy and perform their "banking"

Plato considered the cycle (*yuga*) as two phases: a "divine" one, when the Divinity directly governed the world, and a "human" one, when the world forgot about Heaven and subsisted by inertia. An application of what Plato said is the fourth so-called "Great Year,"[1] the "Atlantis Year," which had its first half (the "divine" phase) in the "Silver Age" and the second half (the "human" phase) in the "Bronze Age." At a more reduced scale, the Order of the Temple's "age" could also be divided in two phases, a "divine" phase, from 1119 to 1187 (in fact we should say the 12th century),[2] and a "human" phase, from 1187 to 1312 (the 13th century).[3] During this second phase the "Lombard bankers" became very active, and the Templars, who also had the function of guarding the spiritual meaning of money, could not stop its depreciation and decadence toward the "materialistic" aspect, and only now, in this second phase, we could assume that some individuals (and not the Order!), who were in contact with money, became, like Judas, tarnished and corrupted by the "satanic" influence.[4]

However, it is impossible to compare the Templars' "banking" function to the "Lombard banking" and only the modern mentality under the suggestion of counter-initiatory forces extrapolated the

---

manoeuvres (it is said that "the organized Jewish communities of Florence, Siena, Pisa and Livorno were political creations of the Medici rulers"). It is also said that some Jews were adopted by the Medici family (who were Catholics), but René Guénon wrote in a letter: *savez-vous que les Médicis étaient d'origine juive? Ils descendaient, comme le nom l'indique d'ailleurs, d'une famille de médecins juifs établis à Florence* (René Guénon, *Fragments Doctrinaux*, Rose-Cross Books, 2013, p. 370).

[1] There are 5 such "Great Years" in a *Manvantara*, each having half the value of the precession of the equinoxes.
[2] The Battle of Hattin (July 4, 1187) and the recapture of Jerusalem by Saladin marked the decadence of the Templars, not to mention how unsuitable the Grand Master of the Knights Templar, Gérard de Ridefort, was, who died two years later. However, the crucial date marking the second phase was the year 1241 when the Mongols (representing the "destructive force" or the "dissolving force" helping the demolition of the traditional spirit) invaded Europe.
[3] The Templar "quality" was one of a very high standard; as the century went by, the lack of qualified knights to replace the ones who died in battles became more and more apparent.
[4] Saint Nilus of Sinai said: "it is not possible for the one who purifies the sins of others to remain untouched."

"greed" and antitraditional practices of the moneylenders and profane bankers to the Order of the Temple.

Sharan Newman declared with unambiguous irony:

> "Everybody knows" that the Templars were rich. They had piles of treasures hidden everywhere. When the order was dissolved, no treasure was found. Therefore, it's still hidden.[1] There is no indication that the Templars ever had mounds of cash and treasure for their own use, especially not in the London and Paris houses.[2]

We must strongly stress that the idea of the Templars' treasure is a pure invention exploited by malevolent forces, and, as in René Guénon's case, where, even now, similar forces strive to denigrate and tarnish his work, they have worked hard through the centuries to the present day to defame the Knights Templar.[3] There are no such things as a materialistic "treasure" and boxes of "documents" containing the "secrets" of the Order, which would have been incompatible with the

---

[1] Sharan Newman, *The Real History Behind the Templars*, Berkley Books, 2007, p. 189. "Everybody knows" is a typical modern expression hiding ignorance, arrogance and malevolence. We decided to quote Sharan Newman for her impartiality and sharp mind, even though she is not at all interested in the traditional spirit.

[2] Newman 201. "For years some people have been assuming that somehow in 1307 all the commanderies in France got wind of the impending arrests and either hid or removed everything of value. Then they all just went to bed and waited for the king's men to come for them" (Newman 202). "The inventories taken in 1308 show they lived a frugal life. Unless many goods had been looted when the Templars were arrested, the inventories show that the brothers had few possessions of comforts" (Evelyn Lord, *The Knights Templar in Britain*, Pearson, 2004, p. 168). "The French Templars were taken completely by surprise and no treasure was found in their houses, nor any of the idols mentioned in the confessions. The implication is that neither treasure nor idols existed, and that the Templars were living in poverty, as their vows required" (Lord 250).

[3] "The treasure of the Templars, if there was any, wouldn't have been in London or Paris in any case, but in Cyprus in the Templar headquarters. On the day of their arrest in Cyprus, an inventory was taken of Templar goods. At Nicosia, along with a lot of crossbows and foodstuffs were 120,000 white bezants (coins made of a mix of silver and some gold). That seems like a lot to me but legends begin early, and a near contemporary chronicler insists that 'no one knows where in the world they hid the rest, nor has anyone been able to find out' (Newman 202). "This is all speculation. There is no evidence for the existence of any treasure" (Lord 169).

traditional spirit to which the Templars belonged. It is true that the Knights, especially those located in the *Temples* of London and Paris, were custodians of money, in the sense of spiritual guardians not of "bankers,"[1] and the fact the kings entrusted them their money and sometimes their lives is an obvious testimony to the Templars' high standard of honesty and purity[2]; but how can a mentality of serfs comprehend what real "nobility" meant?

It is important to understand that to sustain the operations in the Holy Land, the Order of the Temple needed a lot of funds for equipment, to supply the sergeants, the turcopoles and other servants, for horses, food, transportation, etc.[3] and usually what they owned back in Europe were mills, ovens, stores, houses, markets but not money[4]; all the profit from agriculture,[5] mills, fairs and markets was sent to the Holy Land to maintain the Knights' fight for the Cross[6]; in

---

[1] "Most of the time the Templars were more like warehouse guards than bankers" (Newman 199); "the Templars... didn't charge interest on loans and they also didn't lend money left in their keeping" (Newman 200).

[2] "The Templars were trusted by royalty, particularly the kings of France and England, to handle their business affairs" (Newman 201).

[3] "Each knight brother had to have three horses and tack and on squire, a ration of barley for the horse, and armor, as well as regular clothing. He needed his own napkin and washcloth. He also had a cook pot and bowl to measure the barley, drinking cups, two flasks, a bowl and spoon made of horn, and a tent, among other things... The average cost of a warhorse during the twelfth and thirteenth centuries was thirty-six livres. That's more than the value of a good-sized manor. There are many stories about poor knights who sold or mortgaged their patrimony for a good horse... The Templars also hired Turcopoles to fight with them... Added to these, there was the cost of shipping men and equipment from West to East (Newman 196-197).

[4] Lord 49, 68, 70. "It is no coincidence that the land given to the Templars was often on the poorer soils, low-lying marshlands or densely wooded areas that had to be cleared before the land could be planted... They were encouraged in their efforts to reclaim the waste by successive popes" (Lord 57). The Templars, as the Israelis today, "had experience in reclaiming waste in the Holy Land where they had restored Judaean villages destroyed by the Romans to productivity" (*ibid.*).

[5] See Newman 193-194. "Many houses were run by sergeants. Men of fighting age and ability were immediately sent overseas."

[6] Lord 58. Also, "a large part of the 'donations' to the Temples were actually sales" (Newman 198).

the second phase, at the end of the 13th century, these properties were ruined,[1] partly because of lack of men and lack of motivation (Jerusalem was in the Muslims' hands).[2]

We mentioned earlier the Council of Vienne: it was the fifteenth Ecumenical Council of the Roman Catholic Church and was held between 1311 and 1312 in Vienne, France, where, aide from the denunciation of usury, the condemnation of the Knights Templar was the main act of the Council, and it is not fortuitous that it took place in France, since France played a special role in the destruction of the traditional spirit and of the sacred aspect of money. In the second phase of the Templars' "age," King Philippe Auguste already showed a particular thirst for money, and therefore, after expelling the Jews from his lands (but not from France entirely), in 1182, because of their activities as moneylenders, he brought them back in 1198 since their "banking" function provided a lot of profits for himself, through taxes and duties. Later on, another Philippe, King Philippe le Bel, arrested the Jews to seize their assets and expelled them from his French territories on July 22, 1306[3]; he also expelled the "Lombard" bankers, all this being a useful preview for the next step, when Philippe le Bel started destroying the Order of the Temple. At the same time the king debased the coinage; for Dante, Philippe le Bel was driven in his actions by "avarice" and "cupidity," but it is very clear that he was a

---

[1] "In 1308... the Templars' property was unkempt and ruined" (Lord 56).
[2] Lord 126-127. The inventories of Templar property are very instructive. "The prestigious Temple in London had little more than the provincial commandery had. The cellar contained some maple cups, twenty-two silver spoons, some canvas cloths, and four tankards. There were seven horses in the stable, three for farm work. The master had some clothes and bed linen, one gold buckle, and a crossbow without bolts... Even in Paris there were no great caches of jewels or coins... If the Templars were terribly rich, then where was all the money?" (Newman 191).
[3] This is the so-called "Great Exile of 1306"; Philippe le Bel was considered by some as very "pious," but after he took possession of the Jews' properties (houses, lands, etc.) and sold them, he replaced the Jews as moneylender and collected the debts from the Christian defaulters; and, the irony of ironies is that the king declared the prohibition of clipped and debased money, which forced the debtors to pay with genuine coins.

sinister creature who, beyond "cupidity," was engaged in a mortal battle against the traditional spirit.[1]

There is no doubt a strong connection between the alteration of money and the annihilation of the Knights Templar, protectors of the authenticity of coinage, as René Guénon highlighted many times:

> *C'est par là que s'explique, non seulement la destruction de l'Ordre du Temple, mais aussi, plus visiblement encore, ce qu'on a appelé l'altération des monnaies, et ces deux faits sont peut-être liés plus étroitement qu'on ne pourrait le supposer à première vue; en tout cas, si les contemporains de Philippe le Bel lui firent un crime de cette altération, il faut en conclure que, en changeant de sa propre initiative le titre de la monnaie, il dépassait les droits reconnus au pouvoir royal. Il y a là une indication qui est à retenir, car cette question de la monnaie avait, dans l'antiquité et au moyen âge, des aspects tout à fait ignorés des modernes, qui s'en tiennent au simple point de vue "économique"* [2]

---

[1] In August 1290, Philippe le Bel minted a genuine pure gold coin called *Petit Royal assis*, with proper weight; yet in 1295, he minted the "false" *double parisis* made of an alloy of copper with some silver (called *billon*), and next year the *masse d'or* was issued, which was supposed to be a "double florin," but it was actually debased. In 1306, again he dramatically debased the French coinage, which led to rioting in Paris and forced the king to briefly seek refuge in the Paris Temple – headquarters of the Knights Templar, the same Knights he accused next year of a series of invented charges.

[2] René Guénon, *Autorité spirituelle et pouvoir temporel*, Véga, 1976, p. 85; "See *Spiritual Authority and Temporal Power*, where we specially referred to the case of Philip the Fair, and where we suggested that there may be a fairly close connection between the destruction of the Order of the Templars and the alteration of the coinage, something easily understood if it is recognized as at least very plausible that this Order had the function, among others, of exercising spiritual control in this field; we do not want to pursue further here, but we remind that the beginning of the modern deviation could be assigned precisely to this moment" (*Voir* Autorité spirituelle et pouvoir temporel, *p. 111 [85], où nous nous sommes référé plus spécialement au cas de Philippe le Bel, et où nous avons suggéré la possibilité d'un rapport assez étroit entre la destruction de l'Ordre du Temple et l'altération des monnaies, ce qui se comprendrait sans peine si l'on admettait, comme au moins très vraisemblable, que l'Ordre du Temple avait alors, entre autres fonctions, celle d'exercer le contrôle spirituel dans ce domaine; nous n'y insisterons pas davantage, mais nous rappellerons que c'est précisément à ce moment que nous estimons pouvoir faire remonter les débuts de la déviation moderne proprement dite* (Guénon, *Le règne*, p. 149); *Il est intéressant de considérer la succession de ces dates: en 1307, Philippe le Bel,d'accord avec Clément V, fait emprisonner le Grand-Maître et les principaux dignitaires de l'Ordre du Temple (au nombre de 72, dit-on, et c'est là encore un nombre symbolique); en 1308, Henri de Luxembourg est élu*

Therefore, the modern people who strive to perpetuate the imaginary "treasure" of the Knights Templar are not better than King Philippe le Bel: they are trustful successors who, under the suggestion of increasingly aggressive and shameless "satanic" forces, march triumphantly, with evil eyes shining of foolish arrogance, trampling any last traces of the traditional spirit in this agonizing world.

---

empereur; en 1312, l'Ordre du Temple est aboli officiellement; en 1313, l'empereur Henri VII meurt mystérieusement, sans doute empoisonné; en 1314 a lieu le supplice des Templiers dont le procès durait depuis sept ans; la même année, le roi Philippe le Bel et le pape Clément V meurent à leur tour. Le mobile de Philippe le Bel, pour Dante, c'est l'avarice et la cupidité; il y a peut-être une relation plus étroite qu'on ne pourrait le supposer entre deux faits imputables à ce roi: la destruction de l'Ordre du Temple et l'altération des monnaies (René Guénon, *L'ésotérisme de Dante*, Gallimard, 1981, p. 55).

www.ingramcontent.com/pod-product-compliance
Lightning Source LLC
Chambersburg PA
CBHW050142170426
43197CB00011B/1937